Transforming the Authority of the Archive

UNDERGRADUATE PEDAGOGY AND CRITICAL DIGITAL ARCHIVES

Coedited by
Andi Gustavson and Charlotte Nunes

LEVER
PRESS

Lever Press (leverpress.org) is a publisher of pathbreaking scholarship. Supported by a consortium of higher education institutions focused on, and renowned for, excellence in both research and teaching, our press is grounded on three essential commitments: to be a digitally native press, to be a peer-reviewed, open access press that charges no fees to either authors or their institutions, and to be a press aligned with the liberal arts ethos.

The complete manuscript of this work was subjected to a fully closed ("double blind") review process. For more information, please see our Peer Review Commitments and Guidelines at https://www.leverpress.org/peerreview

DOI: https://doi.org/10.3998/mpub.12752519
Print ISBN: 978-1-64315-051-2
Open access ISBN: 978-1-64315-052-9

Library of Congress Control Number: 2023939165

Published in the United States of America by Lever Press, in partnership with Michigan Publishing.

Contents

Acknowledgments

The authors gratefully acknowledge Anne Houston, director of Swarthmore College Libraries and former dean of Lafayette College Libraries, for her support of this volume. We are particularly grateful to the student research assistants at the Lafayette College Libraries department of digital scholarship services who helped bring this project to fruition through their dedication and attention to detail: Jessica Mummert, Xavier Walker, and Kristin Dingelstedt. We thank also Janna Avon and Nora Zimmerman, our colleagues in digital scholarship services who provided supervisory support for student research assistants working on this project.

We are especially indebted to Jamie A. Lee, Associate Professor of Digital Culture, Information, and Society, and their students in the School of Information at the University of Arizona. We are deeply grateful for their generosity in sharing resources and for their strong influence on this project. Our thanks as well to panelists on the 2017 American Studies Association session "Dissenting Documents: A Roundtable on Teaching with Special Collections." Our conversations during the session with Cecily Marcus, Kimberly McKee, Sarah Moazeni, Doran Larson, and Nicole Guidotti-Hernandez inspired us to pursue this edited collection. Thank you to Gabriel Solis, Executive Director of the Texas After Violence

Project, as well as the members of the Board of this organization (Jim Kuhn, Glenna Balch, Celeste Henery, A. Naomi Paik, Betty Snyder, and Walter C. Long), for providing opportunities for us to think and learn about relationships among community archives, campus partnerships, and undergraduate contributions. And our gratitude to Hannah Alpert-Abrams, whose thinking and teaching in the area of critical digital archives has inspired and influenced our own work over the course of many years.

We also wish to acknowledge our families for their love and support: Andy, Henry, and Laurie Uzendoski, and Keith, Gray, Eloise, and Imogene Gaddis. Thank you!

INTRODUCTION

Andi Gustavson and Charlotte Nunes

Writing in 2018, reflecting on digital archives of police violence and in anticipation of the symposium *Architecting Sustainable Futures: Exploring Funding Models in Community-Based Archives*, Jarrett Drake laid out the immense potential of collaborative, community-engaged archiving initiatives: "the opportunity exists to embody the seismic shift in paradigms that we want to see in society."[1] Drake makes explicit that archives reflect the past, but actively shape the present and future as well. As communities build archives with care and intention, they claim agency in defining present realities and forming historical records, thus charting paths to the future that are accountable to the people and histories of these communities. A more multi-faceted, less hegemonic sense of the past produces a more equitable future.

In this edited collection, we address the proliferation in recent years of critical digital archives projects in the undergraduate classroom that are informed by critical archival studies and driven by the values of community-based archiving. As we forefront initiatives that hinge on partnerships with undergraduate students, we consider what reciprocity looks like between undergraduate pedagogy and archival stewardship on campus and beyond. What does this mean for the public service mission of higher education? We argue that projects such as those profiled in this volume transform what college campuses can be to their publics. As academic libraries increasingly offer both physical and digital infrastructure for community-engaged archives initiatives within, without, and across campus bounds, college campuses can serve as integral community resources.

When we set out to compile this collection, we sought perspectives from educators, archivists (both community and institutionally affiliated), and undergraduates involved in efforts to deconstruct and transform the institutional authority of the archive. We started with a series of questions: How can emergent best practices in community-based digital archiving inform productive shifts in undergraduate pedagogy? How can educators transform their pedagogy to better prepare students to ethically engage with the digital archives they encounter and create? How can these transformations newly express the core values of higher education? And how, in turn, can this process manifest the "seismic shifts" in society Drake anticipates in his call to action for community-led archives?

Contributors to this volume detail new roles for archives in undergraduate pedagogy and new roles for undergraduates in archives. While there has long been a place for archival exploration in undergraduate education, especially primary source analysis of items curated by archivists and educators, the models offered here engage students not only in analyzing collections, but also in the manifold challenges of building, stewarding, and communicating about collections. In transforming what archives are to undergraduate education, the projects profiled here transform the authority of the archive, as students and community partners claim powers to curate and create history.

Contributions to this volume represent a wide range of institutions, from small liberal arts colleges (Grinnell College, Lafayette College, Hampshire College) to historically Black colleges and universities (HBCUs: Prairie View A&M University) to Ivy Leagues (Dartmouth College) to large research institutions (University of Texas at Austin, James Madison University). Not all the projects detailed in this collection are primarily affiliated with academic institutions. Contributions by aems emswiler and Jane Field detail collecting efforts that are accountable to people who are incarcerated as well as families and communities disproportionately impacted by punitive criminal justice policies. The projects they describe are community- rather than campus-based, yet both projects have historically involved significant undergraduate labor and leadership, and both offer insight into the interaction between community archives and academic institutions. The edited collection as a whole rests on the premise that archival institutions, often associated with academic libraries, strongly comprise and reflect the identities of the campuses where they are housed. In playing active roles developing archival collections, undergraduates shape how campus pasts are narrated and direct the future of their institutions by setting new norms for who and what values are represented by the student body. The faculty, librarians, and archivists who make available these collections and teach with them in new ways create the educational experiences through which the students claim the authority to engage and reimagine the archives they encounter.

The stories collected here are not always triumphant. Many contributors detail challenges experienced by students, educators, archivists, and community members involved in the grinding forward of new modes of archival authority. Authors describe tensions with college administration and among student collaborators (Jones, Rodrigues, Schnepper, and Woolf), the precarity of new programs established to advance equity, diversity, and inclusion in college archives (Fuentes and Koreman), the emotional strain of engaging with archives of trauma (De Fazio; Field; Alpert-Abrams and Gustavson), difficulties building authentically reciprocal relationships among campus, archive, and community partners (Robinson, Earles, and White; emswiler), obstacles to sustainable collaborative archives initiatives posed by the semester timeline (Lang and Nacca), and issues of contingent labor and institutional hierarchy preventing equitable archival collaborations (Hardesty, Kumbier, and Miller). Yet the contributions to this volume are also rich with thoughtful and creative pedagogical approaches to counter the presumed neutrality of the archive and advocate a shared understanding of the contingency of archival collections. Authors offer theoretically backed case studies that we hope will inspire a new wave of pedagogical engagements with archives, in which students have opportunities to learn about the historically exclusionary nature of archives and contribute to more inclusive initiatives.

OVERVIEW OF THE FIELDS AND DEFINITION OF TERMS

What do we mean when we talk about archives in this collection? While not every archival collection and project described across this volume has a formal affiliation with a campus or public archival institution, all involve primary sources of abiding value to communities depicted in each chapter, and all hinge on infrastructural support from academic libraries, community organizations, or both. We take our cues from the Society of American Archivists on how to use the terms "archive" and "archives."[2] Namely, we consider them more or less interchangeable, with a preference for the term "archives" in reference to archival repositories (whether physical or digital), and to organizations documenting and preserving heritage. We consider the term "the archive" (or "the Archive") as associated with the archival turn in theoretical humanities scholarship. We take Michelle Caswell's point in "'The Archive' Is Not an Archives: On Acknowledging the Intellectual Contributions of Archival Studies" that traditions of theory and practice in both the humanities and archival studies have much to gain from each other, especially in discussions about representation.[3] The contributors to this volume take this exchange to heart, describing in detail how their respective projects address histories of exclusion in archival collections.

This volume is especially informed and inspired by recent scholarship in critical digital archives, critical archival studies at large, and community-based archives. While the term "critical digital archives" provides the most relevant framing for the volume—hence its inclusion in the title of the collection—the related and interrelated fields of critical archival studies and community-based archiving provide essential theoretical grounding for the projects and initiatives collectively described here. With the term "critical digital archives," we follow Clare Battershill et al. who model how to apply a critical humanistic lens to digital archival infrastructure in their essay "Building a Critical Digital Archive."[4] Resting on the critical archival studies premise that no archival collection-building process is neutral or objective, these scholars assert the value of critically modeling archival data in digital projects to highlight perspectives that have not historically been centered in collection-building, but that are very much present in the archives. As Ricardo L. Punzalan and Michelle Caswell observe, "[t]echnology has often been touted for its potential to open up collections and encourage greater access and participation," but "the field must investigate how cultural heritage institutions can create avenues of meaningful access without further promoting the uneven power dynamic that inspired the creation or collection of records of certain communities or groups."[5] Another key contribution to the field of critical digital archives is Itza A. Carbajal and Michelle Caswell's 2021 publication, "Critical Digital Archives: A Review from Archival Studies."[6] The assignments, projects, and initiatives described across this collection are fundamentally concerned with the challenge to model digital archival collections so as to center individual and community voices that are historically under-engaged[7] in the archives. To address this challenge, contributors describe various approaches to substantively, often radically, redistribute archival resources and authority.

This collection is thus fundamentally informed by the broader field of critical archival studies. Critical archival studies builds on work by such figures as Terry Cook, Joan M. Schwartz, and Anne Gilliland, among others. Writing in 2014, Gilliland succinctly summed up what might be understood as the essence of critical archival studies: critical awareness of the contingency of archives, their historic associations with power, and their non-objective, non-neutral nature.

> [P]eeling away the stereotypes and looking back over archival history, one readily discerns that archives have always been dynamic...their rationales, contents, processes, and activities directly reflecting the contingency of archives upon their own juridical, political, social, cultural, and technological contexts. Moreover, archives have historically been closely and unabashedly associated with the exercise, structures, and worldviews of power. While archives and the records they contain do not explicitly intend to be unrepresentative of different perspectives, experiences, and epistemologies, they inevitably and inexorably reflect and legitimize how, when, why, and by whom those records were generated and preserved.[8]

Sharing the premises that archives are dynamic and contingent, never neutral, and that they replicate power, scholars of critical archival studies advocate an approach to building and interpreting archives attuned to values of equity and social justice. Writing in 2016, Punzalan and Caswell acknowledge the influences of the radical social history movements of the 1960s and 1970s as well as critical theory movements during the 1990s on the expansion of archival concepts and practice to account for values of equity and inclusion.[9] They note "a growing call for the archival field to explicitly adopt a social justice mission,"[10] asserting that "archival labor and scholarship have much to contribute to the ways in which social justice is envisioned and enacted, and that, as shapers of the historical record, archivists have a professional obligation to work toward a more equitable future."[11]

In 2017, the special issue "Critical Archival Studies" in the *Journal of Critical Library and Information Studies* gave further shape to the field by establishing a framework to analyze the institutional power and white supremacy within and foundational to many traditional archives, and further, to strive for liberatory practices in archival stewardship.[12] Contributions to the special issue strengthen our understanding of the critical conversations about whose materials archives collect, where historical oppressions are upheld and where they might be dismantled within archival institutions, and about new practices for recreating and re-envisioning the archives of the future. Following these contributions, as well as the work of such scholars as Tonia Sutherland ("'Archival Amnesty': In Search of Black American Transitional and Restorative Justice") and Lae'l Hughes-Watkins ("Moving Toward a Reparative Archive: A Roadmap for a Holistic Approach to Disrupting Homogenous Histories in Academic Repositories and Creating Inclusive Spaces for Marginalized Voices"), authors in this volume operate on the premise that to transform our practice—both archival and pedagogical—is to imagine new ways of relating to old structures or to dispense with those structures altogether.[13]

To answer the call by critical archival studies to dismantle historic hierarchies and chart equitable, emancipatory paths forward for archival collection-building, we turn to the literature on community archives. (The terms "community-led," "community-based," and "community-engaged" archives appear variously throughout this volume, depending on the specifics of the initiatives under discussion.) Many scholars across the field cite the need for community-led collaborations to build more comprehensive collections where gaps and silences exist. They point out the particular utility of community archives to puncture the myth of archival neutrality, leveraging the constructed, contingent nature of archives to make intentional, values-driven interventions in the historical record.[14] As "[c]ommunity archival discourses have expanded the notion of who has the power to process and control archival records,"[15] contributors to this volume engage with sources such as the *Sustainable Futures* project on community-based archiving[16] to detail in their respective chapters the ethical and practical considerations of building and sustaining equitable, reciprocal, and participatory archives projects.

How do we define "community" in the term "community archives"? Much of the literature adopts a straightforward definition of community archives as "independent, grassroots alternatives to mainstream repositories through which communities make collective decisions about what is of enduring value to them."[17] Other scholarship[18] complicates a binary opposition between autonomous community and mainstream archives by defining the field more broadly. For instance, in "'What We Do Crosses over to Activism': The Politics and Practice of Community Archives," the authors "follow archival scholars Andrew Flinn, Mary Stevens, and Elizabeth Shepherd in defining a 'community' as 'any manner of people who come together and present themselves as such.' In turn [the authors] understand a 'community archive' as the product of community efforts to actively document the history and ongoing experiences of members of the source community in order to make their history accessible on 'their own terms.'"[19] Poole demonstrates the vast range of ways in which community archives manifest; they

> show varying degrees of independence and affiliation. Depending upon their geopolitical context, they may overlap with or comprise part of public libraries, local history museums, historical societies, and art galleries, participatory or do-it-yourself (DIY) archives,

> postcolonial archives, memory groups, oral history initiatives, virtual communities, independent or autonomous archives, ethnic archives, activist archives, ethnocultural collections, religious and spiritual orders' archives, First Nations organizations, leisure clubs, and mainstream academic institutions. They evince varying organizational forms, too, based inter alia on age, physical or virtual presence, degree of autonomy or independence, nonprofit status, and sustainability (namely resources and funding).[20]

With a more open, perhaps "unsettled" definition of community archives, there is a risk of "muddying the waters," as Poole writes: "some communities adopt the term...whereas others see it applied to them by scholars, politicians, or policymakers."[21] Yet with such a diversity of community archives evinced across the scholarship and within the bounds of this volume, we also embrace a broad definition of the term. While some of the projects detailed across this collection meet the definition of community archives as autonomous and non-institutionally based, others are explicitly campus-based, representing cohesive efforts by communities within a larger campus community to redress historic exclusions in institutional archives.

Indeed, this volume is pointedly interested in how undergraduate engagements with archives bear out their transformation from upholding hegemonic power to fostering belonging. This transformation is an aspirational goal across the literature in critical digital archives, critical archival studies, and community archives, and it forms the through-line of this collection as well. To achieve this transformation, all areas of archival practice, including appraisal, determination of shared custody agreements, accessioning, description, and sustainability planning, must be participatory; as Lauren Haberstock writes in "Participatory Description: Decolonizing Descriptive Methodologies in Archives," "[k]nowledge production needs to be relational and collaborative if it is going to be representational...[P]articipatory methods need to be process-driven, not results-based, allowing time for respectful and reciprocal relationships to grow."[22] Contributions to this volume detail how participation, collaboration, and more equitable representation are both challenged and achieved across a wide range of undergraduate-engaged digital archives projects.

Thus, informed by scholarship in the fields of critical archival studies and community-based archives, and with a particular emphasis on the digital realm, this volume puts the subject areas of critical digital archives and undergraduate archives-based pedagogy into conversation with each other. Ambitious consortial digital archives initiatives such as Project STAND, Documenting the Now, and the Colored Conventions Project—all of which bring together multiple activist, organizational, and institutional stakeholders, and all of which offer unique opportunities for undergraduate engagement—are out of scope for this volume, which largely highlights projects and initiatives undertaken in more granular contexts of higher education. However, the coeditors gratefully acknowledge the immense influence of these and similar initiatives to establish ethical frameworks for collaboration among diverse contributors and organizations. Similarly, although deep engagement with the field of digital humanities is out of scope for this collection, the principles of "data feminism" as laid out by Catherine D'Ignazio and Lauren Klein provide valuable framing for the intersection of critical digital archiving and undergraduate pedagogy undertaken here. To challenge power, they advise a series of actions including "[c]ompiling counterdata... in the face of missing data or institutional neglect," "imagin[ing] our end point not as 'fairness,' but as co-liberation," and "engag[ing] and empower[ing] newcomers to the field,"[23] in part through innovations in undergraduate pedagogy. The *Archive Journal* project "Undergraduates in the Archives" addresses the challenges, benefits, and logistics of incorporating archives in undergraduate curricula.[24] But no source to date provides a comprehensive study of how critical digital archives and archives-based undergraduate pedagogy interact, inform each other, and even determine new contours in each of these respective fields. Little of the existing scholarship addresses how innovative archives-based pedagogy is itself transforming dynamics of power and privilege that have historically shaped the institutional authority of the archive.

By the same token, with notable exceptions such as "Teaching to Dismantle White Supremacy in Archives" by Michelle Caswell, the scholarship on pedagogy and archival collections does not engage explicitly with the structural factors determining histories of representation and exclusion in archives.[25] The scholarship in this field uses a case study model in which each contribution outlines a lesson plan and includes resources such as sample questioning practices. Groundbreaking works such as *Using Primary Sources: Hands-on Instructional Exercises* edited by Anne Bahde, Heather Smedberg, and Mattie Taormina, and *Past or Portal? Enhancing Undergraduate Learning through Special Collections and Archives* edited by Eleanor Mitchell, Peggy Anne Seiden, and Suzy Taraba,[26] are exciting models for thinking about the recent shift in special collections and archival studies toward primary source literacy and instruction. Collectively, the chapters in this volume build upon pedagogical case studies to make theoretical claims about how archives-based pedagogy can transform the institutional authority of the archive. We bring together the fields of critical digital archives and archives-based pedagogy by considering how to invite undergraduates into the broader critical conversations around digital archives and challenges to institutional authority that are already taking shape on their college campuses and in their worlds.

OVERVIEW OF THE COLLECTION

Each of the contributors to this collection explores the intersection of digital archives and undergraduates within higher education. We bring together chapters that expose hierarchies within higher education and indicate how in teaching undergraduates we might upend, reimagine, or transform the archives and higher education writ large. We recognize the projects and content areas addressed across the collection are selective, and we acknowledge that a rich breadth of digital archives projects and topics are not addressed within the volume. Nevertheless, across the collection, readers will encounter a constructive range of ways to engage with concepts of critical digital archiving and undergraduate pedagogy. Some authors discuss projects where students complete collaborative group work within the structure of the class (De Fazio; Lang and Nacca), while others outline collaborative projects taken on as independent research (Armstrong, Nunes, and Wellnitz; Jones, Schnepper, Rodrigues, and Wolff). Many of the authors describe public-facing digital archives projects that are the results of collaborative undergraduate research lasting beyond the length of a term. At the core of all of these projects is a commitment to experiential learning and authentic audiences—each educator describes the work of leading students from the research process through to the work of engaging or creating digital archives.

All chapters in this collection make explicit the distribution of labor involved in the collaborations described. Contributors provide deep insight into the expertise, technology, and other resources necessary to achieve their goals. Authors surface the unique structures of their programs and projects by describing in detail the various roles played by faculty, archivists, community partners, and students. Contributors thought especially deeply about how to privilege student voices in the programs they built and in the scholarship they produced. Lang and Nacca, and Alpert-Abrams and Gustavson all argue for ethical inclusion of student voices, based on student preferences. In some cases, students divorce their names from public-facing digital archives for privacy reasons, while in other cases students claim their contributions in order to highlight their labor. Several of the pieces include former undergraduate students as coauthors, and emswiler details how their own work as an archivist with the Inside Books Project grew out of experiences in an undergraduate class.

Many of the contributions to this collection highlight student projects that, when completed, become a part of the curriculum for the following year's program or the next semester's class. Across the volume, contributors advocate for librarian and archivist partnerships to gain more solid footing in campus curricula. In their piece on the Historical Accountability Student Research Program at Dartmouth, for example, Myranda Fuentes and Sam Koreman trace the ways student fellows who participate in the program eventually come to see their own relationship to their college and to the historical record change. Fuentes and Koreman—along with Jones, Schnepper, Rodrigues, and Wolff in their piece on Grinnell college, and Armstrong, Nunes, and Wellnitz in theirs on Lafayette College—consider how collaboration with the college archivist leads students to document their own experiences and the experiences of others whose records might redress gaps or silences in the holdings. Lang and Nacca, and De Fazio have found ways to repeatedly iterate on the digital archives they create in order to teach with past students' work as course content and encourage revision and expansion.

Across several of the pieces we see educators, librarians, and archivists advocating for a change in their traditional roles as they undertake critical digital archives projects. Fuentes and Koreman trace the ways that librarians serve as peers, offering assistance or encouragement and "validating a patron's thoughts as worthy of further inquiry" and bolstering student researchers to encounter trauma in the archives by "build[ing] meaningful, trusting relationships with them in preparation for the time(s) when their readiness wavers." These shifting roles often mean supporting our students through difficult emotional experiences as they encounter archives, and both Fuentes and Koreman, and Alpert-Abrams and Gustavson consider the ways to do difficult and important work with students without aggravating trauma. In highlighting these evolving roles for educators, librarians, and archivists, this collection offers examples of the ways that transformative change within archives can begin at the level of the individual relationship, the single class, the new digital project.

The authors represented here highlight a key finding—to teach undergraduates to engage with digital archives is to guide them toward the recognition that archives are institutions that can be questioned, critiqued, and transformed. Jones, Rodrigues, Schnepper, and Wolff remind us that involving students in archival work "can raise student consciousness of the archive as a contested and created site." Robinson works with his students to address critical gaps in the historical record, building his class around collaboration between the archivist and community members at an HBCU. Hardesty, Kumbier, and Miller explore how teaching students to engage with metadata allows them to discover the limitations of digital tools, and how documenting networks of zine creators expanded students' understanding of how to build relationships with the people they researched and within their own research teams.

Contributors directly engage in questions of equity, diversity, and inclusion, challenging students to explicitly tackle social justice work with archives. With Fuentes and Koreman, we learn about the Historical Accountability Project, which explicitly commissions research that addresses diversity and inclusion at Dartmouth. Lang and Nacca explore the possibilities of covering social justice content while also building a class around the attempt to decenter authority. Calling attention to the ways that librarians and archivists are underutilized in semester-long instruction, rectifying that underutilization by embedding a librarian for an entire semester, and engaging other experts, Lang and Nacca "draw attention to how authority is constructed" in order to "show how the best research and social action relies on multiple sources of authority and participants who responsibly claim their own." Hardesty,

Kumbier, and Miller use data about zines collections to center communities of zine creators in ways that don't focus solely on individual zinesters and exclude Black, Indigenous, and people of color (BIPOC) creators. Armstrong, Nunes, and Wellnitz center the voices of LGBTQ+ people at Lafayette College inviting students to work toward equity in representation within archives and highlighting how undergraduate work with digital archives can model new progressive pathways for the archives field.

Of course, several of the authors highlight digital archives and projects that go beyond the curriculum to the broader community and attempt to intervene in injustices in society at large. Robinson, Earles, and White consider how archives projects can enhance relationships of HBCUs with the surrounding communities and alumni networks in which they are situated. De Fazio explores how digital scholarship created with his students to document lynchings throughout Virginia addressed gaps within archival records and led to change in the public memorialization of victims. emswiler focuses on the creation of the Inside Books Project archive and the possibilities of using records documenting censorship to trace the carceral logics the Texas prison system produces and sustains, with the hope that teaching using this digital archive can help students imagine a more "just and liberatory future." And in her reflections on the Texas After Violence Project, Field shows us how inviting undergraduate interns to listen closely to oral histories effectively holds space for those who have encountered state-enacted violence and marks an important step toward dismantling unjust systems. These projects demonstrate how the intersection of digital pedagogy and undergraduate work with collections allows us to imagine new, emancipatory paths forward for the archives we create together. We hope this volume opens up new avenues for collaborative endeavors that transform the authority of the archive by centering the values of equity and undergraduate partnership.

NOTES

1 Jarrett Drake, "Seismic Shifts: On Archival Fact and Fictions," ed. Bergis Jules, Architecting Sustainable Futures: Exploring Funding Models in Community-Based Archives, February 2019, 29. Jarrett Drake, "Seismic Shifts: On Archival Fact and Fictions," *Medium*, August 20, 2018, https://medium.com/community-archives/seismic-shifts-on-archival-fact-and-fictions-6db4d5c655ae

2 "What Are Archives?" Society of American Archivists, September 12, 2016, https://www2.archivists.org/about-archives.

3 Michelle Caswell, "'The Archive' Is Not an Archives: On Acknowledging the Intellectual Contributions of Archival Studies," *UCLA*, June 27, 2021, https://escholarship.org/uc/item/7bn4v1fk.

4 Claire Battershill et al., "Building a Critical Digital Archive," in *Scholarly Adventures in Digital Humanities: Making the Modernist Archives Publishing Project*, 1st ed., New Directions in Book History (Cham: Springer International Publishing, 2017), 69–88, https://doi.org/10.1007/978-3-319-47211-9.

5 Ricardo L. Punzalan and Michelle Caswell, "Critical Directions for Archival Approaches to Social Justice," *The Library Quarterly* 86, no. 1 (January 1, 2016): 34, https://doi.org/10.1086/684145.

6 Carbajal, Itza A., and Michelle Caswell, "Critical Digital Archives: A Review from Archival Studies." *The American Historical Review* 126, no. 3 (September 2021): 1102–20, https://doi.org/10.1093/ahr/rhab359.

7 Association of College and Research Libraries, *Cultures of Collecting: Sustaining Diversity, Equity and Inclusion in Collection Development*, 2021, https://www.youtube.com/watch?v=641k-uyndHA.

8 Anne J. Gilliland, *Conceptualizing 21st-Century Archives* (Chicago: Society of American Archivists, 2017), 38.

9 Punzalan and Caswell, "Critical Directions," 28–29.

10 Punzalan and Caswell, "Critical Directions," 25.

11 Punzalan and Caswell, "Critical Directions," 27.

12 Michelle Caswell, Ricardo Punzalan, and T-Kay Sangwand, "Critical Archival Studies: An Introduction," *Journal of Critical Library and Information Studies* 1, no. 2 (June 27, 2017): 1–8.

13 Tonia Sutherland, "Archival Amnesty: In Search of Black American Transitional and Restorative Justice," *Journal of Critical Library and Information Studies* 1, no. 2 (2017), https://journals.litwinbooks.com/index.php/jclis/article/view/42; Lae'l Hughes-Watkins, "Moving Toward a Reparative Archive: A Roadmap for a Holistic Approach to Disrupting Homogenous Histories in Academic

Repositories and Creating Inclusive Spaces for Marginalized Voices," *Journal of Contemporary Archival Studies* 5, no. 1 (May 16, 2018): 19.

14 For examples, see Alex H. Poole, "The Information Work of Community Archives: A Systematic Literature Review," *Journal of Documentation* 76, no. 3 (January 1, 2020): 658, 664; and Krista McCracken, "Community Archival Practice: Indigenous Grassroots Collaboration at the Shingwauk Residential Schools Centre," *The American Archivist* 78, no. 1 (Spring/Summer 2015): 182.

15 Punzalan and Caswell, "Critical Directions," 30.

16 https://medium.com/community-archives.

17 Michelle Caswell, Christopher Harter, and Bergis Jules, "Diversifying the Digital Historical Record: Integrating Community Archives in National Strategies for Access to Digital Cultural Heritage," *D-Lib Magazine* 23, no. 5/6 (May 2017), https://doi.org/10.1045/may2017-caswell.

18 See, for example, Elspeth H. Brown, "Archival Activism, Symbolic Annihilation, and the LGBTQ2+ Community Archive," *Archivaria* 89 (Spring 2020): 6–32, https://muse.jhu.edu/article/755767.

19 Marika Cifor et al., "'What We Do Crosses over to Activism': The Politics and Practice of Community Archives," *The Public Historian* 40 (2018): 70, https://doi.org/10.1525/TPH.2018.40.2.69.

20 Poole, "The Information Work of Community Archives," 659.

21 Poole, "The Information Work of Community Archives," 659.

22 Lauren Haberstock, "Participatory Description: Decolonizing Descriptive Methodologies in Archives," *Archival Science* 20, no. 2 (June 1, 2020): 131-33, https://doi.org/10.1007/s10502-019-09328-6.

23 Catherine D'Ignazio and Lauren Klein, "2. Collect, Analyze, Imagine, Teach," in *Data Feminism* (March 16, 2020). https://data-feminism.mitpress.mit.edu/pub/ei7cogfn/release/4.

24 Kevin Gotkin et al., "Undergraduates in the Archives," *Archive Journal* (blog), 2012, http://www.archivejournal.net/?p=1500.

25 Michelle Caswell, "Teaching to Dismantle White Supremacy in Archives," *The Library Quarterly* 87, no. 3 (July 2017): 222–35, https://doi.org/10.1086/692299; Anne Gilliland, "Neutrality, Social Justice and the Obligations of Archival Education and Educators in the Twenty-First Century," *Archival Science* 11, no. 3 (November 1, 2011): 193–209, https://doi.org/10.1007/s10502-011-9147-0. Michelle Caswell and Anne Gilliland have explored the role of pedagogy in identifying and dismantling oppression and exclusion within archives but this scholarship considers mostly graduate-level pedagogical approaches within Schools of Information. For example, Anne Gilliland reminds us that service-learning courses like those offered at UCLA's School

of Information focus on a social justice curriculum and encourage students to engage with issues related to ethics, diversity, and to dispense with the myth of neutrality. Gilliland argues that in order to maintain the public's trust in archives we need to teach master of science in information systems (MSIS) students:

there is no level-playing field in terms of how the world of records and archives works to support different communities and perspectives. The needs of some communities and individuals whose identities, lives or welfare are implicated with the record will never be equitably addressed without a proactive archival community that many would argue is incompatible with neutrality, but others would argue is the pursuit of social justice. When one considers some of the other characteristics that are also associated with neutrality (detachment, disinterested- ness, non-engagement, non-involvement, non-participation, and non-intervention- ism), where is the line between neutrality and failing to act to counteract negative aspects related to the power of the record or the archive? Whose trust is it that the archival profession is seeking to maintain through its stance of neutrality?

26 Anne Bahde, Heather Smedberg, and Mattie Taormina, eds., *Using Primary Sources: Hands-on Instructional Exercises* (Santa Barbara, CA: Libraries Unlimited, 2014); Eleanor Mitchell, Peggy Seiden, and Suzy Taraba, eds., *Past or Portal? Enhancing Undergraduate Learning through Special Collections and Archives* (Chicago: Association of College & Research Libraries, 2012).

BIBLIOGRAPHY

American Library Association. "Framework for Information Literacy for Higher Education," February 9, 2015, http://www.ala.org/acrl/standards/ilframework.

Association of College and Research Libraries. *Cultures of Collecting: Sustaining Diversity, Equity and Inclusion in Collection Development*, 2021, YouTube video, https://www.youtube.com/watch?v=641k-uyndHA.

Bahde, Anne, Heather Smedberg, and Mattie Taormina, eds. *Using Primary Sources: Hands-on Instructional Exercises*. Santa Barbara, CA: Libraries Unlimited, 2014.

Battershill, Claire, Helen Southworth, Alice Staveley, Michael Widner, Elizabeth Willson Gordon, and Nicola Wilson. "Building a Critical Digital Archive." In *Scholarly Adventures in Digital Humanities: Making the Modernist Archives*

Publishing Project, 1st ed., 69–88. New Directions in Book History. Cham: Springer International Publishing, 2017. https://doi.org/10.1007/978-3-319-47211-9.

Brown, Elspeth H. "Archival Activism, Symbolic Annihilation, and the LGBTQ2+ Community Archive." *Archivaria* 89 (Spring 2020): 6–32.

Carbajal, Itza A., and Michelle Caswell. "Critical Digital Archives: A Review from Archival Studies." *The American Historical Review* 126, no. 3 (September 2021): 1102–20. https://doi.org/10.1093/ahr/rhab359.

Caswell, Michelle. "Teaching to Dismantle White Supremacy in Archives." *The Library Quarterly* 87, no. 3 (July 2017): 222–35. https://doi.org/10.1086/692299.

Caswell, Michelle. "'The Archive' Is Not an Archives: On Acknowledging the Intellectual Contributions of Archival Studies." *Reconstruction: Studies in Contemporary Culture* 16, no. 1 (2016).

Caswell, Michelle, Christopher Harter, and Bergis Jules. "Diversifying the Digital Historical Record: Integrating Community Archives in National Strategies for Access to Digital Cultural Heritage." *D-Lib Magazine* 23, no. 5/6 (May 2017). https://doi.org/10.1045/may2017-caswell.

Caswell, Michelle, Ricardo Punzalan, and T-Kay Sangwand. "Critical Archival Studies: An Introduction." *Journal of Critical Library and Information Studies* 1, no. 2 (June 27, 2017): 1–8.

Cifor, Marika, Michelle Caswell, Alda Allina Migoni, and Noah Geraci. "'What We Do Crosses over to Activism': The Politics and Practice of Community Archives." *The Public Historian* 40 (2018): 69–95. https://doi.org/10.1525/TPH.2018.40.2.69.

D'Ignazio, Catherine, and Lauren Klein. "2. Collect, Analyze, Imagine, Teach," in *Data Feminism*. Cambridge, MA: MIT Press, 2020. https://data-feminism.mitpress.mit.edu/pub/ei7cogfn/release/4.

Drake, Jarrett, "Seismic Shifts: On Archival Fact and Fictions," *Medium*, August 20, 2018, https://medium.com/community-archives/seismic-shifts-on-archival-fact-and-fictions-6db4d5c655ae

Gilliland, Anne J. *Conceptualizing 21st-Century Archives*. Chicago: Society of American Archivists, 2017.

Gilliland, Anne J. "Neutrality, Social Justice and the Obligations of Archival Education and Educators in the Twenty-First Century." *Archival Science* 11, no. 3 (November 1, 2011): 193–209. https://doi.org/10.1007/s10502-011-9147-0.

Gotkin, Kevin, Benjamin Hebblethwaite, Timothy B. Powell, Suzy Taraba, and Sarah Werner. "Undergraduates in the Archives." *Archive Journal* (blog), 2012. http://www.archivejournal.net/?p=1500.

Haberstock, Lauren. "Participatory Description: Decolonizing Descriptive Methodologies in Archives." *Archival Science* 20, no. 2 (June 1, 2020): 125–38. https://doi.org/10.1007/s10502-019-09328-6.

Hughes-Watkins, Lae'l. "Moving Toward a Reparative Archive: A Roadmap for a Holistic Approach to Disrupting Homogenous Histories in Academic Repositories and Creating Inclusive Spaces for Marginalized Voices." *Journal of Contemporary Archival Studies* 5, no. 1 (May 16, 2018). https://elischolar.library.yale.edu/cgi/viewcontent.cgi?article=1045&context=jcas.

McCracken, Krista. "Community Archival Practice: Indigenous Grassroots Collaboration at the Shingwauk Residential Schools Centre." *The American Archivist* 78, no. 1 (Spring/Summer 2015): 181–91.

Mitchell, Eleanor, Peggy Seiden, and Suzy Taraba, eds. *Past or Portal? Enhancing Undergraduate Learning Through Special Collections and Archives.* Chicago: Association of College and Research Libraries, 2012.

Poole, Alex H. "The Information Work of Community Archives: A Systematic Literature Review." *Journal of Documentation* 76, no. 3 (January 1, 2020): 657–87. https://doi.org/10.1108/JD-07-2019-0140.

Punzalan, Ricardo L., and Michelle Caswell. "Critical Directions for Archival Approaches to Social Justice." *The Library Quarterly* 86, no. 1 (January 1, 2016): 25–42. https://doi.org/10.1086/684145.

Sutherland, Tonia. "Archival Amnesty: In Search of Black American Transitional and Restorative Justice." *Journal of Critical Library and Information Studies* 1, no. 2 (2017). https://journals.litwinbooks.com/index.php/jclis/article/view/42.

Society of American Archivists. "What Are Archives?" September 12, 2016. https://www2.archivists.org/about-archives.

PART I

ARCHIVES AND TRAUMA

CHAPTER ONE

THE ETHICS OF TEACHING UNDERGRADUATES USING DIGITAL ARCHIVES

Hannah Alpert-Abrams and Andi Gustavson

WHY ETHICS

A colleague of ours who works in special collections recently described conducting a one-hour presentation for undergraduate students. The class was focused on the history of colonialism in the Caribbean, and so he had selected a number of documents that were relevant to the topic: historical maps of the region, diagrams and texts related to the sugar trade, and documents about slavery and emancipation. Among the objects he chose was a political cartoon that relied on a racist caricature to represent an enslaved woman. The moment he came to that image in his presentation, he realized he had made a mistake. Rather than providing a window on a history of violence and enslavement, he realized he had reinforced stereotypes and committed violence against the Black students in the class. He felt terrible, he said, but he also didn't know what he could have done differently. Eliding the histories of violence studied by the class and evidenced in the collection did not feel ethical either. Wouldn't excluding these documents be even worse?

When teaching with primary sources, we confront ethical dilemmas as we teach histories of violence, engage with our own biases, and make private information public. Digitizing primary sources does not change this fact, though the distancing effect of the screen may make us feel less complicit in violence and trauma. Digitization can also introduce new ethical dilemmas as we engage with decontextualized records or put documents online. Our goal when teaching with primary sources may be to transform the authority of the archive by disassembling structures of white supremacy, capitalism, and colonialism. As we use digitized sources to diversify, decolonize, and educate, however, we often run the risk of doing more harm than good. Nevertheless, as almost all authors writing about the subject emphasize, fear of making a mistake is no excuse for avoiding teaching contentious subjects, working with histories of violence, and engaging with the troubled pasts of libraries and archives. As Michelle Caswell writes, we must all teach to dismantle white supremacy in the archives.[1]

In this chapter, we review three circumstances under which we see particularly challenging ethical dilemmas arise: teaching histories of trauma with digital archives, teaching the absences in digital archives, and teaching students to build digital archives. In each case, we survey the approaches that we have seen for teaching within these challenging conditions, focusing on those that are relevant to a digital context. We seek to address the specific contexts in which we see these circumstances unfold for archives and libraries: in individually taught or co-taught semester-long classes, in guest instruction within a semester-long class, in one-off workshops and public events, and in digital humanities projects co-developed with faculty and students. We acknowledge that librarians and archivists may have any number of positions within this framework: they may be the people experiencing trauma or those putting vulnerable people at risk; they may be speaking for marginalized communities of which they are a member, or introducing students to histories about which they know very little. We cannot encompass all of these positionalities, but we hope to address many of them here.

The reflections we offer here are by necessity informed by our own backgrounds. We have both worked in libraries and special collections associated with well-resourced public and private research institutions, including the University of Texas and Brown University. We have taught with digitized special collections in a variety of roles, both as classroom instructors and as representatives of collecting institutions. We have both taught with materials that document violence, including records of war, of police brutality, of political oppression, and of domestic violence. We have served as instructors while also being students, contingent workers, and permanent staff. We are both cis-gendered abled white women.

In thinking about the ethics of teaching with digitized primary sources, we follow the work of scholars working in critical library, archives, and information studies who call for a more relational and reciprocal approach to information access. Michelle Caswell and Marika Cifor's framework of radical empathy, for example, positions archival workers in relation to the creators, subjects, users, and communities associated with archival collections.[2] This model calls on archivists to be attentive to the affective experiences of these individuals as we facilitate preservation, organization, and access to a collection. In practice, this work can range from inviting community members into preservation or planning meetings to providing tissues in the reading room for users who might be moved to tears by the content of a collection. These practices, however, are made complicated by the context of teaching with digital materials. Sometimes this is because of the limited time that many instructors have when working with students—a one-hour session, for example, rather than a full semester. Other times, it is because digital pedagogy introduces distance between students, users, and collections, decentering human interactions by way of the screen.

It can often feel, in fact, like our ability to fulfill these obligations and act ethically as instructors in digital spaces is limited by the ways that, in the digital sphere, what we build or teach can move beyond what we can control. As archivists and librarians, we may build a digital archive with the intent to teach it, but might not be present when our pedagogical resources are engaged by others. We run the risk that other educators or audiences will use these digital archives differently than we intended. As instructors, we may teach with digital archives that were created by others, and unintentionally expose our students to primary sources that they are unequipped to interpret or that may cause them harm. We run the risk that we are using others' digital archives differently than we or they might have intended. Finally, we may teach students to create digital archives, turning their learning experiences into public record and potentially exposing the creators of the primary sources to further harm. We run the risk that we are creating digital archives that could unintentionally harm the creators of the records and publicly involve our students in those acts of harm. All of these feelings of risk arise out of a sense that we, as educators, may need to give up some control over the digital archives that we create, teach, and teach our students to create.

This fear over loss of control of digital archives rests on the tension between a sense of responsibility for the impact of racist, violent, or oppressive materials, and the need to cultivate a level of comfort with downstream uses for the digital content we place online. While most instructors do not wish to cause further harm by placing difficult content into digital spaces, we also do not wish to avoid teaching difficult histories out of fear that others might use the content in ways that don't align with our pedagogical goals. There is no way around the tension between these two impulses. We find that the best way forward is to acknowledge with our students that these ideas are in conflict with one another and to guide them, with care, through their own grapplings with them.

Operating as teachers from this place of tension requires that we shift how we understand our relationship to both the materials we steward and the users we instruct. We both were trained in the "show and tell" model of primary source education. This approach, in which students are given limited access to highly curated selections of primary sources, positions the instructor as a gatekeeper who facilitates not only the ways students engage with physical or digital materials, but also how they engage intellectually with complex collections. This model aligns with the priorities of highly-resourced institutions that have historically viewed gatekeeping as a mechanism for maintaining prestige. It also aligns with the workings of white supremacy, which operate in the archive by silencing, erasing, and miscategorizing historical records that conflict with dominant narratives.

Critical library and information studies scholarship, the "archival turn" in literary and cultural studies, and many significant publications in primary source pedagogy have pushed the field far beyond show and tell.[3] For those educators who may have moved beyond show and tell, there are still many pedagogical practices for teaching primary source literacy that attempt to tightly manage students' engagement. These practices include relying too heavily on the content expertise of the educator, curating the items in the classroom or online so that a single interpretive narrative is intended, and prioritizing a setup of physical objects or an online arrangement that separates primary sources from their archival contexts. In many cases, the impulse to rely on teaching practices that rigidly structure the parameters of student engagement or control information comes from a position of privilege.

In the reading room, archivists and librarians have been working hard to dismantle these rigid structures and the fears that inform them. When we turn to digital archives and pedagogy, however, the impulse to control information circulation when teaching resurfaces. As we learn more about the ethical complexities of working with digital materials, including the very real reasons that information should be controlled online, it can be tempting to return to this impulse to control and limit access to historical documents. In thinking about our ethical obligations as primary source instructors working in a digital space, we try instead to focus on empowering students to make responsible decisions as they engage with materials and information structures. This may mean repositioning ourselves as educators of information systems, rather than as curators of information resources. It may also mean carrying this repositioning over into the digital space as we design—or help our students to design—digital resources. When working as educators in the digital space, our goal is to create the conditions that will allow us to trust students to bring their best and most inquisitive selves to bear on the primary source materials they are engaging.

TEACHING HISTORIES OF TRAUMA WITH DIGITAL ARCHIVES

When teaching with records of trauma, instructors must consider their obligation to prevent additional traumatization or violence. While it might be tempting to teach with or digitize horrifying images, such as photographs of lynchings or records of police violence, we should be aware that those images may produce trauma in certain members of the public. We should also be sensitive to the possibility that, once these images are digitized, they can be used for purposes that are beyond our control. In one case, we have seen newspapers use images of violence to illustrate articles about our work, decontextualizing and sensationalizing images that we worked hard to put in context. In another case, images from a collection were used by an organization promoting white supremacy. We must be aware that these possibilities exist when working with students to digitize collections. In some cases, the best choice is not to work with digital documents at all.

The first time I (Hannah) was confronted with the complexities of teaching with digitized primary sources representing histories of violence occurred when I was the project manager for the Guatemalan Historical Archive of the National Police, a digital collection that represents an important and under-acknowledged aspect of US and Central American history. Outreach with the collection was an urgent element of my responsibilities as project manager, and the first thing I did was to develop web-based teaching resources that could be used by myself and by other instructors teaching with the collection. I built a self-driven workshop in Scalar, a web-based publishing platform, which was designed to teach basic archival navigation skills while helping students understand some of the archive's history and the kinds of information it contained.

Developing a teaching resource for the police archive was challenging for many reasons: the collection is enormous, its organizational structure is complex, and the material is written largely in the technical Spanish of a government bureaucracy. US-based students, many of whom may not be familiar with written Spanish, have to learn to see through the collection in order to find meaning in the materials. But the first time I taught with the Scalar workshop I realized that I had underestimated the potentially traumatic impact of working with this collection. Though the histories the archive recorded were distant in time and space, some of the students in the classroom had personal experience with police violence, while others had families directly impacted by state violence in Guatemala. The students were unprepared for the traumatic histories that were revealed, and I had not foreseen this personal and emotional response to the records. This experience had the potential of derailing my lesson plan through the inadvertent retraumatization, secondary traumatization, or wholly new traumatization of the students I was working with.[4] In this section, we consider how instructors can minimize these risks when teaching with digitized collections relating to histories of violence.

Among scholars writing about libraries and archives, discussions of teaching histories of violence have largely centered on relationships: among the people represented by collections, the people facilitating access to the collections, and the people using the collections. Caswell and Cifor, writing about archival practice, call for a shift from individual rights to a "feminist ethics of care," which involves taking account of a creator's wishes in providing access to a document; developing a participant model of co-creatorship; understanding that users may be emotionally connected to an archive's content; or thinking about the "unseen others" who might be impacted by the curation of a collection.[5] Similarly, in the context of information literacy librarianship, Jessie Loyer uses the nêhiyaw (Cree) and Michif (Métis) law of *wâhkôhtowin*, which Loyer defines as reciprocal relationality, to "account for the relational accountability between librarians and students in dealing with traumatic research."[6] This approach to teaching information literacy builds on the premise that for Indigenous students, research is often a process of retraumatization. Following author Zoe Todd, Loyer argues for focusing on radical love as a mechanism for creating student capacity for self-care in the face of traumatizing institutions.[7]

While these approaches stem from different epistemological frameworks, they both place human interaction at the center of the research experience. Indeed, in the case of the police archive described at the beginning of this section, human interaction and individualized care was central to how the Guatemalan archivists mediated interaction with the material: the archive went so far as to have social workers on staff who would be present during each research session in order to help community members process their experience with traumatic content. With the digital archive, we sought to replicate the research experience of the Guatemalan space. But how do we maintain this human-centered approach to teaching undergraduates with primary sources in a digital context?

To answer this question, we turn to the concept of trauma-informed pedagogy, which seeks "to understand how violence, victimization, and other traumatic experiences may have figured in the lives of the individuals involved and to apply that understanding to the provision of services and the design of systems so that they accommodate the needs and vulnerabilities of trauma survivors."[8] In their practice-oriented scholarship on implementing trauma-informed pedagogy, Carello and Butler identify five conditions that are necessary for a trauma-informed teaching environment: ensuring safety, establishing trustworthiness, maximizing choice, maximizing collaboration, and prioritizing empowerment.[9] In what follows, we use their framework for implementation alongside the concept of an "ethics of care" and wâhkôhtowin in order to consider how to apply trauma-informed pedagogy to the context of teaching with digital primary sources.

Preview material

Prior to teaching with a collection, it is necessary for instructors to familiarize themselves with the material and its potentially traumatic content. To do this in a digital space may involve thinking critically about how the content is framed by the digital infrastructure. It may also involve identifying traumatic histories even when they have been actively decentered from a collection, like domestic violence in the correspondence of a celebrated novelist, or racism in the writings of a political leader. When teaching a session on queer book history, for example, I (Hannah) found myself teaching with a collection that both silenced queer identities and used homophobic terminology in the online catalog. I made the collection's structure central to my lesson plan to help students recognize and understand the context for the violent language in the collection. If you are developing a digital teaching resource, you might also develop documentation for instructors that guides them in previewing the collection, identifying potentially traumatic content, and offering context that can help them teach with the material more responsibly. In this case, the challenge is empowering instructors you may never meet to think relationally about their work when they teach the materials you have provided.

Develop content warnings

Content warnings, more popularly referred to as trigger warnings, should accomplish three tasks: they should give students a preview of the traumatic content, its severity, and the extent to which students may be asked to engage with the content. In revising teaching materials associated with the Guatemalan police archive, for example, I added content warnings to an exercise that had students browsing a large collection of records and to an exercise that worked with a specific record. In the first case, the warning alerted students to the range of potentially traumatic content that might appear, usually in the form of a single sentence written in technical language. In the second case, where violence was described in more detail and some violent images were included, the warning specified the kinds of images that would appear. The content warnings appeared on landing pages long before the students arrived at the collection itself. My goal was to affirm the diverse experiences that students might have when engaging with the collection, to help them prepare emotionally for the experience they were about to have, and to empower them to make an informed decision about how they would engage with the project.

Check in

Carello and Butler advise instructors to check in with students about how they are feeling throughout the course of a lesson that touches on traumatic content. This reaffirms the importance of radical empathy built on long-term trusting relationships between instructors and students; it also highlights the difficulties of creating those experiences in a short-term session or a digital environment. Even when teaching a single session, we invite instructors to center vulnerability and emotional honesty when working with students. Library and Information Studies (LIS) scholars have begun to trace the impact of secondary trauma in archivists and trauma-informed approaches to working in archives in ways that we can extend to the classroom and traumatic content.[10]

But we also wonder what it might look like to build this into a digital workshop or teaching-centered repository. Is there a way to design an interface that invites self-reflection and vulnerability? In the Guatemalan police archive workshop, which was a sequential lesson, each section ends with an opportunity for students to reflect not only on the content they engaged with, but also with how they felt about the experience. In a repository, this would be more difficult, but not impossible. We can imagine, for example, embedding short videos where researchers and others reflect on their experiences working with the collection. Or an interactive space for students to share their feelings. Even a few reflection questions that accompany a collection can help students to process their experiences.

Self-direction

Giving students the ability to decide when and how they will engage with traumatic material empowers them to take control of their learning experience. This can mean restructuring a lesson to decenter even the content. For example, the day after the 2016 presidential election I (Andi) was scheduled to teach a class about the Harlem Renaissance. I had planned to include materials related to Nancy Cunard, a white modernist author who compiled an anthology on Black artists and received hate mail for her relationship with Henry Crowder, a Black jazz musician. The hate mail is full of threats of violence and racist slurs and I didn't feel comfortable staging it in the room. I also did not want to elide that hateful history. The faculty member and I decided to keep the hate mail in the room, in its box and folder, on a cart, and off to the side. We let the students know about it, told them why we weren't displaying it, and contextualized it relative to both the Harlem Renaissance and to the current election and white supremacy. We also invited the students to return on their own to consult it in the reading room if they wanted to study it and if they felt prepared to grapple with such racist content.

It's easier to move a box to the side of the room than it is to restructure a digital repository in the face of political events. But we can imagine building responsive interfaces that allow students more self-direction in engaging with racist content and other traumatic materials. A click-through content warning that invites students to stop and reflect before entering a specific sub-collection, for example, might introduce that same visual experience. Particularly violent materials might also be relegated to a password-protected sub-collection that, again, empowered users to make decisions in the ways they engage with content. In the case of the Guatemalan archive, teaching modules offered different levels of engagement with traumatic content; a revision of that workshop might offer alternate tasks for those wary of grappling with certain aspects of the history. There are many ways for students to meet our learning goals, and our aim should be to empower them to choose how they engage with the content and what kind of emotional experience they are equipped to have.

Talk about feelings

When instructors acknowledge, normalize, and discuss feelings of fear, anger, despair, disgust, and hopelessness, including their own feelings, it can help students process their own response.[11] In the classroom, this is another opportunity for reciprocal relationality. Instructors should be careful to share their experiences without centering themselves, particularly if they are not themselves of a community that shares this traumatic history. Furthermore, if students are asked to share their responses, caution should be used in avoiding scenarios where students feel forced to discuss personal histories.

How do we talk about feelings in a digital environment? We find that this is difficult work, and while efforts have been made to describe what this might look like, few have been successful in implementation. We can imagine video interviews, testimonials, and other content that could be built into a repository to accompany a difficult collection, but these may be labor-intensive and introduce additional questions about the ethics of surveillance and privacy. And yet, as we talk and write about trauma-informed pedagogy in digital environments, talking about feelings has come to feel like the most important task. To create a digital pedagogical environment that is human, affirming, empathetic, and caring—to fulfill the obligations articulated by Caswell, Cifor, and Loyer—may ultimately require a rethinking of how digital repositories are designed, how teaching collections are structured, and how lesson plans are created. We look forward to a digital infrastructure that reflects the pedagogical shift toward human-centered design.

TEACHING THE ABSENCES IN DIGITAL ARCHIVES

Our ethical responsibilities in digital collections extend far beyond providing content warnings for only the most violent material. Even when working with collections that do not specifically document trauma, we may nonetheless be teaching materials that reflect histories of oppression stewarded by physical or digital archives that are, themselves, implicated in structures of oppression. Following the American Library Association Guidelines for Primary Source Literacy, we need to help our students "identify, interrogate, and consider the reasons for silences, gaps, contradictions, or evidence of power relationships in the documentary record and how they impact the research process."[12] This work involves being explicit about the daily ways that violence takes place in people's lives and is reflected in the archival record. It also involves helping students see the places where absences exist, interrogate the reasons for those absences, and consider their role in replicating absence when they create digital archives. Here, we offer six principles for teaching absences in the digital archive.

Make power relationships evident

When teaching with digital primary sources, we need to help students see the evidence of power relationships in the institutions within which they encounter those materials. Archives and libraries have often been sites of colonialism and white supremacy, and many of the structures on which our institutions are based reflect that violence. Expressly asking students both to consider the structures framing their engagement with primary sources and to do comparative work between repositories that are addressing these questions in different ways (or not at all) can serve as a starting point for conversations about decolonizing and dismantling white supremacy in the archive.[13] Digitization, in contrast, promises to democratize access, but we must be thoughtful of how it inscribes new forms of authority and creates new barriers to access. For example, violence is present in the language we use to describe collections in finding aids and catalogues, and the structures according to which we organize information; these words and structures are often transferred directly into the digital sphere. We encourage students to extend their analyses beyond the materials themselves to the archival records, repositories, and digital infrastructures that are framing their engagements with the primary sources.

One space where power relations are particularly evident is in the metadata used to describe historical records. Finding aids and catalog records often preserve outdated language that can be experienced as violent, from the misgendering of a historical figure to the use of antiquated subject headings that are now understood to be racist or homophobic.[14] Records written in Indigenous languages, similarly, are almost always presented first through a colonizing language like English, Spanish, or French. Instructors reduce the harm caused by these interfaces by alerting students to their presence and inviting discussion about the historical context of their creation and the reasons they have not been changed (a discussion that might address the professional organizations framing archival practices, the ideologies that underpin conversations about national standards, the role of institutional power in delimiting nationwide standards, and the activism of people working to effect change in these areas).[15] At the same time, when creating digital records with students, instructors might invite their students to develop a more liberatory vocabulary.

Be transparent about archival practices

One way to help students think about the power relationships evident in institutions is to highlight all the work involved in creating and maintaining archives. Expose students to the many decisions that inform our work, making clear that these are places where professional practice intersects with personal decisions and so are spaces where individuals have agency. Expressly discuss collection development policies, acquisition agreements, and deaccessioning guidelines. Highlight decisions about conservation, preservation, access, and funding. When teaching finding aids, databases, or digital archives, point out that there are professional associations that suggest standards for our work but also that these resources were created by real people at a particular point in the recent past with their own identities and biases. Where possible, point out the names of the archivists and the dates they processed the collections, share codes of ethics and professional guidelines, link to professional associations, and use all of these tools to facilitate discussions about the people creating collecting practices that can create silences.

Students often are unaware that collections are not comprehensive, and the scope of a collection can be even more difficult to comprehend in a digital space. The creators of digital archives can make those silences visible through visualization techniques, as Lauren Klein demonstrates by reworking the Thomas Jefferson archives to draw attention to the presence (and absence) of the enslaved Hemmings family.[16] Instructors, meanwhile, can teach students about these limitations by speaking about acquisition practices or developing exercises that invite students to interpret those practices and gaps for themselves.[17]

Teach absence

The organization of our collections rests on cultural biases and creates silences within the cultural record that we want to make explicit when we teach with them. Organizing materials in terms of a single author, for example, tends to preserve people of privilege while erasing other figures from the record. Enslaved and Indigenous people, in particular, may disappear under these kinds of metadata. So might all victims of state violence: as Kirsten Weld writes, archives of the state can preserve the logic of surveillance, social control, and ideological management, forcing us to view citizens first through a criminal lens.[18] Without awareness of these pitfalls, students might think that alternate stories cannot be told or that other kinds of histories do not matter. Digital archives can also create opportunities for students to identify and bring visibility to silenced voices. Projects like "Digital Aponte," which is a digital collection based on a book that has been lost, show how digital spaces can respond to archival absences.[19] Lessons around digital archives might invite students to participate in this kind of restructuring of archival information.

Teaching absence within digital archives requires facilitating discussion about people's identities and the historical and present-day oppression that has an effect on people's lives and the records within collections. Teach intersectionality and select primary sources with inclusivity in mind. Help students build connections and ask questions about gender, sexuality, race, ethnicity, class, religion, ability, and local, regional, and national identities. As Lovisa Brown et al. write in the context of culturally-specific museums, all cultural institutions have an obligation to foster open dialogues about identity.[20] And, as Jasmine Lelis Clark writes, "if you aren't seeing something horrific or problematic, you're seeing revisionism."[21] Especially in a context where libraries, archives, and collections are predominantly white institutions, we have a responsibility to ensure that all communities do not feel erased by the archive.[22]

Intervene to prevent harm

When we teach using digital archives, there are also likely to be moments when we need to respond to comments from our students that enact further harm. Most often, these comments are offered without the intent to harm. Students may be new to discussing hate or oppression, or they may be stumbling as they talk about identities and histories that do not align with their own. We want the classroom to be a space where learning can occur—and this means that we want it to be a space where it is safe to make these kinds of mistakes. But we also need it to be safe for our students who might share some of the identities or experiences being discussed.

When participants come to a session with harmful ideas and minimal preparation, it can be difficult to foster meaningful discussion. This becomes more challenging when students unexpectedly introduce racist, sexist, or ableist thought into a conversation.

Set the parameters for discussions about digital archives at the beginning of the class by reminding students that 1) some topics touch on personal experiences for people in our class; 2) all of us will make missteps—including the instructor; 3) when missteps occur, if it feels safe for you to do so, then please help us learn; and 4) helping us through those moments is part of your job as the instructor. Then, when we encounter moments that could cause harm, it is important to model rephrasing of outdated or oppressive terms, help students contextualize their comments, and gently but immediately interrupt and assist if a line of discussion is likely to cause harm.

End unproductive teaching collaborations

In the library and archives context, we often are partnering with faculty members in instruction sessions. In some cases, faculty can be our allies in preparing students for the conversation, providing historical context, and giving students the language with which to discuss these topics. In other cases, they may be disinterested or even antagonistic toward these conversations. We are not always in a position to contest this on our own, but our institutions can establish expectations for faculty who are bringing students into this environment, set standards for preparing students for difficult conversations, and provide preparatory materials. When a faculty member repeatedly brings classes that are not prepared for the material or for the conversation, we suggest ending that collaborative relationship rather than teaching in ways that do not align with ethical practices.[23]

Invite students to grapple with ethical decision-making

Recognize with your students that histories are complex and we will likely make some missteps, and then encourage students to make the best decisions they can with this complexity in mind. Brown et al. suggest inviting people to add their voices to complex interpretations, handing the challenge of making museum or archival decisions to the visitors—here students—themselves.[24] Students can be involved, for example, in the decision of whether or not to include disturbing images or texts in the digital archives that they create as part of class assignments. These are helpful strategies for inviting students into the process of interpreting the past. We need to teach carefully, however, when we extend these approaches to the ethical work of building digital archives. We want to invite our students to take ownership of their interpretations, but we never want to suggest that there are many sides to histories of hate and violence. We want to recognize that these histories are complex, but we never want to let those layers of complexity prevent us from taking a stance. Teaching students to build an argument about history—especially if they are placing those arguments online—requires recognizing that historical narratives should not be reduced to platitudes about multiple perspectives or complexity.

TEACHING STUDENTS TO BUILD DIGITAL ARCHIVES

One extraordinary opportunity introduced by teaching with digital primary sources is the ability not just to teach students to think critically about the collection, classification, and presentation of historical records, but also to work with them to rebuild those structures in ways that correct for some of the mistakes of the past. Here we can learn from library and information science pedagogy, which has prioritized integrating archival theory with practice for some time, as well as from digital humanities pedagogy, which has focused on building and making in the undergraduate classroom.[25] Teaching students to build digital archives requires embedding ethical questions around privacy, representation, and access into the construction of digital projects that are built for or with students. As in previous sections, we recommend making these questions central to the way these projects are constructed and instructed, allowing student users of digitized primary sources to take ownership (with guidance) of decision-making around the ethical complexity of creating historical memory online.

For example, in one course on digital archives that I (Hannah) co-taught with a faculty instructor, students were asked to work together to write a lib-guide to Indigenous studies materials in one of the collections on our campus. The goal of the assignment was to invite students to help correct for the absence of resources on Indigenous materials in the collection. But as the project unfolded, we encountered a number of challenges. The students decided that they wanted to include scanned images of documents online, but they were unfamiliar with community protocols for image sharing. They were motivated by the possibility of creating real impact for researchers, but were uncertain about the consequences of putting their names, and their work, online. As their vision for the project expanded, we also began to think seriously about access and accessibility: about who the project was for, and about how to ensure that those audiences could engage with the resource meaningfully. This led us to think through the different kinds of engagement that a student researcher, faculty researcher, and community member might have with a digital project, as well as the expectations that the project set around access to technology and visual ability. Based on assignments like this, we propose three principles for working with students to responsibly design digital archives, collections, or exhibitions.

Don't put everything online

Radical empathy in the digital archive means thinking about our responsibilities to the content creators as well as the users of digitized sources. We often think of this obligation as one of legal responsibility: the confusing challenge of understanding and following copyright law, as well as the agreements an archive may have made during the acquisition of a collection.[26] But in some cases, our responsibilities may extend far beyond the limits of the law. For example, a content creator who gave permission for researchers to visit their papers in an archive may not have foreseen the much greater scale of circulation and access that accompanies digitization.

One case where we have encountered this problem is when working with ethnographic records, especially documentation of Indigenous life made by non-Indigenous researchers. Even if the researchers followed appropriate protocols in getting consent to record oral histories or take photographs, that consent may not extend to the digital space. The same might be true in the context of records that contain personal information about an individual that was not public knowledge during their life. Erin Baucom, for example, writes about digitizing records of LGBTQ activists whose sexual identities were often hidden during their lifetimes.[27] Those individuals may not have been involved in the decision to preserve their histories, never mind the decision to put them online. In these cases, we have to think about our obligation to that person's public legacy, but also to their surviving family and friends. Minimizing harm may mean consulting with communities or individuals whose records are contained within the collection as part of a digitization workflow, as well as introducing students to this practice.

In the cases of cultural heritage, legal protections often fail to adhere to the cultural expectations of Indigenous communities in particular. Jane Anderson and Kim Christen have written extensively about Indigenous cultural expectations in the context of digital archives, and argued for a more thoughtful and attentive approach to the digitization of cultural heritage.[28] When digitizing or working with Indigenous records, instructors should be sensitive to these contexts. One way to ensure that we are not violating cultural expectations is to work with collections that have been uploaded to a Mukurtu repository, which enables more complex accessibility strategies.[29] Another is to work with collections that have traditional knowledge (TK) labels, such as the Ancestral Voices collection hosted by the Library of Congress.[30] These labels function like copyright to provide guidelines on appropriate use; while they do not have legal standing, they are assigned through collaboration with affiliated tribes and reflect the tribes' wishes for the reuse of digital instances of their cultural heritage.

In other cases, minimizing harm may mean inviting students to help imagine the shape of a digital project that can engage with the ethics of digital distribution without putting anyone's privacy at risk. Most importantly, in some cases it may mean choosing not to put documents online. While we encourage instructors who are working with students to build digital collections to include students in the decision-making process, it is important to be prepared to protect the privacy of a community or individual when necessary.

Prioritize discussions of privacy

We face two kinds of concerns when considering privacy in the digital archive: the privacy of our students and the privacy of the people whose lives are preserved in the collections.

When putting student work online, we have to balance our desire to provide credit and compensation with a student's right to privacy and to make mistakes in the process of learning. When it comes to credit and compensation, we follow the Student Collaborators' Bill of Rights, a coauthored document published by the UCLA Digital Humanities program.[31] While we encourage those intending to publish student work online to review the document in full, the main argument is that students deserve to be fully aware of the potential consequences of publishing online, to be given the option to opt out of publishing online, to be given credit for their work, and to be compensated appropriately. These guidelines are intended to protect students from exploitation, and also to protect them from the potential dangers of participating in public discourse. Instructors, too, should be aware of those dangers, especially when asking students to participate in work relating to contentious or personal topics.

When thinking about student privacy, we want to consider assignments or activities that ask students to participate in the digital interface of a collection, by writing blog posts, being photographed, creating curated collections, and so on.[32] An additional concern, especially when dealing with issues related to intersectional identities, are activities that encourage students to claim identities in public and digital spaces. Activities designed to help students develop an empathetic relationship with historical events might force them to reveal information that they may have preferred to keep private.[33] We should be cautious about this in general, but in a digital environment, this can have far-reaching consequences. In general, if you are working with students on a project that deals with politically or socially volatile issues, you should avoid asking students to provide any personal information online, require that students use identifiers not associated with their names, and credit all student contributors in ways that do not link them individually to specific parts of a project.

When teaching students to protect privacy within archival records, we are concerned with questions of the privacy of individual creators, heritage, and violence. There are legal protections of personal privacy when a collection contains medical information or when an acquisition contract includes stipulations about privacy, for example. Even when there are no legal regulations, however, we should be wary of working with online records that provide intimate details about individuals who have not given informed consent for those details to be put online.[34] Sara Trotta describes the case of an individual who appeared in an LGBTQ collection under a pseudonym, but whose real name was linked in the metadata. In this case, the individual was effectively 'outed' online; they were able to request that the identifying details be removed, but that is not always possible.[35] Given that we are not always able to retroactively get consent, we have to make guesses about ethical behavior. These choices can be opportunities for learning with our students as well, as they make a collective determination about working with a set of documents.

Center accessibility

When teaching students to build digital projects with primary sources, we must think broadly about who we want to access the records and how we can ensure that our digital platforms enable that access. This may include access for blind or visually impaired students, for students who do not speak English, for students who do not have advanced digital hardware or software, and for students who do not have fast and reliable internet, among many other barriers to access. Designing classes to be accessible to these students is both federal law and ethical practice, and we have an obligation to incorporate it into our work with digital collections.[36]

Similarly, when we are working with our students to create digital archives, we must encourage them to build in ways that are accessible. This means being knowledgeable about and complying with the regulations set forth by the Americans with Disabilities Act, but also thinking holistically about the kinds of engagement we hope to enable through our collections. Factors to consider when evaluating a digital collection include whether the records have been transcribed and described, whether the site's colors contrast effectively, and whether hyperlinks and images include descriptions, among many other design features.[37]

We recommend embedding accessibility training alongside transcription and metadata as a fundamental aspect of learning to work with digital primary sources. When working with already digitized records, online testing can be a useful preliminary step before introducing a class to a digital collection. Be prepared to offer alternative assignments in the case that a student is unable to work with the collection you have chosen. Teach students working with multilingual documents to consider the language of the documents, the metadata, and the web platform. If creating a platform for non-Anglophone documents, it is recommended that the platform have multilingual metadata and a multilingual interface in order to ensure access by affiliated communities. When teaching students to create digital collections, consider how hardware and internet infrastructure can also introduce barriers to access. Ensure materials can be accessed and used on a cell phone or make sure that all students have access to computers outside of class. When building digital collections, lightweight platforms that work off-line or with intermittent wifi, and on cell phones as well as computers, should be the goal. The guidelines provided by the Minimal Computing community can serve as a useful resource.[38]

CONCLUSION

In this chapter, we have sought to identify some key areas where ethical questions arise when teaching with digitized primary sources, as well as to articulate some principles that can help instructors think with their students about the complexity of working with the historical record online. While the instructional frameworks included here are not intended to be definitive, we hope this will serve as a practical resource for instructors, and as a starting point for ongoing conversations about teaching online.

This chapter developed out of our work writing "Teaching with Digital Primary Sources: Literacies, Finding and Evaluating, Citing, Ethics, and Existing Models," a white paper published by the Digital Library Federation's working group on teaching with digital primary sources.[39] In the years since we began that project, the coronavirus pandemic has radically changed the use of digitized sources in libraries, archives, special collections, and college campuses. As instructors rush to adapt to the new online learning environment, thoughtful attention to digital context and its complications is more necessary than ever. While we hope to return to the classroom and the reading room soon, we don't expect that these challenges will be going away.

It is in the context of rapidly increasing use of digitized content that we return to the central principle of this article. The classroom is one space where the authority of the archive can be questioned and transformed. We find that facilitating responsible student engagement with digitized primary sources requires empowering students to take ownership of the ethical questions at the heart of digital research. This is most effective when students consider themselves to be active participants in a community that includes the many writers, users, and practitioners involved in creating and providing access to a historical record. This carries with it a responsibility to do right by the various people whose histories and labor are at stake, including the students themselves. It is then our job as instructors to equip students to think critically about questions of access, representation, violence, trauma, and care. In this way, we must make deliberate choices to minimize harm and maximize opportunities to teach and to heal within our communities.

This work is not easy and this chapter is far from comprehensive. There remain many conversations to have about the nuanced responsibilities that accompany various kinds of infrastructure and interface, historical documents and community representation, descriptive metadata and instructional design. In particular, there is a need to address more thoroughly the distinctions between digitized primary sources and the born-digital sources that are becoming more common in the twenty-first century. We invite ongoing discussion of these topics and the challenges of approaching them responsibly.

NOTES

1 Michelle Caswell, "Teaching to Dismantle White Supremacy in Archives," *The Library Quarterly* 87, no. 3 (July 2017): 222–35, https://doi.org/10.1086/692299.

2 Michelle Caswell and Marika Cifor, "From Human Rights to Feminist Ethics: Radical Empathy in the Archives," *Archivaria* 81 (May 6, 2016): 23–43.

3 For more on this see Anne Bahde, Heather Smedberg, and Mattie Taormina, eds., *Using Primary Sources: Hands-on Instructional Exercises* (Santa Barbara, CA: Libraries Unlimited, 2014); Nancy Bartlett, Elizabeth Gadelha, and Cinda Nofziger, eds., *Teaching Undergraduates with Archives* (Maize Books, 2019), https://doi.org/10.3998/mpub.11499242; Teresa Gray, "Special Collections in the Classroom: Embedding Special Collections in an Undergraduate History Writing Class," *Public Services Quarterly* 16, no. 2 (April 2, 2020): 139–45, https://doi.org/10.1080/15228959.2020.1723461; Jen Hoyer, "Out of the Archives and into the Streets: Teaching with Primary Sources to Cultivate Civic Engagement," *Journal of Contemporary Archival Studies* 7, no. 9 (2020): 18; Chris Marino, "Inquiry-Based Archival Instruction: An Exploratory Study of Affective Impact," *The American Archivist* 81, no. 2 (September 2018): 483–512, https://doi.org/10.17723/0360-9081-81.2.483; Eleanor Mitchell et al., eds., *Past or Portal? Enhancing Undergraduate Learning through Special Collections and Archives* (Chicago: Association of College & Research Libraries, 2012).

4 Janice Carello and Lisa D. Butler, "Potentially Perilous Pedagogies: Teaching Trauma Is Not the Same as Trauma-Informed Teaching," *Journal of Trauma & Dissociation* 15, no. 2 (March 15, 2014): 153–68, https://doi.org/10.1080/15299732.2014.867571.

5 Caswell and Cifor, "From Human Rights to Feminist Ethics," 23–43.

6 Jessie Loyer, "Indigenous Information Literacy: Nêhiyaw Kinship Enabling Self-Care in Research," in *The Politics of Theory and the Practice of Critical Librarianship*, ed. Karen P. Nicholson and Maura Seale (Library Juice Press, 2018), 150.

7 Zoe Todd, "Relationships," in Editors' Forum: Theorizing the Contemporary, *Fieldsights*, Society for Cultural Anthropology, January 21, 2016, https://culanth.org/fieldsights/relationships.

8 Carello and Butler, "Potentially Perilous Pedagogies," 156; Some of our thinking here also comes from a presentation on trauma-informed pedagogy offered by former University of Texas at Austin graduate students,

Lauren White and Sarah Le Pichon, who note that instructors should "limit overall exposure levels and vary the intensity of particularly difficult material." Sarah Le Pichon and Lauren White, "Trauma-Informed Practices in the Higher Education Classroom." Informal presentation (Austin, TX, April 23, 2021).

9 Carello and Butler, "Potentially Perilous Pedagogies."

10 See for example: Nicola Laurent and Kirsten Wright, "A Trauma-Informed Approach to Managing Archives: A New Online Course," *Archives and Manuscripts* 48, no. 1 (January 2, 2020), 1-8, https://doi.org/10.1080/01576895.2019.1705170; Katie Sloan, Jennifer Vanderfluit, and Jennifer Douglas, "Not 'Just My Problem to Handle': Emerging Themes on Secondary Trauma and Archivists," *Journal of Contemporary Archival Studies* 6, no. 1 (July 16, 2019).

11 Carello and Butler, "Potentially Perilous Pedagogies."

12 Association of College and Research Libraries, "Guidelines for Primary Source Literacy," Rare Book and Manuscript Section—Society of American Archivists Joint Task Force on the Development of Guidelines for Primary Source Literacy (American Library Association, February 12, 2018), http://www.ala.org/acrl/sites/ala.org.acrl/files/content/standards/Primary%20Source%20Literacy2018.pdf.

13 Ashley Farmer, "Archiving While Black," The Chronicle of Higher Education, July 22, 2018, https://www.chronicle.com/article/archiving-while-black/.

14 Erin Baucom, "An Exploration into Archival Descriptions of LGBTQ Materials," *The American Archivist* 81, no. 1 (March 2018): 65–83, https://doi.org/10.17723/0360-9081-81.1.65; Jane Anderson and Kimberly Christen, "'Chuck a Copyright on It': Dilemmas of Digital Return and the Possibilities for Traditional Knowledge Licenses and Labels," *Museum Anthropology Review* 7, no. 1–2 (2013): 105–26.

15 Sawyer Broadley and Jill Baron, "Change the Subject – a Documentary about Labels, Libraries, and Activism," https://collections.dartmouth.edu/archive/object/change-subject/change-subject-film; Archives for Black Lives in Philadelphia's Anti-Racist Description Working Group, "Anti-Racist Description Resources," October 2019, https://archivesforblacklives.files.wordpress.com/2019/10/ardr_final.pdf; "Statement of Principles" (2015; repr., Society of American Archivists, October 13, 2021), https://github.com/saa-ts-dacs/dacs/blob/419f93ecc4467be62507b6951a2ee7c21b5fad4d/04_statement_of_principles.md.

16 Lauren F. Klein, "The Image of Absence: Archival Silence, Data Visualization, and James Hemings," American Literature 85, no. 4 (January 1, 2013): 661–88, https://doi.org/10.1215/00029831-2367310.

17 Association of College and Research Libraries' Rare Book and Manuscript Section--Society of American Archivists Joint Task Force on the Development of Guidelines for Primary Source Literacy. "Guidelines for Primary Source Literacy." American Library Association, February 12, 2018. http://www.ala.org/acrl/sites/ala.org.acrl/files/content/standards/Primary%20Source%20Literacy2018.pdf.

18 Kirsten Weld, *Paper Cadavers: The Archives of Dictatorship in Guatemala* (Durham: Duke University Press, 2014).

19 *Digital Aponte*. https://aponte.hosting.nyu.edu/.

20 Brown, Lovisa, Caren Gutierrez, Janine Okmin, and Susan McCullough. "Desegregating Conversations about Race and Identity in Culturally Specific Museums." *Journal of Museum Education* 42, no. 2 (April 3, 2017): 120–31.

21 Jasmine Lellis Clark (lellyjz), "Important topic. When studying history, if you aren't seeing something horrific or problematic, you're seeing revisionism. For me, violent primary sources teach students to be real historians, not just propagandists. Interested to see the responses here," Twitter, November 30, 2018, https://twitter.com/lellyjz/status/1068554151850909698.

22 https://twitter.com/lellyjz/status/1068558579748220928.

23 Kate Crowe (kcrowe), "Basically you have the time/ability to properly contextualize the resources, what were the circumstances within which they were created (public or private, by those w/in or external to community), and are you prepared to deal w violence present in a nuanced & empathetic way," Twitter, November 30, 2018, https://twitter.com/kcrowe/status/1068512772172861441.

24 Brown et al. "Desegregating Conversations about Race and Identity in Culturally Specific Museums."

25 For more information about digital humanities pedagogy, including the forthcoming volume *Debates in Digital Humanities Pedagogy* edited by Brian Croxall and Diane Jakacki, see Debates in Digital Humanities, https://dhdebates.gc.cuny.edu/.

26 For resources relating to copyright law, readers might refer to the Legal Literacies for Text Data Mining Institute, https://buildinglltdm.org/; "Code of Best Practices in Fair Use for Academic and Research Libraries" (Association of Research Libraries, January 2012), https://www.arl.org/wp-content/uploads/2014/01/code-of-best-practices-fair-use.pdf.

27 Baucom, "An Exploration into Archival Descriptions of LGBTQ Materials."

28 For example, see Kimberly A. Christen, "Does Information Really Want to Be Free? Indigenous Knowledge Systems and the Question of Openness," *International Journal of Communication* 6, (November 30, 2012): 24; Anderson and Christen, "'Chuck a Copyright on It.'"

29 The Plateau Peoples' Web Portal is a good example of this: https://plateauportal.libraries.wsu.edu/.

30 Library of Congress Collection: Ancestral Voices. "About this Collection: Rights and Access," https://www.loc.gov/collections/ancestral-voices/about-this-collection/rights-and-access/.

31 Haley Di Pressi et al., "A Student Collaborators' Bill of Rights," HumTech, UCLA, June 8, 2015, https://humtech.ucla.edu/news/a-student-collaborators-bill-of-rights/.

32 Di Pressi et al., "A Student Collaborators' Bill of Rights."

33 Liora Gubkin, "From Empathetic Understanding to Engaged Witnessing: Encountering Trauma in the Holocaust Classroom," *Teaching Theology & Religion* 18, no. 2 (2015): 103–20, https://doi.org/10.1111/teth.12273.

34 For a discussion of testimony and privacy, see J. J. Ghaddar, "The Spectre in the Archive: Truth, Reconciliation, and Indigenous Archival Memory," *Archivaria* 82 (2016): 3-26. https://archivaria.ca/index.php/archivaria/article/view/13579.

35 Sara Trotta (Sar_brarian), "We had someone contact us, (rightly) upset because they had been heavily involved in group activities using a pseudonym but had somehow been identified as a creator in the finding aid using their real name," Twitter, November 30, 2018, https://twitter.com/Sar_brarian/status/1068575932783443968.

36 "Welcome," Digital Accessibility for Archives, https://archivesaccessibilityworkshop.commons.gc.cuny.edu/.

37 For more information on designing for digital accessibility, see for example WebAIM (Web Accessibility in Mind), https://webaim.org/intro/; Web Accessibility Initiative, https://www.w3.org/WAI/; The A11y Project, https://www.a11yproject.com/.

38 Alex Gil, "The User, the Learner and the Machines We Make," Minimal Computing, May 21, 2015, http://go-dh.github.io/mincomp/thoughts/2015/05/21/user-vs-learner/.

39 Brianna Gormly et al., "Teaching with Digital Primary Sources: Literacies, Finding and Evaluating, Citing, Ethics, and Existing Models," *#DLFteach* (October 7, 2019), https://doi.org/10.21428/65a6243c.6b419f2b.

BIBLIOGRAPHY

Anderson, Jane, and Kimberly Christen. "'Chuck a Copyright on It': Dilemmas of Digital Return and the Possibilities for Traditional Knowledge Licenses and Labels." *Museum Anthropology Review* 7, no. 1–2 (2013): 105–26.

Archives for Black Lives in Philadelphia's Anti-Racist Description Working Group. "Anti-Racist Description Resources," October 2019. https://archivesforblacklives.files.wordpress.com/2019/10/ardr_final.pdf.

Association of College and Research Libraries. "Guidelines for Primary Source Literacy." Rare Book and Manuscript Section—Society of American Archivists Joint Task Force on the Development of Guidelines for Primary Source Literacy. American Library Association, February 12, 2018. http://www.ala.org/acrl/sites/ala.org.acrl/files/content/standards/Primary%20Source%20Literacy2018.pdf.

Bahde, Anne, Heather Smedberg, and Mattie Taormina, eds. *Using Primary Sources: Hands-on Instructional Exercises*. Santa Barbara, CA: Libraries Unlimited, 2014.

Bartlett, Nancy, Elizabeth Gadelha, and Cinda Nofziger, eds. *Teaching Undergraduates with Archives*. Maize Books, 2019. https://doi.org/10.3998/mpub.11499242.

Baucom, Erin. "An Exploration into Archival Descriptions of LGBTQ Materials." *The American Archivist* 81, no. 1 (March 2018): 65–83. https://doi.org/10.17723/0360-9081-81.1.65.

Broadley, Sawyer, and Jill Baron. "Change the Subject - a Documentary about Labels, Libraries, and Activism." Accessed October 15, 2020. https://collections.dartmouth.edu/archive/object/change-subject/change-subject-film.

Carello, Janice, and Lisa D. Butler. "Potentially Perilous Pedagogies: Teaching Trauma Is Not the Same as Trauma-Informed Teaching." *Journal of Trauma & Dissociation* 15, no. 2 (March 15, 2014): 153–68. https://doi.org/10.1080/15299732.2014.867571.

Caswell, Michelle. "Teaching to Dismantle White Supremacy in Archives." *The Library Quarterly* 87, no. 3 (July 2017): 222–35. https://doi.org/10.1086/692299.

Caswell, Michelle, and Marika Cifor. "From Human Rights to Feminist Ethics: Radical Empathy in the Archives." *Archivaria* 81 (May 6, 2016): 23–43.

Christen, Kimberly A. "Does Information Really Want to Be Free? Indigenous Knowledge Systems and the Question of Openness." *International Journal of Communication* 6 (November 30, 2012). https://ijoc.org/index.php/ijoc/article/view/1618/828.

Association of Research Libraries. "Code of Best Practices in Fair Use for Academic and Research Libraries." January 2012. https://www.arl.org/wp-content/uploads/2014/01/code-of-best-practices-fair-use.pdf.

Di Pressi, Haley, Stephanie Gorman, Miriam Posner, Raphael Sasayama, and Tori Schmitt. "A Student Collaborators' Bill of Rights." HumTech - UCLA, June 8, 2015. https://humtech.ucla.edu/news/a-student-collaborators-bill-of-rights/.

Farmer, Ashley. "Archiving While Black." *The Chronicle of Higher Education*, July 22, 2018. https://www.chronicle.com/article/archiving-while-black/.

Ghaddar, J.J. "The Spectre in the Archive: Truth, Reconciliation, and Indigenous Archival Memory". *Archivaria* 82 (2016), 3–26. https://archivaria.ca/index.php/archivaria/article/view/13579.

Gil, Alex. "The User, the Learner and the Machines We Make," *Minimal Computing*, May 21, 2015, http://go-dh.github.io/mincomp/thoughts/2015/05/21/user-vs-learner/.

Gormly, B. et al., "Teaching with Digital Primary Sources: Literacies, Finding and Evaluating, Citing, Ethics, and Existing Models," #DLFteach (October 7, 2019), https://doi.org/10.21428/65a6243c.6b419f2b.

Gray, Teresa. "Special Collections in the Classroom: Embedding Special Collections in an Undergraduate History Writing Class." *Public Services Quarterly* 16, no. 2 (April 2, 2020): 139–45. https://doi.org/10.1080/15228959.2020.1723461.

Gubkin, Liora. "From Empathetic Understanding to Engaged Witnessing: Encountering Trauma in the Holocaust Classroom," *Teaching Theology & Religion* 18, no. 2 (2015): 103–20, https://doi.org/10.1111/teth.12273.

Hoyer, Jen. "Out of the Archives and into the Streets: Teaching with Primary Sources to Cultivate Civic Engagement." *Journal of Contemporary Archival Studies* 7, no. 9 (2020): 18.

Klein, Lauren, F. "The Image of Absence: Archival Silence, Data Visualization, and James Hemings." *American Literature* 85, no. 4 (January 1, 2013): 661–88. https://doi.org/10.1215/00029831-2367310.

Laurent, Nicola, and Kirsten Wright. "A Trauma-Informed Approach to Managing Archives: A New Online Course." *Archives and Manuscripts* 48, no. 1 (January 2, 2020). https://doi.org/10.1080/01576895.2019.1705170.

Le Pichon, Sarah, and Lauren White. "Trauma-Informed Practices in the Higher Education Classroom." Austin, TX, April 23, 2021.

Loyer, Jessie. "Indigenous Information Literacy: Nêhiyaw Kinship Enabling Self-Care in Research." In *The Politics of Theory and the Practice of Critical Librarianship*, edited by Karen P. Nicholson and Maura Seale, 145–56. Library Juice Press, 2018.

Marino, Chris. "Inquiry-Based Archival Instruction: An Exploratory Study of Affective Impact." *The American Archivist* 81, no. 2 (September 2018): 483–512. https://doi.org/10.17723/0360-9081-81.2.483.

Mitchell, Eleanor, Peggy Seiden, Suzy Taraba, and Diane Windham Shaw, eds. *Past or Portal? Enhancing Undergraduate Learning through Special Collections and Archives*. Chicago: Association of College & Research Libraries, 2012.

Sloan, Katie, Jennifer Vanderfluit, and Jennifer Douglas. "Not 'Just My Problem to Handle': Emerging Themes on Secondary Trauma and Archivists." *Journal of Contemporary Archival Studies* 6, no. 1 (July 16, 2019): 25.

Society of American Archivists. "Statement of Principles." 2015. Reprint, October 13, 2021. https://github.com/saa-ts-dacs/dacs/blob/419f93ecc4467be62507b6951a2ee7c21b5fad4d/04_statement_of_principles.md.

Todd, Zoe. "Relationships." Society for Cultural Anthropology, January 21, 2016. https://culanth.org/fieldsights/relationships.

Weld, Kirsten. *Paper Cadavers: The Archives of Dictatorship in Guatemala*. Durham: Duke University Press, 2014. https://www.dukeupress.edu/paper-cadavers.

CHAPTER TWO

CAN CRITICAL DIGITAL ARCHIVES ADDRESS "ARCHIVAL AMNESTY" TOWARD LYNCHING? THE RACIAL TERROR: LYNCHING IN VIRGINIA PROJECT

Gianluca De Fazio

INTRODUCTION

In 2015, a *New York Times* editorial titled "Lynching as Racial Terrorism" argued that the issue and history of lynching in the Southern United States "needs to be properly commemorated and more widely discussed before the United States can fully understand the causes and origins of the racial injustice that hobbles the country to this day."[1] The lynching of thousands of people in the South, most of them Black men, represented a form of state-sanctioned terrorism to control, intimidate, and subjugate African American communities after the end of Reconstruction.[2] This foundational aspect of American history has been almost completely expunged from history textbooks,[3] as well as from collective memory and public debate. During Jim Crow, federal, state, and local authorities did little to recognize and react to the ongoing threat of mob violence. When not directly involved in organizing lynching mobs, local officials rarely tried to prevent and punish extra-legal violence. Only recently have political authorities started to publicly address the past role of their institutions in enabling racialized terrorism in the South. After more than one hundred years refusing to confront lynching, in 2020 the US Congress passed the Emmett Till Antilynching Act,[4] a law that would make lynching a federal crime. In addition, various initiatives at the state level have been implemented to address the history of lynching. For instance, the Virginia General Assembly unanimously passed a joint resolution in February 2019 condemning the more than 100 lynchings that took place in the Commonwealth.[5] The resolution explicitly decried the failure of Virginia authorities in trying to prevent lethal mob violence and apprehend lynchers. In the same year, Maryland established a Lynching Truth and Reconciliation Commission to research cases of racially motivated lynchings and hold public meetings.[6]

These initiatives at the federal and state levels are not merely symbolic as they draw attention to a history of racial terrorism that has been largely overlooked in school curricula, government archives, and public debate. Moreover, these legislative actions should be understood within the larger racial reckoning that is developing in the US public sphere, thanks to cultural debate generated by the *1619 Project*,[7] and the activism of the Black Lives Matter movement. One of the movement's central claims, in fact, is that Black history and the Black experience have been expunged from American history. For far too long, media and political institutions, alongside most White communities, have suffered from collective amnesia about the history and ramifications of lynching in the United States. But the oblivion surrounding lynching permeates archival practices and records too.

While historians, social scientists, and activists have documented more than 4,000 lynchings between the end of Reconstruction and World War II,[8] archives have, with a few exceptions, been culpably complicit in failing to document lynching and, more generally, White supremacist violence.[9] As Tonia Sutherland points out, "early 20th century archivists actively collected neither lynching ephemera such as souvenir postcards, nor evidence of lynching in the official records of state governments."[10] This silence is not accidental, but rather the result of biased archival practices that have failed to hold accountable the perpetrators of White supremacist violence.

In response to this erased history, several digital scholars have attempted to document lynching in the United States and tackle what Sutherland calls "archival amnesty," the "intentional turn away from the suffering of human beings, [the] turn away from justice and toward maintaining the status quo."[11] Sutherland's concept calls attention to archivists' failure to properly document White supremacist violence against marginalized groups in the United States. In part, this is the result of Western archival practices that cherish record permanence, "the inherent stability of material that allows it to resist degradation over time."[12] As Sutherland notices, archival permanence neglects the "creation, maintenance, and use of oral records or performed records, the use of which are common in African American and other Black American communities. This strict adherence to the materiality of records, the de-legitimization of alternate forms of record keeping, and the standards of permanence inevitably leads to oblivion."[13] The oblivion about White supremacist violence is thus a central mechanism of how archival amnesty is produced. This is problematic from a scholarly and educational viewpoint, but, crucially, it also undercuts contemporary efforts to attain transitional and restorative justice. Transitional justice refers to the "ways countries emerging from periods of conflict and repression address large-scale or systematic human rights violations so numerous and so serious that the normal justice system will not be able to provide an adequate response."[14] Restorative justice instead focuses on addressing and repairing the harm caused by a crime and "is best accomplished through cooperative processes that allow all willing stakeholders to meet."[15] In the vein of achieving transitional and restorative justice, truth and reconciliation practices are being implemented across the United States, as the ongoing Lynching Truth and Reconciliation Commission in Maryland testifies.[16] However, the oblivion that has historically surrounded the comprehensive documentation of past lynchings is a serious obstacle for achieving racial healing and justice.

In this chapter, I present the digital history project Racial Terror: Lynching in Virginia,[17] one of the many ongoing efforts to document lynching across the United States. Adopting a critical archival studies approach, I examine archives' gaps and silences toward lynching in the context of the state of Virginia. Launched in March 2018, Racial Terror details the stories of the victims of more than one hundred lynchings that occurred in Virginia between 1866 and 1932, and serves as an example of how digital archives can contribute to expose racialized terrorism in the United States. Specifically, Racial Terror provides a key digital resource to inform local communities' efforts to restore the collective memory of lynching victims, thus enabling the development of historical counternarratives about the pervasiveness of White supremacist violence. The Racial Terror project also embraces the key pedagogical mission of teaching students and future generations about the history of lynching in Virginia and its legacy in contemporary society.

In the next section, I outline the critical archival studies framework and discuss how scholars and activists are trying to challenge the "archival amnesty" of racialized terrorism in the United States. Then, I describe the Racial Terror project as a critical digital archive; last, I examine the pedagogical implications of this project for both college and K-12 education in Virginia and nationally.

CRITICAL ARCHIVAL STUDIES

The idea of the archive, digital or physical, as a neutral repository of historical knowledge has been decisively contested in the past two decades. Traditionally, "archivists have perceived themselves as neutral, objective, impartial [...] the very antithesis of power;"[18] however, archival studies scholars and practitioners today challenge the supposed impartiality of the archive. They recognize that archives are social constructs and that their records "wield power over the shape and direction of historical scholarship, collective memory, and national identity, over how we know ourselves as individuals, groups, and societies."[19] Archives, in their selection of what to preserve and what to discard and how to conserve, present, and regulate access to records, advance physical and intellectual infrastructures that are the product of power relationships. Furthermore, archives and their alleged mission of neutrality conceal these power relations and the impact they have on our understanding of past and present socio-political issues.[20]

Recognizing these two key facts, several archivists and scholars have strived to question, improve, and de-naturalize archives, both as institutions and records. In particular, the application of critical theory to archival studies has put at the forefront of academic analysis the role of archives and their records as potential "tools for both oppression and liberation."[21] Caswell, Punzalan, and Sangwand have developed *critical archival studies* as a subfield of archival studies; this new discipline revolves around "those approaches that (1) explain what is unjust with the current state of archival research and practice, (2) posit practical goals for how such research and practice can and should change, and/or (3) provide the norms for such critique."[22] Critical archival studies combine Horkheimer's definition of critical theory (which includes a myriad of critical and cultural theoretical perspectives) and archival studies to develop a research agenda with the emancipatory objective to transform archives and their practices, as well as to inspire social change.[23] A critical approach investigates and questions the production of power structures and their effects on historically oppressed groups that the archives tend to neglect. By recognizing that official narratives often obscure marginalized communities and their perspectives, archives can thus become a key tool "in the recovery of silenced voices as well as in sustaining counternarratives."[24]

Applying this critical approach to documenting lynching reveals how past archival practices have concealed the centrality of racial terrorism and its enduring legacy today. However, it also indicates the potential for contemporary digital archives to subvert the dominant narrative around White supremacist violence and lay the foundation for efforts to bring about racial justice.

ADDRESSING SILENCES AND GAPS IN THE ARCHIVE

While historians and social scientists have extensively researched lynching for the past three decades,[25] a unified database of lynchings that occurred in the United States is still not available.[26] There are several reasons why this is the case, but a significant part of the problem is the lack of comprehensive archival documentation on lynching. The National Association for the Advancement of Colored People Collections at the Library of Congress and at the Tuskegee University in Tuskegee, Alabama, are the only archival collections that contain detailed information about lynching in the United States.[27] Project HAL[28] (Historical American Lynching Data Collection Project) at the University of North Carolina (UNC) Wilmington is a website designed to "accumulate a database of lynchings that took place at any date within the present borders of the United States." Unfortunately, the database is incomplete and has not been updated in years. In 2002, the Maryland State Archives released an online database of Maryland lynching victims called the Judge Lynch's Court.[29] In addition to documenting lynching between 1854 and 1933, the Judge Lynch's Court provides biographical profiles for each victim.

Observing how lynching has been under-documented in the archives, Sutherland argues that "this intentional dearth of archival evidence is tantamount to a tacit provision of clemency" for racialized terrorism.[30] This archival amnesty is neither accidental, nor harmless; on the contrary, by failing to produce and provide the raw material for a counter-narrative to emerge, "American archives have effectively created a master narrative of normativity around Black death."[31] In other words, when archives are silent about the direct involvement of White communities and local authorities in turning mob violence into a spectacle and celebration of White supremacy, they are reproducing a racial ideology that dictates whose lives matter and whose lives are disposable and unworthy of remembrance. In addition to affecting the production and dissemination of historical knowledge, archival erasure obfuscates the evolution of racial violence into new forms of subordination, from the death penalty and mass incarceration, to hate crimes and police brutality.[32]

In the past few years, several museums, memorials and digital projects have started to counter this amnesty, as they are intent on documenting the history of lynching and White supremacist violence. Until recently, the Jim Crow Museum of Racist Memorabilia[33] at Ferris State University was the only museum to include a section on Jim Crow violence and racialized terrorism in the United States. The National Museum of African American History and Culture[34] opened in 2016 at the National Mall in Washington, a section of which is dedicated to the years of segregation and the anti-lynching campaign by Ida B. Wells. In 2018, the Equal Justice Initiative (EJI) inaugurated the National Memorial for Peace and Justice[35] in Montgomery, Alabama, a site "dedicated to the legacy of enslaved black people, people terrorized by lynching, African Americans humiliated by racial segregation and Jim Crow." Three years earlier, the EJI (2015) report *Lynching in America: Confronting the Legacy of Racial Terror* had sparked a public debate on the role of lynching in shaping the African American experience under Jim Crow and its legacy today. This discussion prompted national media to join the conversation and newspapers to publish editorials like the one cited at the beginning of this chapter from the *New York Times*. Other memorials and historical markers have since sprung up throughout the South thanks to the EJI's Community Remembrance Project[36] and other groups' initiatives to recognize the victims of lynching and reflect on the enduring legacy of lynching.

Several digital projects are also tackling the lack of information about lynching. The Center for Studies in Demography and Ecology at the University of Washington Lynching Database,[37] launched in 2015 as a companion to the book *Lynched: The Victims of Southern Mob Violence*, contains a searchable database of 3,935 lynching victims, spanning fourteen southern states between 1877 and 1950.[38] The Monroe Work Today[39] website, released in 2016, provides an extraordinary map of White supremacist collective violence between 1835 and 1964.[40] This map contains information about more than five thousand events of racial lynchings and mob violence against nonwhites in all the continental United States. Started in 2015, A Red Record – Revealing Lynchings Sites in North Carolina[41] is a project based at UNC Chapel Hill that documents and maps lynching in North Carolina between 1865 and 1946. Importantly, it also provides resources for K-12 teachers.[42] *The Baltimore Sun* provides an interactive map of lynching in Maryland, 1854–1933, providing for each victim a brief narrative of the lynching.[43] Many more websites and blog posts also detail individual or area-specific lynchings.

The Racial Terror digital project is part of this larger effort by scholars, activists, media, and institutions to address digitally the archival amnesty that for so long has plagued US archives. As Sutherland highlights, "these documentation efforts are also an attempt to create a historical record, eliminating the possibility of erasure and enabling the possibility of justice."[44] Notably, the promotion of social justice outcomes aligns with a broader trend in archival scholarship, as it is increasingly recognized that "social justice is indeed a worthwhile goal, [...] and that, as shapers of the historical record, archivists have a professional obligation to work toward a more equitable future."[45] Digital history projects that systematically document lynchings and make their information accessible to the public are thus uniquely positioned in fostering the social justice orientation of critical archival scholarship.

THE RACIAL TERROR DIGITAL PROJECT

As a critical digital archive, Racial Terror (Figure 2.1) embraces an emancipatory aspiration of challenging current archival practices and changing societal narratives around lynching. By documenting a key aspect of White supremacist violence, Racial Terror portrays lynching as a Southern institution, a topic that is often silenced, minimized or completely absent, not just in classroom education, but also in the archives.[46] The Racial Terror project, at least in part, tries to address a striking gap in the way lynchings in America have been documented, or, more accurately, under-documented.

In the spring of 2017, I led a research team of six senior students enrolled in an advanced research course in the Justice Studies

Figure 2.1. Racial Terror: Lynching in Virginia – Welcome page.

department at James Madison University (JMU). The team relied on the online newspaper repository of the Library of Congress, Chronicling America,[47] to search and catalog all the news stories they could retrieve about each of the known lynchings that took place in Virginia between 1877 and 1927. Focusing almost exclusively on historical Virginia newspapers, the research team was able to collect more than 600 news articles from 36 newspapers. Based on this research, we were able to improve and update the existing inventories of Virginia lynching victims, critically revealing how the number of White victims of lynching had been overcounted in past inventories. In particular, this project unveiled that "1 in 5 lynching victims in Virginia were white, and not 1 in 4 as previously reported."[48] This finding disputes the argument often displayed by lynching apologists that mob violence was "just" a form of popular justice exerted against all criminals, including White ones. Instead, this study corroborates the notion that lynching was an instrument of racial control toward the Black population in Virginia,[49] as well as in the rest of the South.[50] In the spring of 2019, with another undergraduate research team, we expanded the lynching inventory to cover the period 1866–1932. Among other tasks, students collected newspaper articles regarding these additional cases; they also systematically gathered stories from the *Richmond Planet* and the *Norfolk Journal and Guide*, the two leading historical Black newspapers in Virginia. Both newspapers were vociferously opposed to lynching and instrumental in exposing lynching apologists, as they disseminated a counter-narrative to White mob violence.[51]

The Racial Terror website was released in March of 2018 as a Wordpress site designed and maintained by the JMU Libraries' Digital Projects division. JMU librarians, especially Director of Digital Projects Kevin Hegg and two research assistants, were instrumental in translating collaborative research into user-friendly features for the website. Since its launch, the website has been constantly updated with additional documents, and in August

2020, the website migrated to a new domain, using Campus Press as the main platform. The new relational databases of newspaper articles and lynching victims were created using Airtable software, while the new Data Visualization section uses Tableau. All the tables and data displayed on the website can be freely downloaded in a variety of formats and all the newspaper articles collected can be accessed in a fully searchable relational database (see Figure 2.2).[52] Detailed information about the race, gender, age, accusation of each person lynched in Virginia, and the location where the killing occurred, among other things, is available in the lynching victims page.[53] To visualize the geographical distribution of lethal mob violence in Virginia, the website also hosts an interactive map of Virginia lynchings (see Figure 2.3).[54] Both the map and the lynching victim database are linked to the individual stories of how each lynching came to be. For each person murdered by a mob, we compiled a web page detailing the events leading to the killing and describing what happened in the aftermath of

	Victim Id	Victim Name	Read More	Date	Race	Sex	County	City	Method of Dea
1	VA1866041301	James Holden	LINK	1866-04-13	black	male	Accomack	Pungoteague	Hanged
2	VA1866061901	Unnamed Negro	LINK	1866-06-19	black	male	Nelson	Faber's Mill	Hanged
3	VA1869050301	Joseph R. Holmes	LINK	1869-05-03	black	male	Charlotte	Charlotte Court H...	Shot
4	VA1869061201	Jesse Edwards	LINK	1869-06-12	black	male	Rockbridge	Lexington	Hanged

Figure 2.2. Racial Terror: Lynching in Virginia – Lynching Victims Database.

Figure 2.3. Racial Terror: Lynching in Virginia – Interactive Map of Lynching.

the lynching. Each page also contains the primary documents we collected about that lynching.[55] A section of the website features several rigorous yet accessible essays written by scholars, students and journalists, examining the extent and consequences of racial terror in Virginia, from the end of the Civil War up to the 1930s.[56]

The Racial Terror website houses the most comprehensive and up-to-date catalog of lynching victims in Virginia. Moreover, it tells the largely forgotten stories of the 115 victims of mob violence in the Commonwealth between 1866 and 1932 thus far documented.[57] The overwhelming majority of victims (93 out of 115, 82 percent) were Black men; a Black woman, Charlotte Harris,[58] was lynched in Rockingham County in 1878. Twenty victims were White men and one, Peb Falls, was a White woman,[59] also lynched in Rockingham County in 1897. Compiling an accessible and comprehensive archive of primary sources on Virginia lynching, Racial Terror offers students, scholars, and local communities the tools to explore the often-erased stories of mob violence and to revive the collective memory of lynching victims.

In the next section, I discuss how the Racial Terror project has been used for teaching about lynching in a university setting, and its potential pedagogical value for K-12 education.

THE RACIAL TERROR PROJECT AS A PEDAGOGICAL TOOL

There are three different dimensions to the pedagogical implications of the Racial Terror project. The first refers to the undergraduate research teams that have been actively involved in the construction of the digital archive. The second is the use of the website in senior seminars about lynching at JMU. Finally, the third dimension concerns history and social studies teachers that have used Racial Terror in their K-12 classes, and possible future avenues to address the silence of textbooks on this topic.

Regarding the first dimension, the undergraduate research teams at JMU that conducted the bulk of the research for this project had a unique opportunity to learn fundamental research skills, such as searching and categorizing historical newspaper articles, geo-locating lynching events, and reconstructing lynching narratives based on primary sources. Students also learned about the importance of research protocols and group work. Most importantly, though, these students learned about the social, political, and symbolic meanings of racial terrorism in US history through direct contact with original sources. Rigorous engagement with the existing academic literature is fundamental for students' understanding of the context within which lynching could emerge, proliferate, and become a Southern institution; however, students conducting archival research were able to uncover the individual stories of lynching victims, their humanity, and their agency. Through the reading and collecting of primary sources—mostly White newspaper accounts that often justified mob violence—students gained direct access to the larger political, social, and cultural context that produced and rationalized some of the most barbaric instances of racial injustice in US history. In a sense, these research teams were able to pull back the veil of archival amnesty toward White supremacist violence in Virginia.

In class discussions and evaluations, students consistently pointed out how this was a unique, and empowering, way to learn about a topic they have rarely or never encountered in their curriculum before. There is no doubt that the topic and research work had an emotional impact on the research teams (including myself). Some students signaled an initial discomfort in working with such painful material, and I invited them during class discussions to share their emotions, if they wanted to. I also encouraged everyone to think about what could be some ways in which we could honor the memories of these often-forgotten victims of racialized terrorism. By providing a larger purpose of honoring these lives, students recognized that their assignments were more than just academic exercises; the fact that this was a justice-oriented project made their engagement more meaningful. Crucially, students' participation in the construction of a digital product further motivated them. As they felt that they were part of an impactful project, students' performance and satisfaction with the course were significantly boosted. Students showed a keen interest in reviving the collective memory of lynching victims to inform the conversation about contemporary issues like mass incarceration, police violence, and the death penalty.

Second, I used the Racial Terror website in other senior seminars on racial violence with enlightening results. While students were not directly involved in the collection of primary sources, they were able to access and engage those sources for their final research projects. These projects examined different aspects of lynching in Virginia, focusing on specific cases, time periods, geographical areas, and institutional responses to mob violence. Being able to easily access a digital archive of primary sources helped students to initiate their own in-depth research about the assigned topic, generating insightful research papers, presentations, and class discussions. The digital archive made it possible for students to go beyond academic accounts of lynching and engage with how lynchings were portrayed and often justified in local Virginia newspapers. It also raised several questions as to why racialized mob violence was conspicuously absent from their previous education. In these senior seminars, I always asked my students—whether they were from Virginia or elsewhere—if they were aware of any lynchings that had occurred in their hometown or their counties. Basically, none of the students were aware of any of these stories. Several students were astonished to learn that lynchings took place in the city or county where they grew up, or in nearby locations. They were also startled to learn that the only documented lynching of a Black woman in Virginia had occurred near Harrisonburg, the town where they had been attending college for the past four or more years. Until very recently, there was no collective or institutional memory about this act of racial terrorism in town, or at the university.[60] The history of local White supremacist violence is simply not part of the students' educational or civic experience.[61]

My students' collective experience is hardly unique, and neither should it be surprising. The minimization of lynching and racialized terrorism in US history in secondary and (partially) higher education is well documented.[62] In their analysis of Texas K-12 textbooks, Brown and Brown observed how these

> textbooks generally depicted acts of violence against African Americans as aberrational to the narrative of American democracy. Here, violence is depicted as a 'moment of darkness' where specific actors (e.g., ship captains, slave owners, KKK, Northern workers, southern officials), living in a specific time and place (e.g., the South, the North) acted in ways that were inconsistent with American democratic ideals. However, what is left out and/or silenced from this narrative is how the foundation of

> U.S. democracy (and capitalism) occurred simultaneously with the violence used to repress, cause fear, and lock in place an institutionalized system of political, economic, and social inequality.[63]

The history of systemic racial violence against Blacks and other minorities is what Goldsby called the country's "spectacular secret."[64] To shatter this secret, it is critical to transform the curriculum at the K-12 level. Thanks to the documentation provided in the Racial Terror digital project, some high school teachers in Virginia have started to incorporate lynching in their lecture plans and build units to conduct additional research about cases of mob violence in their counties. Moreover, I am currently working with colleagues in the College of Education and Libraries at JMU to develop a K-12 curriculum on lynchings in Virginia, to be released on the Racial Terror website.[65] The goal is to provide a set of resources, ideas, and strategies for K-12 history and social studies teachers so that they can incorporate the history of racial violence in Virginia and discuss its legacy in the contemporary United States.

The silence about lynching in textbooks and, more generally, education, is not fortuitous. There are several historical and systemic factors behind the minimization of the role of violent oppression against minorities in the US. While it is beyond the scope of this work to review all these factors, the critical archival studies approach adopted in this chapter singled out the specific role archives played in the construction and endurance of this collective amnesia shared by most of the US polity. It also showed the considerable potential critical digital archives have in addressing this archival amnesty to generate a counter-narrative of White supremacist violence. From a pedagogical perspective, students' participation in creating a critical digital archive infused the classroom experience with several questions about the construction of knowledge, collective memory, and identities. It raised issues on how power and White supremacist ideology suffuse and encircle our daily experiences as students, scholars, and citizens. But rather than reinforcing hopelessness, this engaged approach invested students in embracing and promoting an orientation to racial justice for both the past horrors of lynching and its contemporary legacy of police brutality, mass incarceration, and the death penalty.

CONCLUSIONS

In summary, the Racial Terror project follows the call of critical archival studies to challenge current archival practices, deliberately incorporating an emancipatory emphasis. Racial Terror tackles an important gap not just in the public awareness of past lynchings and their legacies, but also in the silences of the archives in collecting evidence of White supremacy and its violent tradition. Thanks to the work of undergraduate research teams and the collaboration with JMU libraries, this project seeks to educate students, teachers, researchers, and local communities on lynching. It also aligns with recent trends in archival research and practice toward embracing social justice goals of documenting human rights violations[66] and state-sanctioned violence.[67] Ultimately, the Racial Terror project is meant to be a pedagogical tool to spark in-class and community-wide discussions on racial violence and collective memory.

Racial Terror is also helping to address the silence surrounding lynching to further some form of restorative justice. As Sutherland poignantly remarked:

> When archival amnesty prevails, the relegation of justice to a state of oblivion is tripartite: (1) there is an historical pattern of failure to document violence against a community; (2) if such documentation existed, it would both constitute a claim for restorative justice and serve as a deterrent against future violence; and (3) without

such documentation, transitional or restorative justice remains perpetually elusive.[68]

Archival amnesty is now being challenged by local activists, teachers, organizations, and institutions that are using the research presented in the website to promote local efforts to memorialize lynching victims. The History of Lynching Working Group[69] of the Dr. Martin Luther King, Jr. (MLK) Commission at the Virginia Legislature has adopted the information contained in the Racial Terror project to start memorializing lynching victims in Virginia. In February 2019, the Virginia General Assembly unanimously passed a joint resolution drafted and put forth by the MLK Commission and the History of Lynching Working Group that acknowledged with profound regret the existence and acceptance of lynching in the Commonwealth. Virginia is the first state to pass such a resolution.

Racial Terror joins a larger effort in which numerous activists, scholars, and organizations such as the EJI are forcefully working to rekindle the collective memory of lynching. Digital scholars are uniquely positioned to address the archives' existing gaps and silences, as they can proactively offer the tools necessary to change the public discourse on White supremacist violence and its pervasiveness and legacy in the United States today.[70] By educating students, scholars, teachers, and communities about racialized terrorism, these projects document a key, yet mostly erased, facet of American history: lynching and the legacy of White supremacist violence. Critical archival projects thus invite practitioners and the larger public to reflect on, and raise questions about, the origins of the gaps and silences in both formal and civic education. As they question archival authority and the power relations that have historically shaped it, critical digital archives provide the pedagogical tools to elaborate a critique of how knowledge is constructed inside and outside of the archive.

NOTES

1 The Editorial Board, "Lynching as Racial Terrorism," *The New York Times*, February 11, 2015, https://www.nytimes.com/2015/02/11/opinion/lynching-as-racial-terrorism.html.

2 Stewart E. Tolnay and E. M. Beck, *A Festival of Violence: An Analysis of Southern Lynchings, 1882–1930* (Chicago: University of Illinois Press, 1995).

3 Anthony L. Brown and Keffrelyn D. Brown, "Strange Fruit Indeed: Interrogating Contemporary Textbook Representations of Racial Violence toward African Americans," *Teachers College Record* 112, no. 1 (2010): 31–67; Anthony L. Brown and Keffrelyn D. Brown, "'A Spectacular Secret:' Understanding the Cultural Memory of Racial Violence in K-12 Official School Textbooks in the Era of Obama," *Race, Gender & Class* 17, no. 3/4 (2010): 111–25.

4 Bobby L. Rush, "Emmett Till Antilynching Act," Pub. L. No. H.R. 35 (2020).

5 "House Joint Resolution 655" (2019), https://lis.virginia.gov/cgi-bin/legp604.exe?191+ful+HJ655.

6 "Home - Maryland Lynching Truth and Reconciliation Commission," https://msa.maryland.gov/lynching-truth-reconciliation/.

7 "The 1619 Project," https://www.nytimes.com/interactive/2019/08/14/magazine/1619-america-slavery.html

8 Equal Justice Initiative, "Lynching in America: Confronting the Legacy of Racial Terror," 2015, https://time.com/wp-content/uploads/2015/02/eji_lynching_in_america_summary.pdf.

9 Tonia Sutherland, "Archival Amnesty: In Search of Black American Transitional and Restorative Justice," *Journal of Critical Library and Information Studies* 1, no. 2 (2017), https://journals.litwinbooks.com/index.php/jclis/article/view/42.

10 Sutherland, "Archival Amnesty," 17.

11 Sutherland, "Archival Amnesty," 7.

12 Society of American Archivists, "SAA Dictionary: Permanence," Dictionary of Archives Terminology, https://dictionary.archivists.org/entry/permanence.html.

13 Sutherland, "Archival Amnesty," 14.

14 "What Is Transitional Justice?" International Center for Transitional Justice, February 22, 2011, https://www.ictj.org/about/transitional-justice.

15 Centre for Justice & Reconciliation, "Lesson 1: What Is Restorative Justice?" Restorative Justice, http://restorativejustice.org/restorative-justice/about-restorative-justice/tutorial-intro-to-restorative-justice/lesson-1-what-is-restorative-justice/.

16 On the proposal to establish a truth and reconciliation commission on lynching, see: Sherrilyn A. Ifill, *On the Courthouse Lawn: Confronting the Legacy of Lynching in the Twenty-First Century* (Boston: Beacon Press, 2018).

17 James Madison University, Racial Terror: Lynching in Virginia, https://sites.lib.jmu.edu/valynchings/.

18 Joan M. Schwartz and Terry Cook, "Archives, Records, and Power: The Making of Modern Memory," *Archival Science* 2, no. 1 (March 1, 2002): 1, https://doi.org/10.1007/BF02435628.

19 Schwartz and Cook, "Archives, Records, and Power," 2.

20 Anne Gilliland explores the connection between the alleged value of neutrality in the archive and its complicity with unjust power structures, when she asks: "where is the line between neutrality and failing to act to counteract negative aspects related to the power of the record or the archive? [...] Can neutrality in fact ever support the interests of all parties to records equally or even equitably?" Anne Gilliland, "Neutrality, Social Justice and the Obligations of Archival Education and Educators in the Twenty-First Century," *Archival Science* 11, no. 3 (November 1, 2011): 207, https://doi.org/10.1007/s10502-011-9147-0.

21 Michelle Caswell, Ricardo Punzalan, and T-Kay Sangwand, "Critical Archival Studies: An Introduction," *Journal of Critical Library and Information Studies* 1, no. 2 (June 27, 2017): 1.

22 Caswell, Punzalan, and Sangwand, "Critical Archival Studies," 2.

23 Caswell, Punzalan, and Sangwand, "Critical Archival Studies," 2.

24 Ricardo L. Punzalan and Michelle Caswell, "Critical Directions for Archival Approaches to Social Justice," *The Library Quarterly* 86, no. 1 (January 1, 2016): 29, https://doi.org/10.1086/684145.

25 Amy Kate Bailey and Stewart E. Tolnay, *Lynched: The Victims of Southern Mob Violence* (Chapel Hill: University of North Carolina Press, 2015); W. Fitzgerald Brundage, *Lynching in the New South: Georgia and Virginia, 1880-1930* (Chicago: University of Illinois Press, 1993); Michael Pfeifer, *Rough Justice: Lynching and American Society, 1874-1947* (Chicago: University of Illinois Press, 2006).

26 Lisa D. Cook, "Converging to a National Lynching Database: Recent Developments and the Way Forward," *Historical Methods: A Journal of Quantitative and Interdisciplinary History* 45, no. 2 (April 1, 2012): 55–63, https://doi.org/10.1080/01615440.2011.639289. But see the latest efforts in Charles Seguin and David Rigby, "National Crimes: A New National Data Set of Lynchings in the United States, 1883 to 1941," *Socius* 5 (January 1, 2019): 1-9, https://doi.org/10.1177/2378023119841780.

27 Sutherland, "Archival Amnesty," 8.

28 Elizabeth Hines and Eliza Steelwater, "Project HAL," UNC Wilmington, http://people.uncw.edu/hinese/HAL/HAL%20Web%20Page.htm#SCOPE%20AND%20PURPOSE%20OF%20PROJECT%20HAL.

29 The Maryland State Archives, "Legacy of Slavery in Maryland: Judge Lynch's Court," Legacy of Slavery in Maryland, http://slavery.msa.maryland.gov/html/casestudies/judge_lynch.html.

30 Sutherland, "Archival Amnesty," 2.

31 Sutherland, "Archival Amnesty," 13.

32 Sutherland, "Archival Amnesty," 13; Manfred Berg, *Popular Justice: A History of Lynching in America* (Lanham: Rowman & Littlefield Publishers, 2015).

33 Ferris State University, Jim Crow Museum of Racist Memorabilia, https://www.ferris.edu/jimcrow/.

34 National Museum of African American History and Culture, Smithsonian Institution, https://nmaahc.si.edu/.

35 "The National Memorial for Peace and Justice," Equal Justice Initiative, Legacy Museum and National Memorial for Peace and Justice, https://museumandmemorial.eji.org/memorial.

36 "Community Remembrance Project Archives," Equal Justice Initiative, https://eji.org/news/tag/community-remembrance-project/.

37 Amy Kate Bailey and Stewart E. Tolnay, CSDE Lynching Database, University of Washington, http://lynching.csde.washington.edu/#/about.

38 Bailey and Tolnay, *Lynched*.

39 Plain Talk History, *Monroe & Florence Work Today*, https://plaintalkhistory.com/monroeandflorencework.

40 Plain Talk History, "Map of White Supremacy's Mob Violence," *Monroe & Florence Work Today*, https://plaintalkhistory.com/monroeandflorencework/explore/.

41 University of North Carolina, A Red Record – Revealing Lynching Sites in North Carolina, University of North Carolina, 2021, http://lynching.web.unc.edu/.

42 See University of North Carolina, "The Map," A Red Record – Revealing Lynching Sites in North Carolina, 2021, http://lynching.web.unc.edu/themap/ and University of North Carolina, "K-12 Resources," A Red Record – Revealing Lynching Sites in North Carolina, 2021, http://lynching.web.unc.edu/k-12-resources/.

43 Jonathan Pitts and Caroline Pate, "Lynchings in Maryland," *The Baltimore Sun*, https://news.baltimoresun.com/maryland-lynchings/.

44 Sutherland, "Archival Amnesty," 17.

45 Punzalan and Carswell, "Critical Directions," 27.

46 Brown and Brown, "Strange Fruit Indeed"; Sutherland, "Archival Amnesty."

47 National Endowment for the Humanities, "Chronicling America," Library of Congress, https://chroniclingamerica.loc.gov/.

48 Gianluca De Fazio, "Improving Lynching Inventories with Local Newspapers: Racial Terror in Virginia, 1877-1927," *Current Research in Digital History* 2 (2019), https://doi.org/10.31835/crdh.2019.04.

49 Brundage, *Lynching in the New South.*

50 Tolnay and Beck, *A Festival of Violence.*

51 Brundage, *Lynching in the New South.*

52 James Madison University, "Articles," Racial Terror: Lynching in Virginia, 2020, http://sites.lib.jmu.edu/valynchings/articles/.

53 James Madison University, "Victims," Racial Terror: Lynching in Virginia, 2020, https://sites.lib.jmu.edu/valynchings/victims/.

54 James Madison University, "Data Visualization," Racial Terror: Lynching in Virginia, 2020, https://sites.lib.jmu.edu/valynchings/data-visualization/.

55 In addition to newspaper articles, some entries include pictures and death certificates. We are currently in the process of digitizing additional archival documents, such as coroners reports and transcripts of trials, to add to the website.

56 James Madison University, "Essays," Racial Terror: Lynching in Virginia, 2020, https://sites.lib.jmu.edu/valynchings/essays/.

57 Like any other catalogue of lynching victims, this is a vast underestimation of the real number of people lynched. As new sources are explored, the number is destined to change.

58 James Madison University, "Charlotte Harris in Rockingham," Racial Terror: Lynching in Virginia, 2020, https://sites.lib.jmu.edu/valynchings/va18780306 01/.

59 James Madison University, "Peb Falls in Rockingham," Racial Terror: Lynching in Virginia, 2020, https://sites.lib.jmu.edu/valynchings/va1897092501/.

60 As a direct result of this project, a local grassroots effort emerged to address the collective amnesia on the lynching of Charlotte Harris, leading to the formation of a community remembrance project. Its members include representatives from local organizations, as well as the city of Harrisonburg and Rockingham County; in September 2020, the Community Remembrance Project unveiled a historical marker in downtown Harrisonburg to memorialize the lynching of Charlotte Harris (Mike Tripp, "New Historical Marker Tells Story of Charlotte Harris' Lynching," *The Harrisonburg Citizen*, September 28, 2020, https://hburgcitizen.com/2020/09/28/new-historical-marker-on-court-square-tells-story-of-charlotte-harris-lynching/.)

61 To cite one more example, a student from Roanoke, Virginia had never heard of the 1893 Roanoke Riot, during which an armed White mob clashed with a state militia called to protect Thomas Smith (James Madison University,

"Thomas Smith in Roanoke," Racial Terror: Lynching in Virginia, 2020, https://sites.lib.jmu.edu/valynchings/va1893092101/), a Black prisoner, from being lynched. Nine people died in the riot and eventually Thomas Smith was taken from jail and lynched. See: Ann Field Alexander, "'Like an Evil Wind': The Roanoke Riot of 1893 and the Lynching of Thomas Smith," *The Virginia Magazine of History and Biography* 100, no. 2 (1992): 173–206. The Roanoke Riot is not taught in local schools and there are no physical markers to remember one of the bloodiest events in Roanoke and Virginia history.

62 Brown and Brown, "Strange Fruit Indeed." Brown and Brown, "Cultural Memory of Racial Violence."

63 Brown and Brown, "Cultural Memory of Racial Violence," 121.

64 Jacqueline Goldsby, *A Spectacular Secret: Lynching in American Life and Literature* (Chicago: University of Chicago Press, 2006).

65 Gianluca De Fazio, Mary Beth Cancienne, Ashley Taylor Jaffee, Kevin Hegg, Elaine Kaye, Nicole Wilson, "Critical Digital Pedagogy and Civic Education: The Experience of the Racial Terror: Lynching in Virginia project," *Scholé. Rivista di Educazione e Studi Culturali* 1 (December 2021): 65-78.

66 Punzalan and Carswell, "Critical Directions," 27.

67 Stacie M. Williams and Jarrett M. Drake, "Power to the People: Documenting Police Violence in Cleveland," *Journal of Critical Library and Information Studies* 1, no. 2 (2017): 1-27.

68 Sutherland, "Archival Amnesty," 15.

69 "History of Lynching in Virginia," Dr. Martin Luther King Jr. Memorial Commission, 2020, http://mlkcommission.dls.virginia.gov/lynchinginvirginia.html.

70 This is especially true for digital history practitioners: Stephen Robertson, "The Differences between Digital Humanities and Digital History," in *Debates in the Digital Humanities 2016*, eds. Matthew K. Gold and Lauren F. Klein (Minneapolis: University of Minnesota Press, 2016), 298–307, https://dhdebates.gc.cuny.edu/read/untitled/section/ed4a1145-7044-42e9-a898-5ff8691b6628

BIBLIOGRAPHY

Alexander, Ann Field. "'Like an Evil Wind': The Roanoke Riot of 1893 and the Lynching of Thomas Smith." *The Virginia Magazine of History and Biography* 100, no. 2 (1992): 173–206.

Bailey, Amy Kate, and Stewart E. Tolnay. *Lynched: The Victims of Southern Mob Violence*. Chapel Hill: University of North Carolina Press, 2015. https://www.jstor.org/stable/10.5149/9781469620886_bailey.

Bailey, Amy Kate, and Stewart E. Tolnay. CSDE Lynching Database. University of Washington. http://lynching.csde.washington.edu/#/about.

Berg, Manfred. *Popular Justice: A History of Lynching in America*. Lanham: Rowman & Littlefield Publishers, 2015.

Brown, Anthony L., and Keffrelyn D. Brown. "'A Spectacular Secret:' Understanding the Cultural Memory of Racial Violence in K-12 Official School Textbooks in the Era of Obama." *Race, Gender & Class* 17, no. 3/4 (2010): 111–25.

Brown, Anthony L., and Keffrelyn D. Brown. "Strange Fruit Indeed: Interrogating Contemporary Textbook Representations of Racial Violence toward African Americans." *Teachers College Record* 112, no. 1 (2010): 31–67.

Brundage, W. Fitzgerald. *Lynching in the New South: Georgia and Virginia, 1880–1930*. Chicago: University of Illinois Press, 1993.

Caswell, Michelle, Ricardo Punzalan, and T-Kay Sangwand. "Critical Archival Studies: An Introduction." *Journal of Critical Library and Information Studies* 1, no. 2 (June 27, 2017): 1–8.

Centre for Justice & Reconciliation. "Lesson 1: What Is Restorative Justice?" Restorative Justice. http://restorativejustice.org/restorative-justice/about-restorative-justice/tutorial-intro-to-restorative-justice/lesson-1-what-is-restorative-justice/.

Cook, Lisa D. "Converging to a National Lynching Database: Recent Developments and the Way Forward." *Historical Methods: A Journal of Quantitative and Interdisciplinary History* 45, no. 2 (April 1, 2012): 55–63. https://doi.org/10.1080/01615440.2011.639289.

De Fazio, Gianluca. "Improving Lynching Inventories with Local Newspapers: Racial Terror in Virginia, 1877–1927." *Current Research in Digital History* 2 (2019). https://doi.org/10.31835/crdh.2019.04.

De Fazio, Gianluca, Mary Beth Cancienne, Ashley Taylor Jaffee, Kevin Hegg, Elaine Kaye, and Nicole Wilson. "Critical Digital Pedagogy and Civic Education: The Experience of the Racial Terror: Lynching in Virginia Project." *Scholé. Rivista Di Educazione e Studi Culturali* 1 (December 2021): 65–78.

Equal Justice Initiative. "Lynching in America: Confronting the Legacy of Racial Terror," 2015. https://time.com/wp-content/uploads/2015/02/eji_lynching_in_america_summary.pdf.

Equal Justice Initiative. "Community Remembrance Project Archives." https://eji.org/news/tag/community-remembrance-project/.

Equal Justice Initiative. "The National Memorial for Peace and Justice." Legacy Museum and National Memorial for Peace and Justice. https://museumandmemorial.eji.org/memorial.

Ferris State University. Jim Crow Museum of Racist Memorabilia. https://www.ferris.edu/jimcrow/.

Gilliland, Anne. "Neutrality, Social Justice and the Obligations of Archival Education and Educators in the Twenty-First Century." *Archival Science* 11, no. 3 (November 1, 2011): 193–209. https://doi.org/10.1007/s10502-011-9147-0.

Goldsby, Jacqueline. *A Spectacular Secret: Lynching in American Life and Literature*. Chicago: University of Chicago Press, 2006.

Hines, Elizabeth, and Eliza Steelwater. "Project HAL." UNC Wilmington. http://people.uncw.edu/hinese/HAL/HAL%20Web%20Page.htm#SCOPE%20AND%20PURPOSE%20OF%20PROJECT%20HAL.

"Home - Maryland Lynching Truth and Reconciliation Commission." https://msa.maryland.gov/lynching-truth-reconciliation/.

House Joint Resolution 655 (2019). https://lis.virginia.gov/cgi-bin/legp604.exe?191+ful+HJ655.

Ifill, Sherrilyn A. *On the Courthouse Lawn: Confronting the Legacy of Lynching in the Twenty-First Century*. Boston: Beacon Press, 2018.

International Center for Transitional Justice. "What Is Transitional Justice?" February 22, 2011. https://www.ictj.org/about/transitional-justice.

Plain Talk History. *Monroe & Florence Work Today*. https://plaintalkhistory.com/monroeandflorencework.

Plain Talk History. "Map of White Supremacy's Mob Violence." *Monroe & Florence Work Today*. https://plaintalkhistory.com/monroeandflorencework/explore/.

Martin Luther King Jr. Memorial Commission. "History of Lynching in Virginia." 2020. http://mlkcommission.dls.virginia.gov/lynchinginvirginia.html.

National Endowment for the Humanities. "Chronicling America." Text. Library of Congress. https://chroniclingamerica.loc.gov/.

National Museum of African American History and Culture. Smithsonian Institution. https://nmaahc.si.edu/.

Pfeifer, Michael. *Rough Justice: Lynching and American Society, 1874–1947*. Chicago: University of Illinois Press, 2006.

Pitts, Jonathan and Caroline Pate, "Lynchings in Maryland," *The Baltimore Sun*, https://news.baltimoresun.com/maryland-lynchings/.

Punzalan, Ricardo L., and Michelle Caswell. "Critical Directions for Archival Approaches to Social Justice." *The Library Quarterly* 86, no. 1 (January 1, 2016): 25–42. https://doi.org/10.1086/684145.

Racial Terror: Lynching in Virginia. James Madison University. https://sites.lib.jmu.edu/valynchings/.

Robertson, Stephen. "The Differences between Digital Humanities and Digital History." In *Debates in the Digital Humanities 2016*, edited by Matthew K. Gold and Lauren F. Klein, 298–307. Minneapolis: University of Minnesota Press, 2016. https://dhdebates.gc.cuny.edu/read/untitled/section/ed4a1145-7044-42e9-a898-5ff8691b6628.

Rush, Bobby L. Emmett Till Antilynching Act, Pub. L. No. H.R. 35 (2020).

Schwartz, Joan M., and Terry Cook. "Archives, Records, and Power: The Making of Modern Memory." *Archival Science* 2, no. 1 (March 1, 2002): 1–19. https://doi.org/10.1007/BF02435628.

Seguin, Charles, and David Rigby. "National Crimes: A New National Data Set of Lynchings in the United States, 1883 to 1941." *Socius* 5 (January 1, 2019): 2378023119841780. https://doi.org/10.1177/2378023119841780.

Society of American Archivists. "SAA Dictionary: Permanence." Dictionary of Archives Terminology, n.d. https://dictionary.archivists.org/entry/permanence.html.

Sutherland, Tonia. "Archival Amnesty: In Search of Black American Transitional and Restorative Justice." *Journal of Critical Library and Information Studies* 1, no. 2 (2017). https://journals.litwinbooks.com/index.php/jclis/article/view/42.

The Editorial Board. "Lynching as Racial Terrorism." *The New York Times*, February 11, 2015. https://www.nytimes.com/2015/02/11/opinion/lynching-as-racial-terrorism.html.

The Maryland State Archives. "Legacy of Slavery in Maryland: Judge Lynch's Court." Legacy of Slavery in Maryland. http://slavery.msa.maryland.gov/html/casestudies/judge_lynch.html.

Tolnay, Stewart E., and E. M. Beck. *A Festival of Violence: An Analysis of Southern Lynchings, 1882–1930*. Chicago: University of Illinois Press, 1995.

Tripp, Mike. "New Historical Marker Tells Story of Charlotte Harris' Lynching." *The Harrisonburg Citizen*, September 28, 2020. https://hburgcitizen.com/2020/09/28/new-historical-marker-on-court-square-tells-story-of-charlotte-harris-lynching/.

University of North Carolina. A Red Record – Revealing Lynching Sites in North Carolina. University of North Carolina. https://lynching.web.unc.edu/.

Williams, Stacie M., and Jarrett M. Drake. "Power to the People: Documenting Police Violence in Cleveland." *Journal of Critical Library and Information Studies* 1, no. 2 (2017): 1–27.

PART II

CONFRONTING INSTITUTIONAL POWER

CHAPTER THREE

INSTITUTIONAL ARCHIVES AND TRANSFORMATIVE UNDERGRADUATE PEDAGOGY: THE HISTORICAL ACCOUNTABILITY STUDENT RESEARCH PROGRAM AT DARTMOUTH COLLEGE

Myranda Fuentes and Sam Koreman

In April 2018, the Dartmouth College Library was granted funding from the Office of the Provost under the auspices of the institution's Inclusive Excellence initiative to expand its pre-existing undergraduate research pilot into the Historical Accountability Student Research Program, a student-directed initiative to examine issues of diversity and inclusion in college history.[1] Institutional, local, and national news outlets were quick to make comparisons between the new initiative and the efforts of numerous universities to confront their historical connections to slavery. These comparisons are well founded, as many institutions have realized that their archives are crucial places to start reckoning with complex and difficult histories in the wake of these slavery projects.

For the librarians and archivists facilitating the Historical Accountability Student Research Program's research in Rauner Special Collections Library, the student-directed nature of Dartmouth's initiative is what will determine the program's success. These student researchers have uncovered compelling stories that have already fed back into the curriculum and connected with the student body through interactive class sessions, outreach events, and better informed reference support. Former fellows have continued their research in the form of published articles, public presentations, and senior thesis research. In formal reflections, students express increased confidence in their research abilities and describe how their archival research has transformed their relationship with their alma mater. We hold that it is through these individualized and transformative student experiences that the program can help foster an environment where diversity thrives, changing culture over time to build a more inclusive Dartmouth College.

In this chapter, we aim to demonstrate that the Historical Accountability Student Research Program provides undergraduates with impactful research experiences that give them the skills necessary to conduct research in special collections repositories while focusing the attention of the Dartmouth Library, and thus the institution, on productive engagement with Dartmouth's history. We begin with a description of the program's structure and objectives to provide a blueprint for others who wish to implement similar research programs. We then address the affective responsibilities of archivists and librarians as part of the program before we explore a historical accountability student research fellow's research process to demonstrate the role students can play in uncovering archival silences and building more inclusive archives. We conclude with meditations on the importance of situating librarians and archivists as mentors of student researchers and the limitations of these programmatic efforts to achieving institutional accountability in isolation.

HISTORICAL ACCOUNTABILITY STUDENT RESEARCH FELLOWSHIP

Fuentes joined the Rauner Special Collections Library team in September 2018 to coordinate the Historical Accountability Student Research Program as the institutional history research specialist. The staff person in this newly created position was tasked with continuing the work of the historical accountability student research fellowship and developing other undergraduate research opportunities centered around issues of diversity and inclusion in Dartmouth history. Today, the program offers three research positions: the fellowship (full-time research), the internship (part-time research), and the externship (off-site research). All three research opportunities derive basic structure, objectives, and criteria for assessment from the former Rauner student research fellowship, an undergraduate research pilot funded by the Dartmouth Center for the Advancement of Learning. As the first and foundational research opportunity under the program, the historical accountability student research fellowship (or "the fellowship") will be used as synecdoche for the entire program.

Like the Rauner student research fellowship, Historical Accountability Student Research Program opportunities operate primarily as an expansion of already extensive use of special collections materials by Dartmouth undergraduates through interactive class sessions with faculty.[2] Class sessions in Rauner Special Collections Library are designed to produce skilled undergraduate users of primary sources through hands-on, student-centered learning, and often incorporate critical engagement with primary sources related to the history and mythos of Dartmouth College long before the establishment of the Historical Accountability Student Research Program. In 2016, Peter Carini published standards and outcomes for developing primary source literacy based on the working model used in Rauner Special Collections Library.[3] The areas of focus that he outlines in his framework—know, interpret, evaluate, use, access, and follow ethical principles—directly influenced many of the fellowship learning objectives, including developing deeper student understanding of the idiosyncratic ways that manuscripts and archives are handled in special collections libraries, evaluating and interpreting primary sources for subjectivities (such as tone and bias), and situating primary source materials in historical context.[4] Special attention is given to the concept "interpret," in the learning objectives, as students are much more likely to encounter archival silences and contradictions that complicate their research when investigating the history of marginalized groups and institutional controversies with the program.[5]

In structure, the Historical Accountability Student Research Program does not seek to achieve its objectives through formalized instruction but operates on an experiential learning model. While experiential learning does just mean "learning by doing," it requires instructional design that incorporates concrete experience, reflective observation, abstract conceptualization, and active experimentation.[6] For most of our student researchers, the fellowship is their first time conducting long-term archival research, which makes the fellowship a new, concrete experience for them by default. The fellows with prior archival research experience have most often gained their experience through study abroad programs, which means the fellowship is their first meaningful engagement with their home institution's repository. To ensure that students are thinking critically about their experiences (reflective observation), asking questions and pinpointing problems about those experiences (abstract conceptualization), and attempting to solve those problems based on their further reflections (active experimentation), the fellowship requires students to document their research process in a weekly reflection journal, which is then used in weekly meetings with the special collections librarian or archivist assigned as their research adviser.[7] These reflections evolve and aggregate into overarching reflections on the entire research experience in an essay due the final week of the term.[8]

In order to hold students accountable to the expectation that their research will culminate in sharable research products, a series of assignments and corresponding criteria for assessment are also due at different stages of the term of residence. The format of this research product (or final performance) is determined by the student and might take the form of a research paper, data visualization, piece of creative writing, or artistic performance; regardless of the chosen format, it must directly and substantially engage with primary source materials consulted during the term. Midway through the fellowship, students create a brief historical write-up featuring primary sources crucial to their research for the special collections blog. The blog post exercise is beneficial as students begin to think about their research presentation, held publicly in the library during the ninth week of the term, and final performance, as it is the first assignment in which they must build an accessible and concise narrative from several weeks of research for public consumption. The original structure of the Historical Accountability Student Research Fellowship is tried and true; all former research fellows indicate that they have had a positive experience with the program and report they would recommend the fellowship to their peers.[9]

Since Fuentes began coordinating the program, two new "systems" of meetings have been implemented for building rapport between librarians and students interested in the program. The first system requires students to meet with the institutional history research specialist at least once before submitting an application to the selection committee.[10] Application portfolios to the fellowship program consist of a brief description of the project (up to three pages in length), list of collection(s) of interest at Rauner and how they will be used, resume or CV, and a letter of recommendation. Scheduled meetings with the institutional history research specialist involve a discussion of the primary source materials available in the archives and how to use library discovery tools to better understand which archival materials are relevant to their project aims. These pre-proposal meetings have been beneficial for the student applicants and selection committee alike by giving students the knowledge necessary to craft more purposeful research proposals with direct ties to library holdings. As a result, the selection committee spends less time assessing if a promising research concept has sufficient records to sustain ten weeks of research and students begin their fellowships confidently with a better sense of where to begin.

The second set of meetings is for students awarded fellowships to become acquainted with other non-program staff in Rauner Special Collections Library. These meetings are designed to help orient students to the reading room. Staff at Rauner Special Collections Library rotate through reference desk shifts and it can be intimidating for a student researching full-time to continually interact with a new person throughout the day. While meetings with students before applying ensure that the institutional history research specialist is a familiar face, these initial meetings with staff can counteract the intimidation factor of being unable to recognize the librarians staffing the desk. In conjunction with pre-proposal meetings, in which students learn early on that not all good ideas have records with which to pursue research inquiry, these staff meetings are invaluable in getting students to cast aside an imagination of "the archive" as the sum total of human knowledge, and instead begin to understand that "the archive" is made up of a series of individual "archives" often limited by storage concerns and years of exclusionary curation (deliberately or otherwise).

The program's Winter 2019 historical accountability student research fellows were the first group of students required to attend a series of individual staff meetings and they greatly influenced their timing, structure, and content. Today, meetings take place regularly with the following library staff:

- rare book cataloger;
- processing specialist(s);
- college archivist and/or acquisitions archivist;
- digital collections and oral history archivist;
- subject specialty librarians (Baker-Berry Library).

The meetings progressively allow for increasing levels of metacommentary on archives and primary source research.

In the first two weeks of the fellowship, students meet with our rare book cataloger and at least one processing specialist for in-depth, interactive sessions about special collections discovery tools. In the first session, our cataloger walks students through effective strategies for using the library catalog (Alma/Primo) and the physical card catalogs and indexes in the reading room. Although he comes equipped with tailored searches based on the students' research proposals, he begins with search terms provided by the students and leads them through several guided searches. This first meeting closely resembles the pre-proposal meetings in content, acting as a refresher even as it demonstrates how to advance beyond the searches that went into formulating their applications.

In the meeting with a processing specialist, students use rules and principles outlined in *Describing Archives: A Content Standard*[11] to process a mock collection, which gives insight into the way information is entered into our archives management system (ArchivesSpace). In this activity, students learn that the decisions one person makes can have lasting effects on how people find and use that collection for years to come. The activity acclimates students to ArchivesSpace in a more indirect way than the meeting with our cataloger, but the concrete nature of that first meeting allows our students to combine those search strategies with the information about how archives are described and organized to extrapolate for themselves how to run expert searches in ArchivesSpace. When students meet with the library's archivists, they have experienced concrete meetings with other librarians and they have a few weeks of reflection journaling behind them, which better prepares them to have more conceptual conversations about assessment, acquisitions, access restrictions, and archival ethics.

Relationships between the archivists and students are especially valuable, as the greatest transformative potential of the fellowship is its ability to change how students see their relationship with the historical record. The research parameters for all Historical Accountability Student Research Program opportunities, including the fellowship, are broadly to research "issues of diversity and inclusion." These parameters often attract students who apply for personal, identity-based reasons; they apply as students of color, as women, as members of the LGBTQ+ community, and as members of the working class. While the former Rauner student research fellowship was successful in teaching students to think archivally, the subject matter addressed under the auspices of the historical accountability student research fellowship more directly encourages participatory archival practice; student researchers have sought to fill archival gaps with their perspectives and those of other Dartmouth community members.[12] These participatory practices allow for the more traditional institutional archive to share authority with student researchers,[13] but also requires librarians and archivists to be aware of their emotional, or affective, responsibilities as students progress through the research process.

ADDRESSING PROGRAMMATIC AFFECTIVE RESPONSIBILITIES

In "From Human Rights to Feminist Ethics: Radical Empathy in the Archives," Caswell and Cifor argue that "archival relationships are essentially affective in nature and that archivists have ethical responsibilities based on these affective relationships."[14] Responsibility is achieved through the practice of radical empathy, a "deep connection between the self and another," which places "affective labour at the centre of the archival endeavor."[15] The work of the historical accountability student research fellowship is predominantly concerned with the affective responsibility between archivist and user. Since the program does not simply happen to attract students from historically underrepresented groups at the institution but also actively recruits these students, the program creates frequent opportunities for library staff and student researchers to interface with one another to facilitate mutual understanding, respect, and empathy among these parties as students find (or do not find) records with which they have personal and emotional connections.

Students will not form deep connections with all library staff over the course of their term of residence, but they will connect with at least one staff person who can help them work through any difficult consequences of their archival interactions and liaise with other people on their behalf if necessary. The beauty of being library staff in these contexts is the ability to be seen as a peer more readily than a professor or other intellectual authority. When a librarian helps or offers advice, we validate a researcher's thoughts as worthy of further inquiry. If a librarian's job is done well, a researcher sees interactions and potentially difficult conversations as dialogue on equal ground. It is easier for library staff and students to apologize and grow together as peers than in the traditional teacher and student relationship.

The series of staff meetings at the start of a fellowship term and weekly one-on-one meetings with a staff research adviser serve to orient students to the tools and strategies of using the reading room, and also to orient them to feel ownership over the physical space that they will occupy for the next ten weeks. Far from just an attempt to alleviate the intimidation of unfamiliar faces, these meetings work to counteract "archival anxiety," or a sense of unease or unwelcome in special collections for individuals who lack research experience or advanced degrees.[16] This anxiety is a major roadblock in getting undergraduates, K–12 students, and non-academics into the reading room outside of class requirements or special events, and these anxieties are easily aggravated the further a patron is from wealth, whiteness, maleness, heterosexuality, and able-bodiedness at institutions built for the historic default of straight white able-bodied men. Fellows are four weeks deep into research when the series of staff meetings conclude, a time in the term when students have usually already encountered a research roadblock, whether in the form of an institutional restriction or gap in the historical record. The recent conceptual conversations about archival ethics intermingle with the experience of their research, which can create anxiety about the preservation of their own records, perspectives, and insights. In other words, students exchange the archival anxiety that renders a reading room unwelcome for an archival anxiety that demands their presence and perspective.

In the words of the fall 2019 historical accountability student research fellow, researching with the program instills the idea of being part of a living history, a notion that not only bodes well for fostering a campus environment that allows for continual and open dialogue with the past at Dartmouth, but underscores the fellowship's ability to build a more inclusive archives in the future by raising archival consciousness among those underrepresented in the archives. Students have not only brought records to the attention of our archivist for acquisitions, but more than a few of these students, such as our Spring 2020 historical accountability student research fellow, have themselves made calls to action among their peers and alumni to offer up records for assessment:[17]

> I've been surprised at some of the resources that have been preserved, and equally surprised at the ones that haven't...According to the [*The Dartmouth*], the [Gay Students Association] had a newsletter in the early 80s, and I know absolutely nothing about it other than the fact that it existed...So if anyone has anything saved, please consider sharing it with Rauner!

The tendency of former researchers to engage in outreach activities on behalf of the library suggests that "[t]hrough the preservation and sharing of a community's records, community members are preserving and reaffirming their community memory and identity."[18] The archival consciousness of student participants in the fellowship also better situates the library to fulfill its affective responsibilities between archivists and the larger community, "for whom the use of records has lasting consequences."[19] The added understanding of in-depth archival research can equip students with the knowledge that centuries of exclusionary archival curation has rendered their perspectives and personal records invaluable; and that they have power in their ability to include or withhold those things from the institution. Students tend to favor the idea of adding to the archives, but the power to opt out is something that cannot be understated.

The role of the librarian or archivist in transforming archival authority at institutions like Dartmouth is to empower their diverse library constituencies to interpret the contents of its largely white male archives on their own terms and, in so doing, encourage them to fill its silences with their own voices. Fortunately, building rapport and trust thereafter is easily accomplished through personal meetings with librarians and archivists, which are neither arduous, time consuming, nor outside the parameters of traditional reference work that library staff already provide. Students will have the confidence and inclination to work wonders in and for institutional archives when librarians and archivists are attentive to both the intellectual and affective needs of their researchers, as this chapter's undergraduate contributor, Sam Koreman, will demonstrate in the section to follow.

CASE STUDY: INSTITUTIONAL HISTORIES OF DISABILITY

(SAM KOREMAN, WINTER 2019 HISTORICAL ACCOUNTABILITY STUDENT RESEARCH FELLOW)

I applied for the historical accountability student research fellowship with the intent to investigate Dartmouth's institutional history of physical disability. More specifically, I wanted to shed light on the history of Dartmouth's community members who were physically disabled. I envisioned a two-part project: 1) a visual and literary representation of disability that would include pictures of community members with disabilities, as well as their stories, articles, or poems; and 2) a written history of policy changes and building alterations at the college in response to different pieces of federal legislation requiring institutions nationwide to meet evolving accessibility standards.

My original research proposal opens with an assessment that disability often feels like an afterthought in discussions of inclusion and diversity on campus, which tend to focus more on identity characteristics related to race, ethnicity, sex, gender, sexuality, and income. I was certain that Dartmouth had been home to students with disabilities in its past and that my project could uncover their stories to provide historical visibility for the Dartmouth community members with disabilities today. During my ten weeks of research in Rauner Special Collections Library, my convictions that individuals with disabilities have historically been present in the Dartmouth community were validated.

Throughout my research experience, I experienced several challenges accessing the information required to answer my original research questions. This section will focus on explaining why areas of the Dartmouth archives were lacking, before highlighting my role in starting to fill in those gaps. During my ten weeks in Rauner Special Collections Library, I realized that archives are not naturally created; archives are purposely constructed, often by those in powerful positions. Historical records detailing the stories of certain minority groups or trends can be more difficult to find due to the simple fact that there are fewer of those stories available in the archives. As my project focused on disability, the archives I dealt with fell prey to this trap. Ultimately, my research experience illustrated that members of minority communities can—and must—use their perspectives to fill in archival gaps in order to provide complete institutional histories.

Early on in my fellowship, I was forced to abandon the idea of constructing a visual and literary history of disability due to the lack of archival material detailing the lived experiences of individuals with disabilities at Dartmouth. After combing through photographic records for canes, wheelchairs, and ramps, and the index of the student newspaper, *The Dartmouth*, for the word "disability," its synonyms, and slurs, I came out almost empty handed: there were no indexed photographs and only one newspaper article written by a student with a disability. At this point, I shifted my focus to the second objective: a written history of accessibility changes at the college. Tackling this objective ultimately allowed me to access indirect accounts of experiences with disability at Dartmouth in the archives, and first-person accounts of the experiences with disability at Dartmouth outside of the archives.

While my first thread of inquiry was abandoned as a result of too many dead ends, switching my focus to crafting a written history of disability did not make the hunt for records any easier. The crux of this series of searches came down to uncertainty about which collections and departmental records would contain information about disability. To use a cliché, the process was like looking for a needle in a haystack. Outside of committees with names containing keywords like "disabled," "disability," or "handicapped," it proved extremely difficult to track down which files mentioned disability. Any information related to disability that predated these committees was also difficult to find.

Using this scattered approach, I discovered my earliest chronological mention of disability in the archives—a series of letters from high-level business staff and administration members in 1967 (see Figures 3.1, and 3.2 a and b). These letters frame accessibility as a way to capitalize on students with disabilities as an economic opportunity.[20] Despite the strange context for this exchange of letters, the most important thing about it is its useful secondhand account of students with disabilities. The administrators discuss three wheelchair users admitted to the college in previous decades

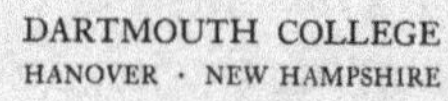

DARTMOUTH COLLEGE
HANOVER · NEW HAMPSHIRE

DARTMOUTH COLLEGE BUSINESS MANAGER RECEIVED FEB 15 1967 Noted Refer to Ans'd File John Scotford

February 14, 1967

FROM John Scotford

TO President Dickey, Richard Olmsted, Edward Chamberlain, Dr. Jackson

re: Extending the opportunity of a Dartmouth education to a hithertofore untapped minority group -- crippled students

When I visited the campus of Southern Illinois University last year I was struck by the effort that institution had made to encourage crippled students to attend SIU. First floor rooms were reserved for them in some dormitories, ramps for wheelchairs had been placed at strategic points about the campus. They had a special office set up to handle their problems. I do not know if many state colleges do this or are required to do it to meet the needs of their citizens, but I know of no Ivy League schools or other independent liberal arts colleges which make a point of making their campuses livable for crippled students. I have not noticed many crippled students at Dartmouth. I can think of only two recently. Undoubtedly there are many who would qualify for admission. Many are highly motivated. Many must want to go to a school like Dartmouth. Are we missing a bet in not making it easy for them to attend? Can we steal a march on our competition by making a few simple alterations in present buildings and planning future buildings with them in mind?

JS

JRSjr:nb

Figure 3.1. Memo from John R. Scotford to Dartmouth administrators, Feb. 14, 1967.

and concede that the institution had made a series of mistakes regarding how they treated each of these students.[21] Unfortunately, I never uncovered the greater institutional context for these letters.

In a search for context, I abandoned my scattered approach and began researching the committees that formed to implement federal disability legislation. I discovered that my two original project ideas were interrelated in the archive; my written history of accessibility changes was the gateway into narratives of disability at Dartmouth. My research into the records of the Advisory Counsel to the Handicapped, later renamed the Committee on the Handicapped, was particularly illuminating for various

DARTMOUTH COLLEGE BUSINESS MANAGER RECEIVED FEB 23 1967

DARTMOUTH COLLEGE
HANOVER · NEW HAMPSHIRE

February 20, 1967

FROM Mr. Dickerson

TO Mr. John Scotford

cc: Messrs. Dickey, Olmsted, Chamberlain, Jackson

President Dickey has shared with me your memorandum of February 14 and suggested that I in turn share with you the experience that we have had with crippled students.

One naturally reacts warmly to a proposal like yours because of the humaneness which lies behind it. Let's talk about it the next time we are together.

In my experience in Admissions and in deaning Freshmen, we have had three paraplegic students at Dartmouth.

The first was a son of an alumnus, who had long had Dartmouth as an aspiration, and who had academic promise, but at the time of admission was diagnosed as having an incurable disease. There is no point in dwelling on the detail. He did not live to finish his Dartmouth undergraduate career. Our sentimental gesture in deciding to admit him to Dartmouth meant a great deal to his parents. As time goes on I am assailed by increasing doubts, with relation to the boy himself, whether the decision was kind or wise.

The second case was ████ of Hanover who became a paraplegic in his last year in high school as a result of an automobile accident.

The whole Hanover community poured out its sympathy to ████, and especially the hospital and clinic who went all out in providing services, which I take it were mostly free, since their family was without resources. ████'s high school record would not have supported his admission to Dartmouth but we arranged for him to enroll experimentally in Dartmouth classes to see how it worked out, as a special non-matriculated student. It didn't work out at all. The clinic-hospital people got him admitted to a rehabilitation center down in the South. He wasn't happy there and left soon. As I see this one in hindsight, too many warmhearted compassionate people gave ████ too much sympathy at that crucial point when the severely handicapped person has to develop that super self-discipline which is needed for a handicapped person to overcome his handicaps.

The third wheelchair case was that of a very bright, possibly brilliant,

Figure 3.2a. Memo from Albert I. Dickerson to John R. Scotford, Feb. 20, 1967, p.1.

secondhand accounts and even two firsthand accounts of experiences with disability.

In 1977, this committee formed to address accessibility issues in response to Section 504 of the Rehabilitation Act of 1973, which required organizations all across the nation to make significant changes to internal policies and physical plans.[22] Two members of

-2-

student in his final year at St. Paul's School in Concord. He became a paraplegic as the result of an automobile accident. He spent the ensuing months in the hospital here, was tutored by members of the Dartmouth faculty and qualified for his diploma in June at St. Paul's. He matriculated in September and spent, I believe, two years here, with frequent interruptions caused by the sores and infections which some paraplegics suffer because of the lack of circulation below the waist. Many warmhearted people made many efforts to help him overcome his difficulties and handicaps of transportation, logistics and all the rest. But the rigors of the Hanover winters and Dartmouth's layout and physical structure made life very difficult. It was very hard for him to program his courses because he had to take into account the when and where the courses were given, and he was unable to take courses that he wanted to take, or that he should have taken at a given time because he couldn't get from the 9 o'clock class in Filene to a 10 o'clock class on the fourth floor of Dartmouth Hall. And he found it a lonely life and a conspicuous one, being the only paraplegic on the scene. So he transferred to a university in Illinois which I presume is the one that you visited, where they make a specialty of providing arrangements for handicapped students. He left, at least half expecting to return to graduate from Dartmouth; but he finished there with a distinguished record; will probably get his Ph.D. this year and go into teaching.

I wonder whether you are correct in assuming that there are many crippled students who would qualify for admission to Dartmouth. Whatever people may assume about admissions officers, the wells of compassion flow as freely in their breasts as they do in those of other people. The fact that in the 20 years in which I have been very closely in touch with Dartmouth admissions there have been only three severely crippled cases who were serious candidates for admission to Dartmouth makes me question this. During the same period, there have been five students admitted who were blind or almost blind, the latest of whom is a Freshman who got -- and I am convinced earned -- three A's for his first term.

Of course if we became advertised as an institution specializing in facilities for crippled students, we would get many more applications from candidates of this kind. However, as suggested above, I question whether we have the climate or structure to encourage such specialization. I hope and trust that Dartmouth will continue its present concern for serving disadvantaged students. My present hunch is that we can utilize our particular environment, and the resources that we can muster, more effectively in serving other types of disadvantaged students than we could in becoming a specialized institution for the service of crippled students. But let's talk about it.

AID:dsw

Albert I. Dickerson

Figure 3.2b. Memo from Albert I. Dickerson to John R. Scotford, Feb. 20, 1967, p.2.

the committee were wheelchair users: Richard Luplow, Lecturer of Russian Literature, and David Eckels, a college alumnus who later returned to work for Alumni Relations. While none of the official documents explicitly mention that these men were wheelchair

To Tom — Then file: Handicap Com, CR

Dartmouth College HANOVER · NEW HAMPSHIRE · 03755

Comparative Literature

RECEIVED 1979

PDP BMD CPC

08/23/79

To: Alvin Richard

From: Richard Luplow

Subject: Review of Completed Architectural Modifications To Comply with Section 504

I have checked the architectural modifications completed through August 22, 1979, from my wheelchair perspective and offer the following comments and recommendations.

The ramps at Steele Hall and at the Hanover Inn and the ramped walkway to Clement Hall are adequate, although the walkway to Clement is unusually long and rather steep. The Personnel Office should be made aware that <u>unaided</u> access for certain handicapped people would be difficult or dangerous, especially in bad weather.

The modified bathroom in Streeter dormitory seems adequate with one exception (this also applies to the bathroom in Dana): The door handles are of the standard round, smooth type and are not usable at all by a quadraplegic; they would cause difficulty for anyone in a wheelchair or for someone with impaired hand function. Such handles should be routinely replaced with rectangular bar-type handles. If the bathroom is for both sexes, as in Dana, inside locking can be achieved with a simple slide latch of some sort.

The bathroom at Dana additionally appears to be deficient in the placement of so-called "grab bars" around the toilet. There is a seemingly useless bar <u>behind</u> the toilet (a most strange location) and there is a bar along <u>only</u> one side of the toilet instead of both sides. I think even a person on crutches with a broken leg would have trouble with that arrangement. Getting <u>to</u> the bathroom in Dana, moreover, involves traversing some rather narrow library stacks; this could be made somewhat more feasible if the semi-circular shelf just opposite the bathroom door and also the identical shelf on the opposite side of that stack, where one turns toward or from the elevator, were both removed.

Finally, regarding the long driveway/walkway leading to the Dana-Gilman entrance: The walkway had a small step at the bottom which has been ramped--this was obviously no problem; however, the walkway itself is much too steep and long to be usable by a wheelchair confined person without assistance. The only alternative I can think of is a reserved parking spot at the bottom left side of the walkway; this could be used by the campus bus or by someone with a van. (This arrangement would of course

Figure 3.3a. Memo from Richard Luplow to Alvin Richard, Aug. 23, 1979 p.1.

Luplow Review
Page Two

accommodate only one student with private transportation.) Such a parking spot would be feasible only if there are loud, firm signs making clear that the driveway/walkway is no longer to be used for loading/unloading and the like. It was quite effectively blocked, for example, by a U.P.S. truck when I tried to use it (with help) in my wheelchair.

Incidentally, the Committee on the Handicapped should be made aware that many of the ramps now on campus (for example, at Baker Library), although adequate as far as I am personally concerned, are much steeper than federal specifications call for. In the unlikely event of a check by some federal folk, the ramps could be found legally unsuitable and Dartmouth in this respect in non-complience.

cc: Robert Barnum
Ann Becker
Marjorie Boley
Cary Clark
Heidi Dietchi-Cooper
Gordon DeWitt
William Durant, Jr.
David Eckels
Ethel Garrity
Robert Kleck
Richard Plummer
Alfred Quirk

Figure 3.3b. Memo from Richard Luplow to Alvin Richard, Aug. 23, 1979 p.2.

users, several memos authored by Luplow and Eckels are clear about their wheelchair use (see Figure 3.3 a and b).[23] These personal accounts of the wheelchair user experience at Dartmouth proved to be some of the most important and helpful information to my research, but problems related to accessing sufficient information persisted.

The majority of the committee's meeting minutes focused on architectural changes, but the federal mandate required the committee to conduct a series of departmental self-evaluations. The self-evaluations asked department chairs to answer questions about the department's experience teaching students with disabilities in the past and for them to reflect on how a student with disabilities would experience coursework. These self-evaluations offer valuable insights into how different areas of the institution thought about accessibility. Dartmouth professors representing

Dartmouth College HANOVER · NEW HAMPSHIRE · 03755

Math/Social Science Program TEL. (603) 646-2554

April 25, 1978

To: Subcommittee for Program Accessibility

From: Robert Z. Norman, Chairman Math Social Science

I am pleased to reply to your communication of March 27 concerning the meeting of needs of handicapped. I find it simpler to respond not by answering the six questions you sent me but by telling you the nature of our major, the problems that might be encountered with it by handicapped students and the feasibility of resolving them, our experience with handicapped students, and questions related to the implementation of the three priority stages of improving facilities for the handicapped. I hope this mode of reply meets with your approval.

The Program in Mathematics and the Social Sciences involves the application of mathematical concepts in the various social sciences. The details of our requirements can be found in the O.R.C. None of our requirements should put any handicapped individual at a disadvantage. Many of our students make heavy use of the computer, and I would imagine blind students would probably be at a disadvantage there. I do not know how to redress this inequity, which could limit some of the options available. Even with a most capable reader it seems to me a blind person would have trouble taking full advantage of the computer. No computer work is required for the major.

Some of our courses, mainly MSS 61 and 65, use the computer fairly heavily but the others MSS 62, 63, and 80 and the Thesis course MSS 88 do not require it, and computer use is the only activity I believe might cause a problem in our courses for a handicapped person, specifically a blind person.

Our experience with handicapped students in the Program is limited to one student, ████████, who graduated in 1977. ███ was a psychology major but he was in MSS 63 last winter. ███ was a very capable deaf student whose speech was difficult to understand, especially at first. ███ gave a few pointers to me (the instructor), which were essentially to face the class when I spoke (I'm happy to say I almost always do anyway), to write key words and sentences on the board, and enunciate clearly. These suggestions were helpful to everyone, not just ███.

███ made use of notes taken by others, as he had to concentrate on reading lips sufficiently that his note taking was minimal. He often made suggestions to his note takers on errors and omissions in their notes.

Figure 3.4a. Math and Social Science Program accessibility self-evaluation, Apr. 25, 1978, p.1.

academic departments wrote pages upon pages discussing ad hoc accessibility accommodations they offered students and stories about their students with disabilities (see Figure 3.4 a and b).[24] Ultimately, the stories told in these letters represented the best

Subcommittee for Program Accessibility
April 25, 1978
Page 2

Otherwise ███ needed no extraordinary assistance. He was the top student in the class; his class project was a truly outstanding imaginative work setting forth a completely new theory of learning.

As for facility alterations, since most of the Program's activities are in Bradley and Silsby, Phase II will make us completely accessible to wheelchairs. Since our Program is quite small we could accomodate a student limited to wheelchair access by holding classes in Wilder or Fairchild, which are included in Phase I.

Sincerely yours,

Robert Z. Norman

Robert Z. Norman
Chairman Math Social Science

RZN:ak

Figure 3.4b. Math and Social Science Program accessibility self-evaluation, Apr. 25, 1978, p.2.

evidence that students with disabilities found ways to thrive at Dartmouth.

While the departmental self-evaluations are an invaluable window into the lived experiences of Dartmouth community members with disabilities, my project still felt incomplete without more direct, firsthand accounts. In an attempt to integrate more personal stories, I found it necessary to leave special collections in search of supplemental sources. My success uncovering secondhand accounts fortunately gave me numerous leads for external sources and contacts. However, I learned there were many legal and ethical factors to consider before I could reach out to any one person identified in the primary sources. Federal privacy laws such as the Health Insurance Portability and Accountability Act and Family Educational Rights and Privacy Act (FERPA) prevented my access to student files in the Dean of the college records and medical records of living students and alumni, meaning I could not consult these internal records about identified individuals in unrestricted collections. In cases when I did have lists of names, it was sometimes ambiguous in the records about which individuals were physically disabled. For example, the records of the Section 504 Committee on the Handicapped, formed in 1986, identified several students in its membership and included documents with correlated formatting, which suggested at least one member of the committee experienced low vision. However, I could not go down the list of students asking if they were the student who required the accommodation.

After I confirmed that the author of the singular indexed article in *The Dartmouth* documenting a student's experience with disability on campus is a prominent disability activist today, I was finally able to reach out to an alumnus to discuss his experiences. The most interesting commentary from this alumnus addressed how Dartmouth worked to provide him with as much of a "normal" college experience as possible. For example, Dartmouth allowed this alumnus to live in his coeducational fraternity's house with the ventilator that he used while sleeping from 1987 to 1989, even though many hospitals well into the early 2000s would not allow him to stay overnight anywhere but in the intensive care unit due to fears that someone would tamper with the ventilator. This story supported another main takeaway from my research: prior to the implementation of the Americans with Disabilities Act of 1990 (ADA), Dartmouth made remarkably personalized accommodations on an ad hoc basis. Once the ADA was implemented, disability accommodations on campus would have to become more standardized.

Although I had a preference for student perspectives when seeking out external firsthand accounts, I decided to reach out to a staff person mentioned in committee records who was still employed in the Office of Planning, Design, and Construction after consulting with special collections librarians as to the appropriateness of initiating communication. I was fortunate to receive a reply to my email and we scheduled a meeting in which I was shown records that were not located in Rauner Special Collections Library (but probably should be). There were a few letters related to the perceived conflict between accessibility and preserving college aesthetics, a well-documented controversy that became very important to my research. These records contained the most candid discussions of internal committee tension, including one scathing letter written by Dave Eckels to the head college architect about a denied request for additional signs.[25] Throughout my research, my interest in Eckels continued to grow as he was perhaps the single most important person in all of the accessibility changes that occurred in the entire town of Hanover; ultimately, I dedicated my research to him.

After returning from the Office of Planning, Design, and Construction, I consulted Eckels's alumni file, records transferred from the Alumni Relations Office after the death of an alumnus. The file contains indispensable records related to Eckels' involvement on the disability committees, news articles about his disability, and most importantly for my research project, an image of Eckels on Memorial Track Field (see Figure 3.5). This photograph was the only image of a Dartmouth community member in a wheelchair that I was able to find during my entire ten weeks of research and it was beyond satisfying to fulfill one of my original aims before my fellowship's conclusion.

The first-person accounts brought to my attention as part of these external research efforts were by far the most important and influential portions of my project; the gaps that had so frustrated my research project in the beginning had become smaller. While completing this research in special collections, I grew increasingly aware of the power that archivists have through curating the historical record, but my need to leave the archives for supplemental information underscored my own power in shaping the archives of the future. No one archivist has the bandwidth to track down every missing story from the archive. When I found missing records in the Office of Planning, Design, and Construction, I then brought those records to the attention of the college archivist. Students who have an interest in building more robust institutional history assist archivists through identification of overlooked histories,

Figure 3.5. David T. Eckels for the December 1985 issue of the Dartmouth Alumni Magazine. Photo by Nancy Wasserman.

interpretation of extant primary sources (which creates new research that can, in turn, be added to the archives), and contribution of records of our own.

An able-bodied person's interpretation of Eckels' story could be different from my own, and while this difference is not bad or invalid, it would be comparatively limited. I was able to relate to the stories of the community members with disabilities in these documents because of my experiences as a disabled person on Dartmouth's campus today.[26] Should a student with a disability thirty years from now decide to continue my research, they will have their own unique experience and perspective. By comparing my perspective to those I study in my final paper, this future student will be able to more easily track institutional progress. Over time, these issues and their accompanying perspectives will change and evolve. Inclusion of diverse, first-person student perspectives is necessary for a complete institutional picture.

CONCLUSION

The Historical Accountability Student Research Program at Dartmouth College gives undergraduates the tools they need to advance the values of equity, diversity, and inclusion in their own community through its experiential learning opportunities in the college archives. While the program has enabled special collections librarians to engage in public conversations about difficult institutional history both within the library and with other institutional departments, it is arguable that encouraging students to lead these conversations has a higher chance of enacting lasting institutional change; fellowship research has repeatedly underscored the fact that student-run organizations and events have historically been more effective at creating a more inclusive environment than initiatives and events led solely by staff and administrators in the institution's history. We hope that readers will take our learning objectives, criteria for assessment, and program structure to build out programs of their own, or at least recognize that critical engagement with institutional history requires only a reframing of the work librarians already do.

In this chapter, we have centered discussion about the Historical Accountability Student Research Program around its status as an experiential learning program, in part because experiential learning is crucial to understanding the program's core objectives. While students from historically underrepresented groups at the institution do participate in the program, the focus on individual learning experiences does come at the expense of meaningful exploration into the "historical accountability" component of the program. The program's stated research parameters of addressing issues of diversity and inclusion do mostly include instances in which the institution permitted, perpetuated, or upheld systems of oppression or exclusion, but we want to end with a brief reflection on institutional accountability to articulate the Historical Accountability Student Research Program's role in achieving accountability at Dartmouth.

The phrase "historical accountability" is a bold choice in name—almost shockingly so—in its suggestion that the institution must be held accountable to its past; reparations, or at least actions beyond mere apology, should be central to the concept of historical accountability. When program staff are asked if the program as it exists now is capable of accomplishing accountability for the institution, the answer is always decidedly "no," but that does not necessarily mean we are dealing with a misnomer. The strength of the Historical Accountability Student Research Program lies more in coming to understand the things for which Dartmouth should be held accountable and, more importantly, what accountability might look like for different groups or individuals.

An institution can only claim to be truly confronting and learning from its past once we dispel the myth that self-awareness and honesty is accountability—knowing that some wrong has been done does not mean an apology has been made. What I hope comes from the program is that its research be viewed as a constant call to action, not only to librarians and student participants, but to the individuals and offices at the institution with the power to enact more immediate change.

NOTES

1 Susan J. Boutwell, "Telling Dartmouth's Stories, Some Still to Be Discovered," Dartmouth News, April 18, 2018, https://news.dartmouth.edu/news/2018/04/telling-dartmouths-stories-some-still-be-discovered.

2 In the seed grant application for the Rauner student research fellowship, Morgan Swan, special collections librarian for teaching and scholarly engagement, indicates that special collections teaching staff at Dartmouth had connected 44 percent of the undergraduate student body to special collections materials in 2016.

3 Peter Carini, "Information Literacy for Archives and Special Collections: Defining Outcomes," *Portal: Libraries and the Academy* 16, no. 1 (January 2016): 191–206, https://doi.org/10.1353/pla.2016.0006.

4 See appendices for the program's Learning Objectives and Criteria for Assessment documentation.

5 Carini, "Information Literacy for Archives and Special Collections," 198–200.

6 Pete McDonnell, ed., "Preface," in *The Experiential Library: Transforming Academic and Research Libraries through the Power of Experiential Learning* (Chandos Publishing, 2017), xxvii–xxxiv, https://doi.org/10.1016/B978-0-08-100775-4.00022-4.

7 David Kolb, "Concrete/Reflective/Abstract/Active," SUNY Cortland FACULTYWEB Service, https://web.cortland.edu/andersmd/learning/Kolb.htm.

8 Dartmouth College operates year-round in four 10-week quarters or terms, giving undergraduate students 16 terms to complete their studies. Students are required to enroll in classes for 12 of those 16 terms. The fellowship is designed for undergraduates to complete during any one of their four "off" terms.

9 Qualtrics, Data Summary of Historical Accountability Student Research Fellowship Exit Survey.

10 The selection committee is chaired by the institutional history research specialist and comprises one special collections librarian, two subject specialty librarians, and one representative from the Office of Pluralism and

Leadership. The Office of Pluralism and Leadership at Dartmouth College provides advising, education, training, and leadership development programming to students to foster a campus environment that "values difference and contributes to a socially just world."

11 Society of American Archivists. "Describing Archives: A Content Standard (DACS)." 30 November 2022. https://www2.archivists.org/groups/technical-subcommittee-on-describing-archives-a-content-standard-dacs.

12 Reflective assignments under the program take on a less pedagogical role in the context of participatory archival practices. In cases when students seek perspectives beyond themselves, they usually conduct interviews with members of the community identified in primary documents. In Winter 2021, the digital collections and oral history archivist began introducing student researchers to oral history methodologies, which has facilitated the accession of student interviews into the Dartmouth College Archives.

13 Ana Roeschley and Jeonghyun Kim, "'Something That Feels Like a Community': The Role of Personal Stories in Building Community-Based Participatory Archives," *Archival Science* 19, no. 1 (March 1, 2019): 30, https://doi.org/10.1007/s10502-019-09302-2.

14 Michelle Caswell and Marika Cifor, "From Human Rights to Feminist Ethics: Radical Empathy in the Archives," *Archivaria* 81 (May 6, 2016): 25.

15 Caswell and Cifor, "From Human Rights to Feminist Ethics," 30, 41.

16 C. J. Anderson and C. Brand, "'Out of the Vault': Engaging Students in Experiential Learning Through Special Collections and Archives," in *The Experiential Library: Transforming Academic and Research Libraries Through the Power of Experiential Learning*, ed. Pete McDonnell (Chandos Publishing, 2017), 91, https://doi.org/10.1016/B978-0-08-100775-4.00007-8.

17 Pete Williams, ed., "Student Research on Dartmouth LGBTQIA History," *Green Light: Newsletter of the Dartmouth LGBTQIA+ Alum Association* 25, no. 1 (June 2020): 8.

18 Ana Roeschley and Jeonghyun Kim, "'Something That Feels Like a Community,'" 30.

19 Caswell and Cifor, "From Human Rights to Feminist Ethics," 30, 41.

20 John Scotford, "Letter to President Dickey, Richard Olmsted, Edward Chamberlain, and Dr. Jackson Re: Extending the Opportunity of a Dartmouth Education to a Hithertofore Untapped Minority Group—Crippled Students," February 14, 1967, Rauner Special Collections Library, Dartmouth College, Hanover, New Hampshire.

21 Albert I. Dickerson, "Letter to John Scotford," February 20, 1967, Rauner Special Collections Library, Dartmouth College, Hanover, New Hampshire.

22 "Section 504 of the Rehabilitation Act of 1973," 29 U.S.C. § 794 (1973).

23 Richard Luplow, "Letter to Alvin Richard," August 23, 1979, Rauner Special Collections Library, Dartmouth College, Hanover, New Hampshire.

24 Robert Z. Norman, "Letter to Subcommittee for Program Accessibility," April 25, 1978, Rauner Special Collections Library, Dartmouth College, Hanover, New Hampshire.

25 David T. Eckels, "Letter to George T. Hathorn," May 12, 1994, Dartmouth College Office of Planning Records, Rauner Special Collections Library, Dartmouth College, Hanover, New Hampshire.

26 Throughout this section, I make it a point to use person-first language when referring to other persons with disabilities. This is largely to conform with standard style guides in academia. However, when referring to myself, I choose not to use person-first language. As I know that I am a person, I feel no need for others to reaffirm my personhood. Obviously, I am a person. I am a disabled person.

BIBLIOGRAPHY

Anderson, C. J., and C. Brand. "'Out of the Vault': Engaging Students in Experiential Learning Through Special Collections and Archives." In *The Experiential Library: Transforming Academic and Research Libraries Through the Power of Experiential Learning*, edited by Pete McDonnell, 89–101. Chandos Publishing, 2017. https://doi.org/10.1016/B978-0-08-100775-4.00007-8.

Boutwell, Susan J. "Telling Dartmouth's Stories, Some Still to Be Discovered." Dartmouth News, April 18, 2018. https://news.dartmouth.edu/news/2018/04/telling-dartmouths-stories-some-still-be-discovered.

Carini, Peter. "Information Literacy for Archives and Special Collections: Defining Outcomes." *Portal: Libraries and the Academy* 16, no. 1 (January 2016): 191–206. https://doi.org/10.1353/pla.2016.0006.

Caswell, Michelle, and Marika Cifor. "From Human Rights to Feminist Ethics: Radical Empathy in the Archives." *Archivaria* 81 (May 6, 2016): 23–43.

Dickerson, Albert I. "Letter to John Scotford," February 20, 1967. Rauner Special Collections Library, Dartmouth College, Hanover, New Hampshire.

Eckels, David T. "Letter to George T. Hathorn," May 12, 1994. Dartmouth College Office of Planning Records, Rauner Special Collections Library, Dartmouth College, Hanover, New Hampshire.

Kolb, David. "Concrete/Reflective/Abstract/Active." SUNY Cortland FACULTYWEB Service. https://web.cortland.edu/andersmd/learning/Kolb.htm.

Luplow, Richard. "Letter to Alvin Richard," August 23, 1979. Rauner Special Collections Library, Dartmouth College, Hanover, New Hampshire.

McDonnell, Pete, ed. "Preface." In *The Experiential Library: Transforming Academic and Research Libraries through the Power of Experiential Learning*, edited by Pete McDonnell, xxvii–xxxiv. Chandos Publishing, 2017. https://doi.org/10.1016/B978-0-08-100775-4.00022-4.

Norman, Robert Z. "Letter to Subcommittee for Program Accessibility," April 25, 1978. Rauner Special Collections Library, Dartmouth College, Hanover, New Hampshire.

Roeschley, Ana, and Jeonghyun Kim. "'Something That Feels Like a Community': The Role of Personal Stories in Building Community-Based Participatory Archives." *Archival Science* 19, no. 1 (March 1, 2019): 27–49. https://doi.org/10.1007/s10502-019-09302-2.

Scotford, John. "Letter to President Dickey, Richard Olmsted, Edward Chamberlain, and Dr. Jackson Re: Extending the Opportunity of a Dartmouth Education to a Hithertofore Untapped Minority Group—Crippled Students," February 14, 1967. Rauner Special Collections Library, Dartmouth College, Hanover, New Hampshire.

Society of American Archivists. "Describing Archives: A Content Standard (DACS)." 30 November 2022. https://www2.archivists.org/groups/technical-subcommittee-on-describing-archives-a-content-standard-dacs

Williams, Pete, ed. "Student Research on Dartmouth LGBTQIA History." *Green Light: Newsletter of the Dartmouth LGBTQIA+ Alum Association* 25, no. 1 (June 2020): 8.

CHAPTER FOUR

QUEER PASTS, QUEER FUTURES: THE LAFAYETTE COLLEGE QUEER ARCHIVES PROJECT

Mary A. Armstrong, Charlotte Nunes, and Jennifer Wellnitz

INTRODUCTION

This chapter features perspectives from three key contributors—faculty director, digital scholarship librarian, and student researcher—on the creation of the Lafayette College Queer Archives Project (QAP) at Lafayette College in Easton, Pennsylvania. The QAP is a collaborative, interdisciplinary initiative designed to illuminate Lafayette's Queer history, advance teaching, learning, and research in the area of Queer studies, and promote positive institutional transformation. The project encompasses curricular and oral history components, as well as a unique digital humanities project that was honored with the 2020 Center for Research Libraries Primary Source Award in Access.[1] In this chapter, we narrate the origination of the QAP. We detail how we make use of the structural features of the web-based publishing platform Scalar[2] in order to make visible hidden and under-archived elements of Lafayette's LGBTQ+ past and to structure user engagement with these materials as a distinctively non-linear, Queer experience.

The QAP is informed by recent scholarship in Queer archives studies and academic librarianship emphasizing the relationship between privilege and archival representation. As the coauthors of "Information Maintenance as a Practice of Care" write, "[p]ower inheres in the acts of identifying, classifying, and ordering information. People who are privileged to define information of importance and dictate how it is organized and shared have disproportionate influence on the shape and dynamics of society."[3] In their survey of founders of such community archives as the ONE National Gay and Lesbian Archives at the University of South California and the Transgender Living Archives, Michelle Caswell et al. identify both the "profoundly negative affective consequences of absence and misrepresentation in...archives and the positive effect of complex and autonomous forms of representation in community-driven archives."[4] Jamie A. Lee of the Arizona Queer Archives details such positive effects, arguing that "'legibility' play[s] a role in 'legitimacy.'" They highlight "the important role that LGBTQ-identified archives...can play across generations...in non-dominant communities to legitimate lived and living histories that are often erased, obscured, and marginalized."[5] In conversation with these voices, our aim for the culmination of the QAP is ambitious—nothing less than to actively reshape Lafayette's social, curricular, and institutional futures so as to manifest, as community archivist Jarrett Drake puts it, "the seismic shift in paradigms that we want to see in society."[6]

The QAP is animated by the following questions: how can institutions of higher education—which are historically both products of and replicators of privilege—be truly transformed? Can such transformation move beyond "inclusion," a process that leaves established, hierarchical power relations intact? How can archives-based undergraduate pedagogies contribute to the work of moving marginalized voices to the center? Located at the nexus of pedagogical innovation, archival engagement, and pioneering digital scholarship, the QAP works toward such radical institutional change. The QAP intervenes in an institution that has (historically) been slow to support and often unambiguously hostile to LGBTQ+ people. The project collaboratively deploys undergraduate pedagogy and the curriculum, student engagement in the archives, and use of digital humanities scholarship to leverage that change. It has, at its very center, the voices and stories of the LGBTQ+ people who have lived Lafayette's sometimes quite painful history.

PERSPECTIVE 1—FACULTY DIRECTOR: MARY A. ARMSTRONG, CHARLES A. DANA PROFESSOR OF WOMEN'S, GENDER & SEXUALITY STUDIES AND ENGLISH, AND PROGRAM CHAIR, WOMEN'S, GENDER AND SEXUALITY STUDIES

Curricular and Institutional Change

When I developed Lafayette College's first course in sexuality studies in 2011, I had no idea that my students and I were heading for transformative work with the college archives or that the course would be the starting point for the QAP. As the relatively new chair of the Women's, Gender and Sexuality Studies (WGSS) program Studies program, the original purpose of my WGS 340: Sexuality Studies class was to intervene—as swiftly as possible—in a college curriculum that did not offer students the opportunity to engage in LGBTQ+ studies in any substantive way. Historically a conservative institution, Lafayette's approach to sexuality studies was a perfect version of what education theorist Elliot Eisner has termed the "null curriculum."[7] This particular null curriculum—that is, the Queer studies content with which students were not given the opportunity to engage—was more than a failure to offer important intellectual content to students. The absence of LGBTQ+ studies sent a message about institutional values, signaling clearly that LGBTQ+ histories, cultures, and issues were not sufficiently important to include in the college's most essential work, that is, the business of teaching and learning. The absence of sexuality-related courses banished both Queer history and Queer people to invisibility, inside and outside of the classroom.

QAP's close connections to both the classroom and the archives is shaped by this context. In many ways, WGS 340 was the origin point for the QAP because initial course goals were overtly political as well as pedagogical. When I designed the class, I was clear-eyed about the political nature of the curriculum and eager to deploy it ideologically.[8] Adding a sexuality studies course was a necessary part of developing a more viable WGS program, but the development of WGS 340 was also an intentional intervention in the institution, an instructional decision that aimed for effects that were liberatory and campus-wide, as well as intellectual and classroom-based.

WGS 340: Sexuality Studies is an advanced interdisciplinary class that is, like many higher-level LGBTQ+ studies courses, anchored in the work of French historian and theorist Michel Foucault. Foucault's thinking shapes the course, framing other materials and also functioning as a main reference point for class discussions. Students spend the first three weeks of class intensively reading *The History of Sexuality Vol. I: An Introduction*, with an emphasis on the historically constructed, contingent nature of seemingly self-evident, "natural" sexual identities. Like most courses of this kind, one goal is for students to understand that gender and sexual identities are (re)constructed over time through the intertwined workings of emergent discourses and morphing institutions. These identities arise and dissipate as power, language, and institutions interact. I designed WGS 340 to focus, in particular, on institutions' role in the creation and shaping of modern gender/sexual identities.[9]

The first iteration of the course was successful, judging by 2011 standards for LGBTQ+ Studies at Lafayette. The course "made" with a total enrollment of nine students—an achievement in and of itself. Several LGBTQ+ identified student participants came out to me during or after the class, and most reported I was the first person at Lafayette to whom they had disclosed their Queer sexual or gender identities. This indicates that the course created a much-needed safe space on campus. LGBTQ+ and allied students uniformly expressed appreciation for the class in both its contents and climate-changing senses. Word began to get around that this was a challenging but interesting course.

But the first iteration of the class also revealed an important limitation. Sexuality Studies necessarily spends a great deal of time on theory, and deploys a considerable amount of historical and contemporary examples of how gendered/sexual identities are socially produced. There is also heavy emphasis on intersectionality as a key analytic. Class materials move energetically across many examples of how other identity categories, such as race and ethnicity, intersect with discourses around sexuality and how these categories have mutually constitutive effects. Amid theory, historical examples, and intersectional analytics focusing on race, I also wanted my students to *directly* discover and explore how discourses of sexuality move and shift within institutions, and to see and understand how such processes are currently happening all around them.

Into the Archives—Undergraduate Research as Product and Catalyst for Change

As I was considering possible revisions to the course, a new variable entered the equation in the person of a Lafayette alumnus. Riley Temple, a member of the class of 1971, is one of the earliest African American graduates of Lafayette, an Emeritus Member of the Lafayette Board of Trustees, and an out gay man. Coincidentally, Temple arranged to meet with then-Provost Wendy Hill to discuss what it would mean for the college to begin to attend to its Queer past. Soon after, the (now Emerita) Director of Special Collections & College Archives Diane Shaw and I were invited to meet with the provost to discuss Temple's visit and his request for more attentiveness to Lafayette's LGBTQ+ history. It soon became obvious that connecting WGS 340 to the college archives would be the perfect place to spark an intervention that was both curricular and institutional.

Higher education archives are situated in specific institutions, supported by a particular constellation of resources, and embedded in contexts that shape what it means for an instructor to engage with both archival materials and archivists. In the case of WGS 340, several local institutional factors influenced my ability to partner with Lafayette's special collections and college archives in order to develop a pedagogical strategy for my students to explore the college's "history of sexuality." Some salient characteristics of Lafayette were:

- *Teaching partnerships between faculty and archivists/librarians are routine at Lafayette.* Archivists and librarians hold faculty status, reflecting the institution's recognition of their capacity as co-instructors and normalizing their engagement in teaching praxis.
- As part of a small, well-resourced, private liberal arts college, *the archives are well resourced as well.* Archivists are highly trained, materials are available and well-organized, and there is a functional, welcoming space where classes can take place. The liberal arts model also encourages individual instruction for students in this space.
- The Lafayette archives *has been historically committed to diversity and to the collection and preservation of materials related to underrepresented groups.* Notably, in 2002, the archives collected oral histories from Lafayette's first women alumnae (the college began to admit women in 1971) and African American alumni from the 1960s and 1970s.
- Despite a demonstrated commitment to diversifying collections, such diversification was selective: the archives *had no specific projects, collections, or areas of focus related to LGBTQ+ issues.* Lafayette's Queer history, as such, was not present in the archives.

These characteristics help illustrate that pedagogical interventions involving higher education archives are shaped not only by actors' intentions, but also by relevant local institutional features such as cultures of co-instruction, availability and kinds of resources, institutional type, and already existing or absent ideological and political commitments (both curricular and archival). Understanding how pedagogical interventions and student work can change a higher education archive means actively taking the characteristics of any *particular* institution and archive into account. In Lafayette's case, the college archives had a strong record of successful pedagogical involvement. However, the archives also had implicitly but authoritatively declared that gender and race mattered when it came to more intentionally recording the college's discriminatory past and that Queer issues and lives did not.

Bringing my students into conversation with the archives began with questions. While I of course wanted my students to acquire standard archives-related skills (i.e., strengthen their capacity to work with primary sources), I was especially interested in formulating a way to enable them to put Foucault's ideas into radical praxis. I wrote to the Director of Special Collections, Diane Shaw, and college archivist Elaine Stomber, querying them about possibilities because I was anxious to know whether there were any LGBTQ+/sexuality studies materials and artifacts in the archives at all. I asked four questions:

1. Could the college archives support student research on sexual identities, including LGBTQ history, on campus?
2. Did we have the documentation to help students explore the history of sexuality at Lafayette?
3. Would the records in the college archives help students understand how institutions organize sexuality?
4. And would those documents uncover the mechanisms by which they do so?

I wanted my undergraduate students to recognize and reframe the archives' past representational and preservationist decisions through projects that uncovered "new" artifacts and reoriented archival materials that addressed Queer stories, histories, and lives. But before such an undertaking could begin, I had to believe that it was reasonable to try. What materials and artifacts pertaining to LGBTQ+ life specifically and sexual cultures generally were extant and concealed in the Lafayette archives? In an institution historically hostile to LGBTQ+ people, had any LGBTQ+ related artifacts survived at all?

The willingness of the archives to collaborate on this liberatory project was significant, and connects the QAP with the emergent insights associated with critical archival studies, a field of archival studies that emphasizes "collective critical thinking about ways to resist reinforcing oppression based on race, class, gender, sexuality, and ability in the archives."[10] This critical approach clarifies the many connections between archival practice and the dynamics of power, oppression, and liberation that have focused our work.[11] Archives may actively participate in their own deconstruction and revision, or resist those processes. Archives have the power to support or hinder, to seek or shroud searches for certain materials and documents. And, like the null curriculum, the actions of archives often take place through inaction. The insidious inertia generated by unexamined, default perspectives in which the experience of dominant groups stand in for "experience" itself can effectively block other representations of identities, history and power while seeming to do "nothing."

Research is always *technically* possible when archives are accessible, but the cooperation and interest of colleagues who control access and have intimate knowledge of archival contents influence how a revisionist project moves forward. In the case of WGS 340, archivists at Lafayette embraced the participation of undergraduates in the revision of the archives and welcomed a project that interrupted the invisibility of the college's LGBTQ+ history. College archivists began developing possible nodes of the collection where the history of sexuality—particularly LGBTQ+ issues—might be identified as places for students to start looking. These included materials pertaining to themes such as LGBTQ+ student clubs, Title IX, sexual assault policies, AIDS, college domestic partner benefits, and so on (see Figure 4.1). A very hazy outline of materials began to surface in preparation for the second iteration of WGS 340.

When that iteration came around, WGS 340 students had a new option for their final assignment, a possibility that emerged from the intersection of several variables: an alumnus's outside intervention, the college archive's interest in self-critique and alteration, and an instructor's pedagogical desire for students to directly encounter the intertwined workings of discourse, identities, power, and institutions. Students could choose to write a standard research paper, but they also had the option of participating in

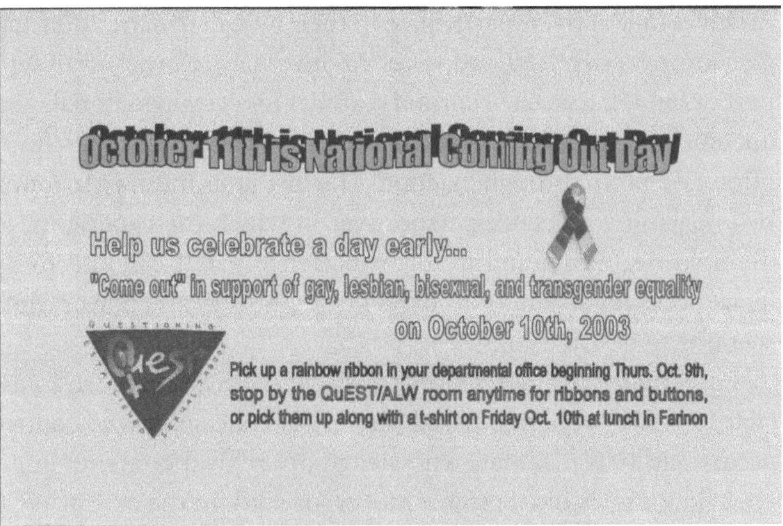

Figure 4.1. Flier to invite Lafayette College campus participation in October 2003 events hosted by QuEST (Questioning Established Sexual Taboos), observing National Coming Out Day.

something new: "The History of Sexuality at Lafayette College: The Archives Project." The archival assignment option offered WGS 340 students

> the opportunity to pursue a Lafayette-centered topic in which you discover and analyze topics concerning sexual identities (including but not limited to LGBTQ identities) on campus. Your work will explore a narrative, historical, and/or political aspect of sexuality on campus and be centered on a theme.
>
> You will design project/do research in the Lafayette Archives (Skillman Library) and partner with the College as it works to better understand and preserve its own rich history around sexual identities, particularly LGBTQ history on campus.

In essence, the assignment asked students to revise the archives' presentation of Lafayette's history of sexuality and alter the contents and organization of that history relative to the archives' collections, holdings, and areas of emphasis. Students were encouraged to see the basic materials presented by the archives not as endpoints but as doorways to new questions and the unearthing of additional materials. It was made explicit that the institutional power of the archives was under scrutiny and the archives was not a static collection of materials to be used in the conventional sense, but also a place and an ideological nexus we would intentionally work to transform.

The new WGS 340 assignment option was also designed to link student work back to the archives, looping newly discovered artifacts *and* related student analyses back into the archives itself. Every student who selected the new archival assignment had the option to (voluntarily) contribute their research project to the archives; the archives, in turn, agreed to add those student papers. This meant that every student project could act as a permanent disruption to the archival status quo. These students would expand knowledge of LGBTQ+ history and sexuality issues but also leverage their research as mechanisms for transforming archival content and, in most cases, contributing sharp critiques of both archival and institutional practices. From that first set of papers, projects spanned a wide range of sexuality-related topics including *Black Manifesto to QuEST Manifesto* (Shanequa Lassiter '14), *The Language of Sexual Health at Lafayette College 1970–2014* (Hollis Miller '14), *LGBTQ and the Princeton Review* (Deja Washington '14), and *The Emergence of Lafayette College's Sexual Harassment Policy* (Kathryn White '14).

Through this new assignment, WGS 340 intervened in the archives in two critical ways. First, students intentionally located and synthesized materials meant to shift how the archives recognized and organized artifacts relative to the significance of sexuality-related issues and LGBTQ+ communities and experiences. Second, the option of adding their own interventive research directly to the archives ruptured the boundary between the classroom and the archives, placing students' challenges to archival decision-making within the bounds of the archives as well. Student research was not a product of updated archival materials but a force that disrupted lines of power and became a transformative artifact in and of itself—one that was permanently capable of disrupting the archival status quo. In short, unlike many final research papers, archived WGS 340 projects were neither synthetic in purpose nor temporary in lifespan. They became long-lasting tools for change.

Queer Oral History

Because the research praxis of WGS 340 was rooted in theory, students saw their work in the archives as much more than simply locating new materials or adding to the collection. The critical context provided by the course enabled them to recognize shifting discourses around sexuality and sexual/gender identities, as well as the relationships of those discourses to formal and informal structures of power. As they unearthed new artifacts and themes, students sharpened their capacity to think critically about the framing of sexuality within the institution of the college over time. Students who chose to add their own research to the archives evidenced a particularly strong sense of the deep intervention they were making. Slowly, after several iterations of WGS 340, the archives' relationship to sexuality studies-related materials shifted. The interventions of student researchers—elevated by course content and energetically abetted by the archives staff—began to generate a collection of materials and artifacts directly associated with the college's history of sexuality and LGBTQ+ lives.

There were, however, limitations to WGS 340's capacity to challenge archival authority around sexuality and Queer lives. Lafayette's history around sexuality and LGBTQ+ issues has been a dark one—so dark that in 1992 the college was recognized by the *Princeton Review* as the most homophobic institution in the United States.

Using logic, imagination, and research, and guided by active archivist allies, students gleaned what they could from the archives relative to sexuality and Queer history. Yet given the institution's long neglect of LGBTQ+ issues there was, predictably, a relatively limited amount of material. We needed to open new avenues for research and enable further interventions in transforming the archives. We needed more information.

The QAP LGBTQ+ Oral History Project developed from this need. Pedagogical interventions into the archives were necessarily limited to what had been somehow already preserved and collected, confining LGBTQ+-related archival work to past record-keeping decisions made by the archives. Because no formal attempts had been made to document Lafayette's history of sexuality generally or LGBTQ+ history specifically, salient materials had largely entered the archives as "stowaway artifacts" piggy-backed onto content that had been retained for other reasons. The idea behind an oral history project with alumni was to move the project away

1992 EDITION

THE PRINCETON REVIEW

THE
STUDENT ACCESS
GUIDE TO
THE BEST
COLLEGES

1992 EDITION

BY TOM MELTZER,
ZACH KNOWER, AND
JOHN KATZMAN

VILLARD BOOKS NEW YORK 1992

Figure 4.2. Excerpt from the 1992 edition of *The Princeton Review: The Student Access Guide to the Best Colleges* putting Lafayette College at the top of a list of the nation's most homophobic campuses.

■ *Gays out of closet:*

Bryn Mawr College
Grinnell College
Simon's Rock of Bard College
Rhode Island School of Design
Goddard College
Bard College
Reed College
Hampshire College
Sarah Lawrence College
Bennington College
New College–University of South Florida
Wesleyan University
Vassar College
Juilliard School
Oberlin College
Beloit College
Tufts University
Smith College
Parsons School of Design
Carleton College

■ *Gays still in closet:*

Lafayette College
Washington and Lee University
Rose-Hulman Institute of Technology
Randolph-Macon College
Rhodes College
College of Holy Cross
Villanova University
Brigham Young University
Wofford College
Clarkson University
Muhlenberg College
University of Dayton
Baylor University
Colorado School of Mines
Seton Hall University
Wittenberg University
Franklin and Marshall College
DePauw University
Claremont–Claremont McKenna
Manhattanville College

■ *Gay community accepted:*

Deep Springs College
Bennington College
New College–University of South Florida
Eugene Lang College
Reed College
Simon's Rock of Bard College
Marlboro College
Bryn Mawr College
Goddard College
College of the Atlantic
Hampshire College
Bard College
Rhode Island School of Design
Parsons School of Design
Sarah Lawrence College
Grinnell College
Smith College
Vassar College
Oberlin College
Juilliard School

■ *Homophobic:*

Lafayette College
Baylor University
Rose-Hulman Institute of Technology
Washington and Lee University
Brigham Young University
Randolph-Macon College
Bucknell University
Morehouse College
Hampden-Sydney College
Furman University
Clemson University
Fairfield University
Villanova University
Providence College
Colorado School of Mines
University of North Dakota
Wofford College
College of Holy Cross
University of Notre Dame
Clarkson University

from a reliance on accidental Queer history. In addition, an oral history project would push the college archives to surrender representational authority to Lafayette's LGBTQ+ community. Queer history at the college could emerge in terms of lived, local LGBTQ+ experience, rather than in terms of archival choice-making or the specific interests of student researchers.

The Lafayette college archives' existing commitment to active engagement with alums from historically marginalized groups (first women graduates and early African American graduates) offered a precedent for launching an LGBTQ+ oral history project at Lafayette. As the QAP turned toward oral history, WGS 340 shifted once again. Students now needed access to the critical debates around the *particular* workings of power and value relative to oral history and Queer lives. I again revised the course to include materials on queering the archives, and on the history and theory behind LGBTQ+ oral history and Queer archives work.[12]

The introduction of oral history interviews powerfully reshaped and expanded the QAP. Structurally, the oral histories added entirely new strata of information about the college's past and its Queer history. The reflections, recollections, and observations of Queer alums, faculty, and staff who had lived the college's LGBTQ+ history guided student research into new places and transformed the content of their work. More profoundly, oral history offered the QAP a particularly rich and productively disruptive mode for transforming the archives. Offering intimate-yet-public narratives that are always "rich with multiple truths," oral history interviews necessarily reflect the shifting nature of human subjectivity and embodied experience, representing particularly powerful ways to engage in archival transformation.[13] The evolving, inherently ambiguous narratives of our LGBTQ+ oral history interviews elevated the QAP from a project that aimed to "fill in gaps" in a linear chronology to one which expanded the record but also productively destabilized and challenged assumptions around the nature of Queer experience, identity, and history.

As the QAP LGBTQ+ oral history project unfolded and transcripts began coming in, our work took on new complexity and depth. It was at this point Lafayette's archivists and I began to consider how we might make these important new materials widely accessible. We wanted to make the LGBTQ+ oral histories available in a standard way, just as other oral history collections from the Lafayette archives were. But we also wanted to go beyond that and make our work in queering the archives—including ongoing transformative student work—public facing and available more broadly for use by other educators and researchers. Having developed a fairly broad collection of emergent LGBTQ+ materials and a slowly-growing collection of LGBTQ+ oral histories, we believed this was a moment to take the archives beyond its own walls. We turned at this point to the development of a Queer digital humanities project, a lofty goal that coincided fortuitously with the arrival of Dr. Nunes.

PERSPECTIVE 2—DIGITAL SCHOLARSHIP LIBRARIAN: CHARLOTTE NUNES, DIRECTOR OF LAFAYETTE COLLEGE LIBRARIES DIGITAL SCHOLARSHIP SERVICES

When I arrived at Lafayette in August of 2016, the QAP was already well under way, as Dr. Armstrong detailed previously. As the QAP faculty director, she had convened an enthusiastic faculty advisory committee to help guide the project. Along with former Director of Special Collections & College Archives, Diane Shaw, and college archivist, Elaine Stomber, Dr. Armstrong had completed the Institutional Review Board process and was actively collecting oral histories to be preserved in the college archives. For some time, the advisory committee had been contemplating a digital humanities (DH) project anchored in the QAP oral histories. As a new member of the committee with a background in digital scholarship technologies, I was happy to consult on some options. We had in mind a highly flexible DH project that would interweave oral histories, archival materials, and undergraduate interpretive research to tell new stories and make new arguments about Queer history at Lafayette.

We considered TimelineJS but determined that although we would indeed want a timeline functionality as part of our DH project, that couldn't be the extent of the project—we needed something more multimodal and multi-linear. The digital exhibit platform Omeka was a possibility; its hierarchical structure, composed of items and thematic collections, gives useful shape to many successful DH projects. Ultimately, we chose the platform Scalar for our project for a number of reasons. In particular, Scalar's aggressively non-linear approach to content meshed with our vision of the site as Queer in form, as well as content. In Scalar, contents are heavily networked and interconnected across the site, rather than being hierarchically nested. We determined that for us this was important in thinking ahead to how the site could be used for research and teaching that approaches history-building critically and iteratively.

We also liked the values behind Scalar. Like TimelineJS and Omeka, Scalar is an open-source software project created and supported by an institution of higher education. Scalar is stewarded by the Alliance for Networking Visual Culture at the University of Southern California. This alliance has a number of archive, library, and university press partners, and is an important player in the field of open access academic library publishing. We liked that Scalar is driven by values of higher education and cultural heritage, and that it has good traction in the way of robust user communities in the fields of DH and open access scholarly communications.

In addition to shared values, Scalar offered specific features that were important to us. Scalar integrates TimelineJS to offer a timeline layout option for content, which supported our goal of creating new historical narratives. Scalar has comprehensive options for metadata—that basic information you need to

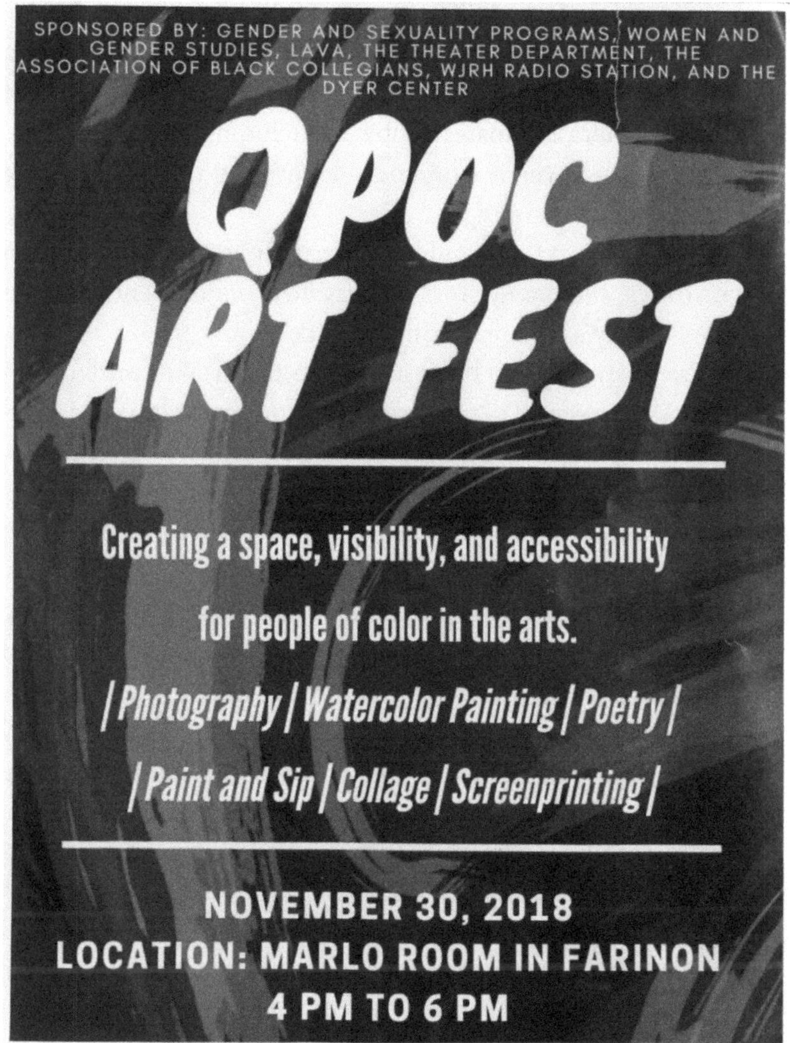

Figure 4.3. Flier to advertise a 2018 Arts Fest hosted by the Lafayette College student group Queer People of Color (QPOC).

orient yourself to a digital asset so it doesn't exist in a vacuum, but relates to a context. In Scalar you can select fields from multiple metadata schemas used by libraries and archives to describe primary source materials. This was appealing to us since the site would incorporate a range of materials such as oral histories, photographs, event posters, meeting agendas, newspaper articles, various ephemera and material objects including leaflets, buttons, and t-shirts, and even a quilt commemorating the admission of women to Lafayette in 1970.

For a DH project that would be inherently archival, anchored in oral histories, and highly cross-linked and cross-referential, Scalar emerged clearly as the platform of choice.

The next step was to build a team to undertake constructing the QAP DH project. There was no question that this would be an invaluable experiential learning opportunity for talented undergraduate students to create new knowledge while building skills in digital content management. Dr. Armstrong recruited a team of students who had taken courses with her in the WGSS program at Lafayette. These students came to the work with a strong general sense of the conceptual and historical issues involved in building the project. Meanwhile, I communicated with members of my department to determine what tasks they could reasonably take on given their other responsibilities in Digital Scholarship Services. By the time we launched the project in April of 2019, Adam Malantonio (digital initiatives developer), Nora Egloff (digital repository librarian), Paul Miller (visual resources curator), and Janna Avon (digital initiatives librarian) had all played key roles in the project, from configuring the Scalar software and addressing server-side issues, to providing training on audio editing workflows for oral histories, to offering consultations on the nuts and bolts of adding content to Scalar. The QAP DH site is a truly collaborative team effort, and the depth and complexity of the site's final iteration is a reflection of the many layers of expertise required to construct a digital project driven by such a complex and ambitious vision.

During the first several months of the project, the undergraduate researchers wrangled with nuts and bolts of the site. Over the course of two workshop sessions per week, we learned the ins and outs of Scalar. We needed a data model, a style guide, and metadata guidelines, and we would need to create all of these from scratch in order to actualize our unique vision for the project. Cue many a lengthy discussion hashing out the component elements of our data model and how they would interact. We made endless minute decisions about fonts, formats, file names, title conventions, date conventions, metadata field definitions, rules for acronyms, and more. Attending to these seemingly endless minutiae was essential to setting a strong prototype for the site that would enable future researchers on the site to contribute seamlessly, with a clear sense of parameters, and create a cohesive whole.

Playing an active decision-making role as we set the foundation of the site was also essential for the students to develop a sense of ownership of the project. This, in turn, supported the goal to support young professionals interested in library work. By scaling up the professionalization opportunities we offer students to participate in digital archives projects, and by improving communication to the student body about the archives-related professionalization opportunities we currently offer, the QAP has made an active investment in the diversity of the archives profession. No matter what fields students enter professionally, their experience with the QAP helps them develop skills for engaging in collaborative, respectful teamwork. Ideally their encounter with archives work exposes them to the contingency of the historical record, and provides opportunities for them to seek equity—both important outcomes of undergraduate education at an institution like Lafayette, where the college values statement on diversity and inclusion calls for "an environment in which difference is valued, equity is sought, and inclusiveness is practiced."

While many campus units do important work to advance these values, libraries and college archives are uniquely situated to enact them. If a community's history doesn't have accessible archival documentation, it's harder to conduct research that centers the community in the historical record. Therefore, the archives profession has a particular responsibility to seek equity by supporting initiatives that offer a corrective to past acquisitions policies that may not have centered what archivist Yusef Omowale calls "minoritized life."[14] For student researchers on the QAP DH project, the process of building the site was a visceral encounter with archival absence. As they realized the apparent dearth of materials on Queer history in the college archives, they were frustrated—even disillusioned—by the inherently incomplete, inherently exclusive nature of archives. Yet as creators of the site committed to make visible hidden and under-archived elements of Lafayette's Queer past, the students could claim ownership of this historical record and play an active role in constructing it from their perspective.

The QAP team found several ways to deliberately build the QAP DH site's digital archives to account for Queer histories. They scoured decades-worth of the digitized Lafayette student newspaper, solicited primary source materials from interviewees, and perhaps most importantly, partnered with archivists Elaine and Diane to identify materials pertinent to Lafayette's Queer histories that were distributed across diffuse collections.

Although the college archives include no centralized collections on Queer history at Lafayette, the archivists' sleuthing surfaced a host of materials that we could bring together digitally in the QAP DH site. This dynamic gives credence to Omowale's concern that in archives, "inclusion is dialectically tied to exclusion." Omowale argues that underrepresented lives and communities "should not echo articulations that we do not already exist in the archive. We are not marginal or other to the archive, but integral to it. We may be silenced or made invisible, but we have always been present."[15] As students recognized these truths, they internalized the constructed nature of history as both a problem (in that it can be exclusionary) and an opportunity: they are agents in its construction.

Friday
April 29, 1988

The Lafayette

page 5

AIDS panel comes to Lafayette for discussion

by Melissa Lennon

Lafayette students and concerned Easton residents filled Colton Chapel Tuesday night to participate in a panel discussion about Acquired Immune Deficiency Syndrome, or AIDS.

The Chapel was packed with people listening to, and asking questions of, Ms. Alice Clark, from the medical profession; a Reverend Calhoun, who helps AIDS sufferers deal with their disease and David, an actual AIDS victim. Most questions asked by the audience were directed towards David.

The actual way or time he contracted AIDS was difficult to pinpoint. Besides the generally well known ways of contracting the disease, by semen, vaginal secretions or blood of an infected person coming in contact with the blood of an uninfected person, all the panel members cited other high risk behavior such as drinking and experimenting with drugs.

Ms. Clark was especially concerned with high school and college-age people because of the their lack of education on the facts about AIDS and its transmission. David reiteratd the need for increased education. He also stressed throughout the program that AIDS patients are people too. He explained that it is not actually AIDS that kills, but the disease that one contracts because of the deficiency in the immune system that actually constitutes the illness.

David had twice before been hospitalized for pneumonia. This, he said, was very frightening, because of the treatment he received. The doctors and nurses wore masks and gloves when administering care, and this left David with a feeling of isolation.

The Reverend's main concern in society's handling of the AIDS crisis has to do with treating AIDS victims as fellow human beings. They are not social outcasts and should not be abandoned. David added that love and understanding, not condemnation, is what AIDS patients need.

In the Lehigh Valley there is an organization called the AIDS Service Center. It provides support and care for family and friends of PWA's (Persons With AIDS). They train buddies to support AIDS patients, conduct a support group and also a therapy group.

STRAIGHT EDGE

(Continued from Page 4)

bigger problem.

In conclusion, the next few months will be very interesting. The American voters will have a choice between a qualified candidate and the Governor of Massachusetts (or JoJo the Dog-faced Boy — you never know). Of course, perhaps neither candidate is that wonderful. There's always 1992. There's also 2008 if you're willing to wait for the Straight Edge Guy. A columnist can dream, can't he!

Honors Convocation held Saturday

by Heidi Ludwick

The Academy Awards of Lafayette College were presetned to students Saturday, April 23, 1988 at the annual All-College Honors Convocation. Usually held in February, the event proved to be a success due in large to improvements made by members of the Subcommittee on Honors Convocation: Ellen Hurwitz, chairman; David A. Portlock, Assistant Dean of Academic Services; George G. Sause, Consultant for the Faculty Committee on Honors and Academic Awards; and Lara Culley '89.

Held in the Morris R. Williams Center for the Arts, the afternoon ceremony opened with remarks by Christopher Wilson, Chairman of the Faculty Committee on Honors and Academic Awards, and President of the College, David W. Ellis. Featured speaker, William S. Andrews, class of '71 and past recipient of the George Wharton Pepper Prize, highlightetd the celebration by reflecting on his experiences at Lafayette College. During his presentation, he discussed the value of honors to him, recognized a positive relation between the faculty and students in the past, and emphasized not only academics, but the importance of the Lafayette experience as a whole.

The ceremony continued with the awarding of prizes for academic excellence, leadership, character, citizenship, and professional promise in various fields of study including engineering, chemistry, English, languages, and military science. Presenting the awards were Dean of Academic Services, Alan W. Childs, and Chairman of the Subcommittee on Honors Convocation, Ellen Hurwitz. Sigma Alpha Epsilon was honored during the ceremony with a trophy for highest academic achievement for a social living group. According to Lara Culley, everyone received certificates for their awards and some students received cash prizes for excellence.

Following the ceremony, students and faculty contineud the celebration at a reception held in the Williams Center lobby. Faculty, students, and guests socialized, congratulated winners, and talked to Andrews while nibbling on cheese and punch and enjoying the background music performed by Lafayette students, Paul Glvin, violin, Courtney Ryan, cello, Colleen Mailhot, flute, and Kevin LaBar, piano.

TRUSTEES FUND

(Continued from Page 1)

those who support the college in a leadership capacity, and its inner Marquis Circle. In 1987, Hugel was inducted into Lafayette's Societe d'Honneur, a group which honors the college's 32 most distinguished benefactors.

Lawrence J. Ramer, a 1950 graduate of Lafayette, is chairman of the board of Pacific Coast Cement Corporation. A member of the college's board of trustees since 1976, Ramer was vice chair of the board's financial policy committee and also served two terms as chair of the Marquis Society.

Participating student artists are Ann T. Augustine, Clayton B. Evans, Hugh R. Jeffers II, Mary Kathleen Hooper, Daryl A. Madi, Paul Miller, and David B. Nemetz. Faculty members Ed Kerns and Tom Burke have also donated works.

The project is co-sponsored by three student organizations: the Apartheid Awareness Group, the Association of Black Collegians, and Theta Delta Chi Fraternity. Co-chairs are Tamar Oberman; Evans; and William Wagner, president of Theta Delta Chi Fraternity.

The public is invited to attend the exhibit. Persons wishing to donate to the fund may send a check made out to "Lafayette College-Art Against Apartheid" to the Association of Black Collegians, Box 4020, Lafayette College, Easton, Pa. 18042. For more information, contact Oberman, 215-559-0689; Evans, 215-252-9643; or Wagner, 215-252-9160.

SUPERIOR

(Continued from Page 1)

The winners of the 1987-88 Superior Teaching Awards received a certificate from Student Government as well as flowers. In addition, both Professor Bukics and Professor McCreary will get their names engraved on two plaques in Marquis Hall for permanent recognition.

Figure 4.4. Article published in *The Lafayette* student newspaper on April 29th, 1988 detailing an AIDS panel that came to Lafayette College.

PERSPECTIVE 3—STUDENT RESEARCHER: JENNIFER WELLNITZ, 2019, FORMER QAP LEAD STUDENT RESEARCHER

As one of the first student researchers on the QAP team, I found that working on the project was a highlight of my undergraduate experience at Lafayette. I was offered the opportunity to join the project at the end of my sophomore year, after taking Dr. Armstrong's WGS 340: Sexuality Studies class (WGS 340 is referenced extensively on the QAP site), and I actually turned down a research opportunity in my major field of computer science in order to join the QAP team. That decision was a defining moment in my college career and working on the QAP has been the most meaningful thing I've done as an undergraduate.

One of the key benefits of working on the QAP was gaining experience in the field of DH, an area in which I had no prior knowledge. Working on a DH project was eye-opening. I had never considered the role technological advancements could play in the preservation and study of oral histories specifically, or in humanities fields more broadly. Though my main area of study in college was in a STEM field, I have always enjoyed working in the humanities. Being able to combine these interests in a meaningful way was an incredible experience. It gave me the ability to work at the center of a project that felt significant to me for both personal and political reasons while leveraging the skills I had already honed outside of the project as a computer science major.

I was also able to use my experience with computer science in new ways on the QAP site. For example, some of the boilerplate text from the Scalar platform needed to be adjusted in order to accurately reflect our data model and to clearly convey the purpose behind the different Scalar components. For example, in place of Scalar's generic general designation "Tagged," I created designations for "Themes" and even more granular "Keywords." This adjustment became one of my responsibilities on the team, and with the help of the Scalar developers at the University of Southern

California, I was able to employ some of my computer science skills to accomplish these goals and directly enhance the project.

As Dr. Nunes discusses in the previous section of this chapter, one of the central issues for the development of the QAP was choosing our platform. Unless a project builds its own web platform from scratch, any data model will be shaped and limited by the capabilities of the platform selected. Hence, the early stages of designing a data model were inextricably tied to the critical process of choosing our platform. Ultimately, because of the complex nature of the data we wished to catalog and the interconnected relationships we wanted to highlight, we chose Scalar due to its flexibility and highly "relational" nature. In short, our choice of platform was informed by our concept for the data model, and our data model was informed by the capabilities of our platform.

My computer science background helped prepare me for developing a working and sensible data model early in the process of creating the QAP DH site. This process took the majority of the working time for my first four months on the team and it remained a large part of my day-to-day efforts over the year and a half that I worked on the project. We wanted to develop a model that was flexible yet coherent, and which could express the nuance and complexity of the relationships inherent in the material we were trying to document. Oftentimes, when engaged in content-based work such as uploading new archival artifacts, we would discover holes or inconsistencies in the way the model was constructed and be forced to spend the rest of our working time for that session reevaluating the structure and then implementing adjustments to make our model more consistent. Ultimately, we landed on a complex but fairly easily understandable data model that complexly networked related archival artifacts with the LGBTQ+ oral histories at the heart of the site.

Because our data model was inevitably shaped and constrained by the capabilities of our platform, we based the various components of our model on the available functionality in Scalar.

Two specific capabilities of the Scalar platform were key to constructing our data model for the QAP: "tags" and "paths." Tags and paths both connect materials in the QAP site. "Tags" form bi-directional, direct links between two pages. "Paths" are links that create a sequential ordering of pages, and can be used to tell a story or make a structured argument using the materials on the site. "Paths" are useful when interpretation is necessary to analyze items relative to each other or to form a narrative about the relationships among various materials on the site.

Oral history interviews with Lafayette LGBTQ+ alumni are the core of the QAP DH site. These narratives are given their own central place in the structure, where they are organized chronologically. As the bedrock of the project, they drive the content of the site and generate the archival materials associated with the QAP. With these interviews at the epicenter, we divided our data model into three main components: "Themes," "Keywords," and "Interpretive Paths." Both Themes and Keywords make use of Scalar's "Tags" feature and both are generated from the content of the interviews. Themes represent broader, more conceptual ideas that tie interviews and archival items together; examples include Gender Discrimination, Religion, and Trans Identities. Keywords represent more granular topics referenced in interviews and are also supported by archival materials; examples include specific on-campus entities (such as the English Department) and the AIDS Quilt. Both Themes and Keywords organize the materials on the site. On the Scalar dashboard, archival items *are tagged by* the page representing the Theme in question and archival items *tag* the page representing a Keyword. A change in JavaScript enabled us to tweak some of Scalar's boilerplate text to make the language of the site less confusing. "This page is tagged by" became "Themes" and "This page is a tag of" became "Keywords."

Scalar's Interpretive Paths function offered us an opportunity to represent abstractions and conceptual gaps within the site. While many archival artifacts can be seen as representing something relatively concrete (such as a specific on-campus event that corresponds to a Keyword), it is difficult to find artifacts that depict important concepts such as isolation, visibility, or climate. These hard-to-capture ideas are, however, central to exploring the Queer experience, especially at an institution where silence around LGBTQ+ lives has been a predominant theme. Interpretive Paths can be employed to create interpretive essays that tie together several items on the site—both archival objects and interviews—to explore a more complex or nuanced idea than could be captured with a basic Theme or Keyword. Current examples of Interpretive Paths on the site address concepts like "Climate" and "Community."

Taken as a whole, our data model could be conceptualized like this (Figure 4.5):

QAP Data Model Element	Scalar Implementation	Examples
Interpretive Path	A media-rich, thesis-driven "path" through the site synthesizes content from across the site (oral history interviews and archival artifacts) in order to tell a story or make an argument about Queer history at Lafayette College.	Sample Path topics: • In/visibility • Passing • Diversity • Allyship
Theme	An intermediary page that corresponds to one of the broad conceptual themes that shape the site. A Theme page can **be a tag of** any number of related interviews, interview clips, and archival artifacts. Themes are generated by the oral history interviews.	Sample Themes: • LGBTQ+ student groups • Greek Life • Campus Events • Interviews
Keyword	An intermediary page that corresponds to a specific, granular concept. A Keyword can **be tagged by** any number of related interviews, interview clips, and archival artifacts. Keywords are generated by the oral history interviews.	Sample Keywords: • AIDS Quilt • Pardee Hall • Women's & Gender Studies Program
QAP Oral History Interviews & Related Archival Artifacts		

Figure 4.5. The Queer Archives Project data model.

Ultimately, my involvement in the QAP was a defining and rewarding feature of my undergraduate career. Whereas my regular course work rarely allowed me to engage in topics that felt personally meaningful, working on this project afforded me the ability to create tangible and long-lasting change (on both the historical and academic levels) to Queer history, even if the scope was the history of only one college. In most of my college experience, the self-contained nature of classroom work made it feel like a purely intellectual exercise, but QAP work produced an actual product from which others could learn as well.

As a Queer person myself, my involvement in this project had a great deal of personal meaning. My first days in the Lafayette College archives during my early involvement in the project showed me a piece of Lafayette College I never knew existed. It highlighted for me both that I am not alone—that others have come before me and that others will come after me—and that since I had never seen this history, it is likely that most of my peers hadn't seen it either. It is vital for Queer undergraduate students to feel a sense of belonging within the institution that is a part of nearly every aspect of their lives. The ability to preserve the narratives of other Queer people and to center and validate the worthiness of oral history and of Queer studies as an academic discipline made my participation in this project feel all the more rewarding, both in terms of posterity and in terms of the accessibility of Lafayette's Queer history to the students of my class year and years to come. I was glad to be able to participate in research that felt important both from an academic perspective and from a social and personal one as well.

CONCLUSION

As exemplified by Wellnitz's reflection, student contributors to the QAP move toward an iterative mode of archive-building that values collaborative process, that routinely reflects on its limits, and that acts to account for those limits. This work is a profound experiential learning opportunity for *all* students to value difference and seek equity that simultaneously supports progressive movements in the archives field at large. In addition, as Kelly Miller and Michelle Morton argue, working on projects such as the QAP can have an especially powerful and empowering effect on students from non-dominant communities, who "recognize themselves and their communities in the collections, thus increasing the potential for transformative educational experiences."[16]

While the archives field is well-positioned to help students achieve important outcomes of undergraduate education, archives-based undergraduate experiential learning is also highly effective in advancing important movements toward equity in archival practice. In "'To Suddenly Discover Yourself Existing': Uncovering the Impact of Community Archives," Michelle Caswell, Marika Cifor, and Mario H. Ramirez offer the term "representational belonging" to encapsulate the broad-reaching impact of community-based archives to "empower people who have been marginalized by...memory institutions to have the autonomy and authority to establish, enact, and reflect on their presence in ways that are complex, meaningful, substantive, and positive to them in a variety of symbolic contexts."[17] No matter how they identify personally with LGBTQ+ communities at Lafayette, students working on the QAP help to facilitate representational belonging in the archives. The QAP transforms Lafayette's archival practice by centering the value of equity in archival representation. The transformation of archival practice manifested by the QAP, alongside the curricular innovations to which it is fundamentally linked, combine to drive meaningful institutional transformations at Lafayette College and model a transformative approach to both archival and educational change.

NOTES

1 https://www.crl.edu/primary-source-awards
2 Visit the Queer Archives Project Scalar site at qap.lafayette.edu.
3 The Information Maintainers, D. Olson, J. Meyerson, M. A. Parsons, J. Castro, M. Lassere, D. J. Wright, H. Arnold, A. S. Galvan, P. Hswe, B. Nowviskie, A. Russell, L. Vinsel, & A. Acker (2019). *Information Maintenance as a Practice of Care*. Zenodo. https://doi.org/10.5281/zenodo.3251131
4 Michelle Caswell et al., "'To Be Able to Imagine Otherwise': Community Archives and the Importance of Representation," *Archives and Records* 38, no. 1 (January 2, 2017): 6, https://doi.org/10.1080/23257962.2016.1260445.
5 Jamie Ann Lee, "Archival Legibility: Sustainability through Storytelling across Generations," *Medium*, August 13, 2018, https://medium.com/community-archives/archival-legibility-legitimacy-sustainability-through-storytelling-across-generations-d0849a4f346d.
6 Jarrett Drake, "Seismic Shifts: On Archival Fact and Fictions," *Medium*, August 20, 2018, https://medium.com/community-archives/seismic-shifts-on-archival-fact-and-fictions-6db4d5c655ae.
7 Elliot W. Eisner, *The Educational Imagination: On the Design and Evaluation of School Programs*, 2nd ed. (New York: Macmillan, 1979).
8 William F. Pinar and C. A. Bowers, "Politics of Curriculum: Origins, Controversies, and Significance of Critical Perspectives," *Review of Research in Education* 18 (1992): 163–90, https://doi.org/10.2307/1167299.
9 Michel Foucault, *The History of Sexuality: An Introduction* (Knopf Doubleday Publishing Group, 2012).
10 Jamie Ann Lee, *Producing the Archival Body* (Routledge, 2020), 11.
11 Caswell et al., "Critical Archival Studies;" Marika Cifor and Stacy Wood, "Critical Feminism in the Archives," *Journal of Critical Library and Information Studies* 1, no. 2 (May 3, 2017), https://doi.org/10.24242/jclis.v1i2.27; Joan M. Schwartz and Terry Cook, "Archives, Records, and Power: The Making of Modern Memory," *Archival Science* 2, no. 1 (March 1, 2002): 1–19, https://doi.org/10.1007/BF02435628.
12 Kevin P. Murphy, Jennifer L. Pierce, and Jason Ruiz, "What Makes Queer Oral History Different," *Oral History Review* 43, no. 1 (December 1, 2016): 1–24, https://doi.org/10.1093/ohr/ohw022; Nan Alamilla Boyd and Horacio N. Roque Ramírez, eds., *Bodies of Evidence: The Practice of Queer Oral History*, Oxford Oral History Series (Oxford University Press, 2012).

13 Jamie A. Lee, "In Critical Condition: (Un)Becoming Bodies in Archival Acts of Truth Telling," *Archivaria*, no. 88 (Fall 2019): 168.

14 Yusef Omowale, "We Already Are," *Medium*, September 3, 2018, https://medium.com/community-archives/we-already-are-52438b863e31.

15 Omowale, "We Already Are."

16 Kelly Miller and Michelle Morton, "Hidden Learning: Undergraduates at Work in the Archives," *Archive Journal* (September 9, 2012). https://www.archivejournal.net/notes/hidden-learning/

17 Michelle Caswell, Marika Cifor, and Mario H. Ramirez, "'To Suddenly Discover Yourself Existing': Uncovering the Impact of Community Archives," *The American Archivist* 79, no. 1 (Spring/Summer 2016): 56–81.

BIBLIOGRAPHY

Boyd, Nan Alamilla, and Horacio N. Roque Ramírez, eds. *Bodies of Evidence: The Practice of Queer Oral History*. Oxford Oral History Series. Oxford University Press, 2012. https://ezproxy.lafayette.edu/login?url=https://search.ebscohost.com/login.aspx?direct=true&db=cat00869a&AN=llc.b2076228&site=eds-live.

Caswell, Michelle, Marika Cifor, and Mario H. Ramirez. "'To Suddenly Discover Yourself Existing': Uncovering the Impact of Community Archives." *The American Archivist* 79, no. 1 (Spring/Summer 2016): 56–81.

Caswell, Michelle, Alda Allina Migoni, Noah Geraci, and Marika Cifor. "'To Be Able to Imagine Otherwise': Community Archives and the Importance of Representation." *Archives and Records* 38, no. 1 (January 2, 2017): 5–26. https://doi.org/10.1080/23257962.2016.1260445.

Cifor, Marika, and Stacy Wood. "Critical Feminism in the Archives." *Journal of Critical Library and Information Studies* 1, no. 2 (May 3, 2017). https://doi.org/10.24242/jclis.v1i2.27.

Drake, Jarrett. "Seismic Shifts: On Archival Fact and Fictions," *Medium*, August 20, 2018, https://medium.com/community-archives/seismic-shifts-on-archival-fact-and-fictions-6db4d5c655ae.

Eisner, Elliot W. *The Educational Imagination: On the Design and Evaluation of School Programs*. 2nd ed. New York: Macmillan, 1979. https://ezproxy.lafayette.edu/login?url=https://search.ebscohost.com/login.aspx?direct=true&db=cat00869a&AN=llc.b10528 07&site=eds-live.

Foucault, Michel. *The History of Sexuality: An Introduction*. Knopf Doubleday Publishing Group, 2012.

Lee, Jamie A. "Archival Legibility: Sustainability through Storytelling across Generations." *Medium*, August 13, 2018, https://medium.com/community-archives/archival-legibility-legitimacy-sustainability-through-storytelling-across-generations-d0849a4f346d

Lee, Jamie A. "In Critical Condition: (Un)Becoming Bodies in Archival Acts of Truth Telling." *Archivaria*, no. 88 (Fall 2019): 162–95.

Lee, Jamie A. *Producing the Archival Body*. Routledge, 2020.

Miller, Kelly, and Michelle Morton. "Hidden Learning: Undergraduates at Work in the Archives." *Archive Journal*, September 9, 2012. https://www.archivejournal.net/notes/hidden-learning/

Murphy, Kevin P., Jennifer L. Pierce, and Jason Ruiz. "What Makes Queer Oral History Different." *Oral History Review* 43, no. 1 (December 1, 2016): 1–24. https://doi.org/10.1093/ohr/ohw022.

Omowale, Yusef. "We Already Are." *Medium*, September 3, 2018. https://medium.com/community-archives/we-already-are-52438b863e31.

Pinar, William F., and C. A. Bowers. "Politics of Curriculum: Origins, Controversies, and Significance of Critical Perspectives." *Review of Research in Education* 18 (1992): 163–90. https://doi.org/10.2307/1167299.

Schwartz, Joan M., and Terry Cook. "Archives, Records, and Power: The Making of Modern Memory." *Archival Science* 2, no. 1 (March 1, 2002): 1–19. https://doi.org/10.1007/BF02435628.

The Information Maintainers, Olson, D., Meyerson, J., Parsons, M. A., Castro, J., Lassere, M., Wright, D. J., Arnold, H., Galvan, A. S., Hswe, P, Nowviskie, B., Russell, A., Vinsel, L., & Acker, A. (2019). Information Maintenance as a Practice of Care. Zenodo. https://doi.org/10.5281/zenodo.3251131.

CHAPTER FIVE

LEARNING WITH ZINE COLLECTIONS IN "BEYOND THE RIOT: ZINES IN ARCHIVES AND DIGITAL SPACE"

Michele Hardesty, Alana Kumbier, and Nora Claire Miller

INTRODUCTION

The story of girl zines of the 1990s is a story laden with trouble. As the dominant story of girl zines goes, young women used zines to build community and to participate in a feminist social movement called riot grrrl. White women authors and artists, who made zines to connect with each other and to communicate their politics, perspectives and desires, are at the center of this story. Zines, also known as fanzines, are self-produced, self-published magazines, assembled cheaply and circulated in small numbers within specific subcultures—from periodicals traded by science fiction fans starting in the 1930s, to the punk zines of the late '70s. As primary sources, zines can be read as photocopied time capsules of people's daily lives and social scenes, unmediated by editors. Punks embraced zines due to the DIY nature of the medium. Zines were easy to create, cheap to reproduce, and could be distributed at concerts, record stores, or through the mail. In the 1990s, a new genre of zines emerged, often referred to as "girl zines." In their 1997 anthology *A Girl's Guide to Taking Over the World: Writings from the Girl Zine Revolution*, editors Karen Green and Tristan Taormino define girl zines as "do-it-yourself publications made primarily by girls and women."[1] Green and Taormino's definition aligns with that provided by Sarah Dyer, publisher of *Action Girl Newsletter*, a directory of girl zines. In an interview with Taormino, Dyer notes that riot grrrl zines are only part of a larger class of "zines by girls which are specifically about being a girl and the 'female experience.'"[2]

Girl zine creators told stories that troubled the popular sentiment that feminists had achieved their aims during the second wave. Girl zine creators enacted a feminist politics that countered the social suppression of survivors' narratives, as they shared experiences of sexism, sexual abuse, assault, harassment, and mental illness. They celebrated girlhood and drew attention to music, movies, comics, books, and art made by and for girls and women. As creators shared their experiences and perspectives, they forged social connections and fostered feminist political consciousness. In particular, as the dominant story goes, zines, and the social networks they enabled, were instrumental to the formation and documentation of a highly-idealized feminist social movement, riot grrrl.

The trouble is that this story is often treated as *the* story of feminist zines in the 1990s.[3] This history has been bolstered by the availability of feminist zines in archival and library collections. Many of these collections are composed of white zine creators' personal papers and zine collections, which in turn become the source material for histories focused on the experiences of white creators and participants in '90s feminisms. Historiography then informs what people look for and expect to find in zine collections: the scholarship points readers back to the same well-known creators, whose work becomes source material for more scholarship, and this cycle of shared referents contributes to the symbolic annihilation or rendering-exceptional of BIPOC zine creators.[4] While it is important to affirm the value of these collections, the zines they hold, and the work zine creators produced, it is also important to deconstruct the dominant story, and tell more stories about feminist and queer zine cultures of the 1990s. This is a critique that has been brought to the fore by Mimi Thi Nguyen and followed by Janice Radway.[5] In a history that centers the experiences and cultural production of middle-class white girls, Nguyen asks, "how then could experience yield revolutionary knowledge about race, where the dominant experience was whiteness?"[6] Archives hold and can help us articulate other stories, but we need methodologies and frameworks like Nguyen's to enable this work. How can we learn about 1990s feminist and queer zine networks and politics through these collections, and how can we work within their limits, pay attention to multiple, co-present networks, and think at the level of scenes to make different knowledges possible?

This chapter tells the story of three linked projects through which we pursued this work: a digital humanities (DH) research project called "Zine Scenes;" undergraduate collaborator Nora Claire Miller's DH project "Locating Zines;" and an undergraduate humanities seminar called "Beyond the Riot: Zines in Archives and Digital Space." In "Zine Scenes," we used DH methodologies and network analysis technologies to study zines on a scene level, rather than a granular (creator- or title-specific) one. After compiling a large database of metadata on zines in local archives, we pursued several digital interventions with the data. We repurposed text-adventure game-developing software, as well as more traditional network analysis technologies, to help us identify lesser-known zine scenes. Visualizing the myriad connections between zine creators helped us understand the complex social movements of zines and zine makers, within and outside of riot grrrl. Our maps also gave us a sense of the scopes, and limitations, of the different archival collections we were working with.

We used this research to develop and teach our seminar, "Beyond the Riot," with a wider network of collaborators, in 2016. In the seminar, we worked with students to analyze zines, collections, and the archives themselves. We posed questions and made critiques, enabled by recent scholarship around zines, archives, and riot grrrl historiography. We acknowledged the racialization of most of the collections we engaged, with their over-representation of materials by white creators and from white donors. We did not offer students a remedy to the problems of limited representation and archival silences. Instead, we asked students to consider how social relations produced these absences and exclusions—and why creators of color might resist inclusion in collections. Here, we encountered trouble as we taught with decades-old sources that evidenced oppressive discourses around race, gender, and sexuality, and were products of a feminism organized around notions of girlhood that felt generationally- and racially-specific. To make matters even more vexing, we resisted the promise that the class would "correct" the problems of non-representative archival collections.[7] We offered the students digital tools, theorizations, and strategies with which to think outside the structuring logics of the collections (e.g., focusing on donors, on girl/grrrl focused zines) and away from the recuperation or the production of a legible historic narrative. Though the class focused on engaging zines, collections, and scenes, our approach equipped students with questions, critiques, methodologies, and ethics they could bring to research in other sites of historic queer and feminist knowledge production.

Ultimately, we would find that network visualization, mapping, and annotation tools could help us to perceive overlapping zine scenes, but what was more difficult to represent were the disputes, conflicts, and incommensurabilities. Moreover, instead of pursuing a *better tool*, we often found that zines and zine culture resonated better when the tools reached their limits or when they didn't really work at all. More importantly, this project that started with collecting metadata and ended with research and visualizations of zinester networks—in which the network nodes kept expanding—raised crucial questions about how we build relationships with those we research, and our research teams themselves. By the end of the project and the semester, students and members of the teaching team had engaged in dialogue with records creators, institutional archivists, digital archivists, community archivists, collection donors, and DH scholars. These dialogues enabled all participants to question and learn from each other, share interpretations, make arguments, and negotiate divergent perspectives on zine archives, scenes, and histories. No archival collection, scholar, archivist, or teacher held a privileged evidential or interpretive position.

SETTING THE SCENES: THE DOMINANT STORY AND ITS ARCHIVAL MANIFESTATIONS

Kate Eichhorn, Mimi Thi Nguyen, and Janice Radway have pointed out how the explosion of feminist zine production and scene-making in the 1990s has made a rapid transit into library and archival collections, followed by a significant burst in scholarship. Within a few years of our reading and making them, feminist zine creators were donating their collections to academic archives and libraries and to community-based collections, including most prominently the Barnard Zine Library, the Sallie Bingham Center for Women's Research and Culture at Duke University, and the Sophia Smith Collection (SSC) at Smith College.[8] In 2009, archivist Lisa Darms founded the Riot Grrrl Collection at the Fales Library and Special Collections at New York University, establishing a key hub for the personal collections of participants in riot grrrl, which include zines. Donors and archivists often made these collections available to researchers soon after they were processed, choosing accessibility over restriction. The same zines we had read and made in our domestic spaces were, in a matter of less than five years, in the custody of archivists and librarians.

This choice had consequences for knowledge production, as scholars have employed these collections to theorize zine creators' rhetorical interventions, zines and/as feminist activism, and as archival activism. For example, Alison Piepmeier analyzes zine making as a third wave feminist praxis, attending to the materiality of zine makers' cultural and political production, in *Girl Zines: Making Media, Doing Feminism* (2009); and Adela C. Licona theorizes how feminists of color collaboratively produce zines, knowledges, coalitions, and social relations in *Zines in Third Space: Radical Cooperation and Borderlands Rhetoric* (2012).[9] In *The Archival Turn in Feminism: Outrage in Order* (2013), Kate Eichhorn contextualizes zines' rapid transit into archives in terms of a longer history of women's archives, which she argues have traditionally sought to validate feminist activism and shore up its records, while making those records available for renewed movement building.[10]

In the case of girl, grrrl, and feminist zine archival collections, the swift move from creation, to donation, to processing, use, and scholarly and popular publication started happening within a decade, rather than across feminist generations.[11] Participants in '90s feminist and queer zine communities could learn about the existence of these collections, and about emergent movement histories, from peers who had become donors, archivists, and researchers. And they could, in turn, shape those collections—and histories—through donations, scholarship, online forums, and critique.

The Riot Grrrl Collection is the site of one such intervention. In 2012, Nguyen and the People of Color Zine Project (POCZP) donated a set of facsimiles of BIPOC-made zines to the Riot Grrrl Collection, as the "Mimi Thi Nguyen, in Collaboration with the People of Color Zine Project, 1992–1998" Collection.[12] Nguyen and Daniela Capistrano, founder of the POCZP, made the donation as a strategic intervention, to "'diversify' their holdings in hurried anticipation of the publication of selected documents in a published collection."[13] Nguyen and Capistrano's collaborative donation might seem to remedy a gap, to mediate an absence of BIPOC representation in the official Riot Grrrl record. But the presence of BIPOC zines in a collection is not enough. Nguyen recalls other feminist historical retrospectives, which "'hold a place' for women of color to say their piece, but in such a way that contains their critique and segregates it from the story of the movement's contribution[.]" She asks, with both archiving and scholarship in mind, "What if their critique *was* the contribution?"[14] What historical knowledge is made possible by attending to critique, to absences, to exclusions in collections?

Alana's and Michele's knowledge about zine culture in the 1990s, and our awareness of zine collections in libraries and archives, derives from personal experience. To put this another way, we had insider knowledge from making zines and forming relationships with other zine creators. While living in Springfield, Missouri as a college student, Alana made and traded zines. As a young white woman, Alana felt included in the cultural and political scenes girl zines represented. At the same time, they felt an acute awareness of their peripheral location in the Bible Belt, as someone geographically isolated from in-person girl/grrrl solidarity. As their LGBTQ+ friends shared personal zines and issues of *Diseased Pariah News,* Alana became aware of queer zines as a genre that connected more closely with who they were becoming. Reading queer zines helped them to navigate a friend's HIV/AIDS death and come into their own subjectivity as a sick and queer person. After a hiatus from zine communities, Alana re-engaged with zine cultures in the late aughts, returning to zine making and becoming a zine librarian.

Michele discovered zines in the same way that many white teenagers did in small towns and suburbs circa 1991—*Sassy* magazine and its "Zine-of-the-Month" feature. But for 14-year-old Michele, *Sassy* became a gateway that helped introduce her to the thriving punk scene and multiplicitous zine culture of Minneapolis and St. Paul and their surrounding towns and suburbs. Michele started a zine almost immediately after learning of their existence, and kept her zine going until her second year of college; zines for Michele were a mode of connection. She sold her zine at her high school, distributed it in stores all over the Twin Cities metro area, and traded zines with other zinesters around the country and world, and she asked those in her networks to contribute. When she stopped making zines in college, she shifted to researching them for her undergraduate senior thesis in the English Department of the University of Wisconsin-Madison, which compared avant-garde little magazines and punk zines, and for which she received a research travel grant. Her experience in the late 1990s illustrates the lack of a pause that exists for young people between making zines and accessing them in archives; however, it also illustrates how much has changed. While there were special collections in 1998–99 (namely, the Factsheet Five Collection at the Albany State Library, and small collections like the ones at the Wisconsin Historical Society and the New York Public Library), and some zinesters were starting zine libraries at their colleges, most zines collections were DIY zine libraries and infoshops (such as the Long Haul Infoshop in Berkeley, Epicenter Zone in San Francisco, and the Anarchist Black Cross (ABC)/No Rio Zine Library in New York City). The wave of feminist zine collections was yet to come.

As zine readers, makers, scholars, and teachers, we have been excited by the availability of zine collections for use, and profoundly affected by Nguyen's writing about the histories we can deconstruct and articulate with these collections.[15] We were compelled by Nguyen's assertion that BIPOC zines indicate "the practice of another, co-present scene or movement that conversed and collided with the already-known story, but with alternate investments and forms of critique."[16] We noted Nguyen's emphasis on the scene and the collective, in both her scholarship and the collaborative aspect of the Nguyen and POCZP collection at Fales. Nguyen's approach signaled the importance of thinking away from a particular creator or donor, toward co-present scenes. Accordingly, we sought to use zine archives to tell a more complex story than the one we had read, about a limited number of white participants and riot grrrl scenes. We envisioned ways to make visible the complex, overlapping and intersecting zine worlds we had experienced as zinesters, while attending to the limitations of our youthful perspectives and entire worlds of which we were not a part. At the same time, we were a core team of white individuals at private liberal arts colleges and predominantly white institutions (PWIs). We were committed to deconstructing and displacing the whiteness of the archives and of academia, but what did that mean in practice? Three problematic scenarios confronted us: given the lack of BIPOC-authored zines in the local collections, might the different narratives we bring to light simply be narratives in which white authors are still dominant? How, we wondered, could data from archives help remediate or interrupt what Nguyen describes as the aesthetic of individualism promoted by both riot grrrl and its historiography, which she argues eclipsed, and eclipses, "the structural determinations that constitute the historical present"?[17] Further, how could we examine the disputatious nature of zine scenes on a macro level?

INVESTIGATING COLLECTIONS AND COLLECTING DATA

Inventory Becomes Analysis: Gathering Metadata

When we began the DH research project called "Zine Scenes" with the core team of Alana, Michele, and Leslie Fields, archivist from Mount Holyoke, we knew that we wanted to engage meaningfully not just with individual zines, but also with zine archives. Western Massachusetts is a hub for such archives, housed both in academic institutions and in community spaces. Not only that, but collections that fit the dominant story were key strengths when we started "Zine Scenes": what was then called the "Girl Zines Collection," part of the SSC at Smith College, and, at Mount

Holyoke Archives and Special Collections, the zine collection of alumna Margaret Rooks, a member of DC Riot Grrrl and a founder of Pioneer Valley Riot Grrrl. Additionally, we researched and taught from zine collections that embodied key differences in location and access. Two zine collections we worked with are housed in archives at Smith College and Mount Holyoke College; another, smaller collection of zines (open to readers but non-circulating) is held at the Hampshire College Library, and another collection is held at Flywheel Arts Collective, a nonprofit, volunteer-run community arts space, and is open when the venue is open for shows or events.

The first zine collection we chose to focus on for our preliminary research was housed in the SSC. That archive contained what was then called the "Girl Zines Collection": 20 boxes of zines, many of which were donated by Tristan Taormino and Karen Green, who had obtained the zines while compiling *A Girl's Guide to Taking Over the World.*[18] Given our interest in breaking out of the very frame represented by Taormino and Green's book, which foregrounded the zines of white, middle-class girls and women, we wondered if the collection could support our work, or what it could reveal.

To answer this question, we needed to turn to the zines themselves. The SSC provided a cursory finding aid, listing only zine titles and dates of publication. We knew, in order to get a sense of the scope of the collection, that we needed to make our own, more detailed inventory through which we could record key details about the Girl Zines Collection. So, we built a metadata collector: a Google Form with some twenty-eight categories which prompted the cataloger to record zine titles and authors, but also information like genres and even subject tags. Our metadata collector was modeled after xZINECOREx, a metadata standard developed by zine librarians and archivists in both institutional and DIY collections.[19] xZINECOREx was a helpful initial framework, because it helped us describe individual zines in more depth. But we ultimately wanted to make sense of zines not as isolated objects, but also in relation to other zines, zine creators, bands, and communities. In other words, we wanted to understand zines in the context of social networks. So, we sought to gather information about paratexts—whether the zine had been sent through the mail, the names on contributor lists, whether the zine contained ads, and if so, what those ads were for.

To record this metadata, Nora Claire Miller, a second-year creative writing student at Hampshire College, joined our team as a cataloger during the summer of 2015. Nora, who had no formal experience working in archives, liked to make their own zines and distribute them anonymously around town, and had done a research project on '90s zines for Michele's class, Post-1945 US Literatures, the year prior. Nora came to the project with a perspective that was different from Alana's and Michele's: a zine creator in the 2010's looking at 1990s zines as historical artifacts. This distanced perspective proved valuable, and Nora often noticed details that Alana and Michele took for granted.

At first, we had envisioned the metadata collector as a tool that would help us get to know the collections, and highlight what would be promising for teaching. But that summer, we found that our metadata collector could also be a powerful pedagogical tool. Early on, Nora started to notice things about zines that made them hard to catalog, but also exemplified what was distinctive about them. The metadata collector asked catalogers to record subject tags—things like "feminism" and "vegetarianism" and "sexual assault." Nora had trouble assigning zines to categories and choosing descriptive keywords, not only because of the particularity of the zines themselves, but also because of the discrepancy between vocabularies of girlhood and queerness, for example, in 1995 and today.

The goal of the metadata collector was, in some ways, to produce an interpretable data set from the Girl Zines Collection. But Nora soon came to realize that the idea of aggregate data, in the context of zine cataloging, was not at all straightforward. The way Nora saw it, the zines they were looking at embodied the ideals of the punk and feminist movements they emerged within, movements which rejected normative notions of authority in publishing. Author names, often pseudonyms, jokes, or just temporary, sometimes changed between issues of the same zine—at one point "Whitney" of the zine *Alien* briefly became "Whitknee" and then "Whit Knee." Many zines listed no date of publication, and the dates that were listed were in nonstandard forms, or included neologisms like "Rocktober" instead of "October." For some reason, writers of several different otherwise English-language zines listed their publication dates in French.

Zinesters built their own relationships to authorship and time, one that resisted formal organization. Housed in an academic archive, a place where order and sense-making feel paramount, the zines seemed to be in direct opposition to their surroundings. Nora was left wondering how to make data points out of writings which, at their very essence, rejected being labeled.

Nora found that the metadata could not be standardized without harming the zines' content. When *Alien*'s author signed their name "Whitknee" as opposed to "Whitney," that zine now had two authors in the catalog—and cataloging it any other way would diminish the author's ability to name themselves. Similarly, the metadata spreadsheet includes a category for genre, but many zines did not stably fit into any genre. Was *Kelp*, for instance, which contained both music reviews and personal writing, considered a "personal zine" or a "music zine"? The question of genre was further complicated by the way vocabularies change with time. As with changing words for girlhood and queerness, the way zine creators considered genre was particular to the moment, and social scene, in which a zine was written. Should terms like "fanzine" and "perzine," used by zine creators to describe their own works, be entered into the catalog in place of more legible signifiers like "music zine" and "personal zine"? Was it a violation of the zine creator's ability to self-determine their relationship to genre if a cataloger, twenty years after a zine was written, added an anachronistic subject term that would make a collection more searchable for researchers in the present day?[20]

As other student catalogers joined the team, using the metadata collector we had developed at the SSC to catalog zines at Mount Holyoke, Flywheel, and Hampshire, they, too, asked questions about the power of authorship in the process of archiving. We had initially envisioned the metadata collector as a research tool. But as we worked with students to gather data from local collections in preparation for our class, we came to see the metadata collector as a creation in and of itself, one that was eye-opening and troublesome, incomplete and yet eminently usable. We liked that trouble. We didn't want it to be too clean or complete—the data set was as complicated as the stories it was helping us to tell.

From Metadata to DH: "Locating Zines"

Up to their ears in data entry, Nora wondered what stories could be gleaned from the data set itself, not individuated into its component zines, but rather as an aggregate. In an attempt to answer this question, Nora applied for, and won, an undergraduate research fellowship from Five College Digital Humanities. Nora embarked on a yearlong project called "Locating Zines" with the goal of digitally visualizing and mapping '90s zine networks.

Nora started out by trying to map location trends between the zines in the SSC. Because many zines were their own envelopes—taped shut, addressed and stamped on the back covers, and then sent in the mail—it was possible to glean some information about where and when a zine might have been written. Nora combed the postmark stamps for dates, and transcribed return addresses. They then used this data to make time- and location-based maps on CartoDB, a dynamic GIS mapping software with a slider which showed incidence over time. The map showed hubs of zines in

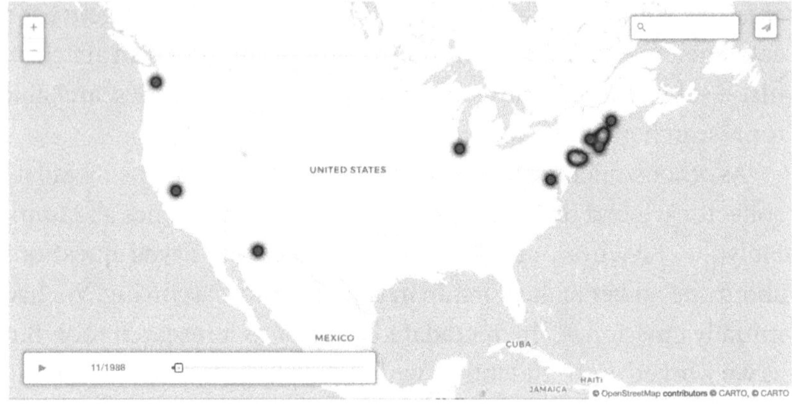

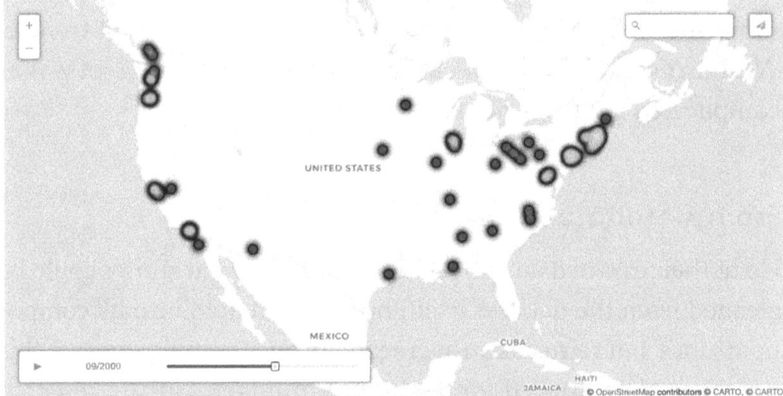

Figure 5.1a and b. Map of zines in the Sophia Smith Collection by location; produced by Nora Claire Miller using CartoDB. The full time-lapse version can be found in the digital edition of this book, available at https://doi.org/10.3998/mpub.12752519.

New York City, Olympia, Washington, and Washington, DC (see Figure 5.1a and b).

Nora quickly realized that their ability to find location-based trends was limited by the collection they were working with. For instance, Tinúviel, whose zine collection comprised the bulk of the zines in the Girl Zines Collection, ran record labels out of New York

City and Olympia, Washington—the two most prominent hubs on Nora's map. Making a GIS map of a specific collection told Nora a lot about the person to whom the zines had belonged, but did not provide much insight into the broader structures of zine culture. However, Nora's attempt at GIS mapping also showed them that, in order to truly understand zine culture, they had to understand its social networks.

The data provided interesting opportunities to explore such networks. In cataloging, Nora noticed that many of the zines in the SSC mentioned, or reviewed, other zines. Reading through these lists of zine reviews, Nora wondered what these connections might reveal about networks of zine creators. They began informally tracking these recommendations, and eventually added an official category to the metadata collector called "Mentions of Other Zines." Nora's adaptation highlighted, for Michele and Alana, the perspective of someone who had not been immersed in zine cultures in the 1990s. When Nora noticed the potential that mentions could hold for mapping zines, we felt we were watching their own research question emerge. Nora's ability to explore zines on their own terms improved our thinking as a collective, and affirmed their status as a co-investigator on the project.

That summer, when they weren't biking to and from the archives, Nora had been watching the TV show "The L Word," on which the character Alice Pieszecki creates something called "The Chart"—a map of the romantic and sexual relationships between the queer women in Alice's social circle. The Chart, made up of names connected by lines, seeks to understand a complex web of human relationships by treating those relationships as data. Alice's chart reminded Nora of the work of cataloging zines—trying to use a scientific process to make sense of social information. Nora, after weeks of tracking which zines mentioned one another, endeavored to create a chart of their own: a network map of zines.

Nora created their map using an app called Twine, an app designed to build simple, text-based online games. Twine games, which often take the form of choose-your-own-adventure stories, are composed of text passages connected via clickable hyperlinks. Earlier on in the project, Michele and Alana had introduced Nora to the medium, and proposed that Nora use Twine to make a digital simulation of a zine archive for the Zine Scenes project. Using the data set they had been working on, Nora had prototyped a game. The Twine game opened onto a list of zines in the SSC, each of which was a hyperlink. When a user clicked on a zine title, they were brought to a new page where they could read cataloged information about that zine, and could also click hyperlinks to look at entries for other zines that zine had mentioned (Figure 5.2).

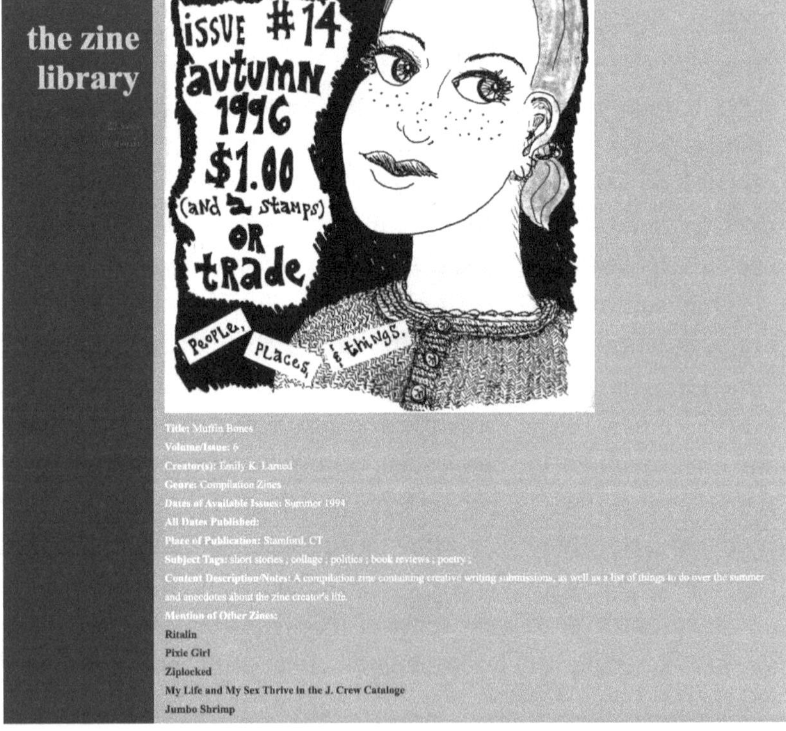

Figure 5.2. This page from "the zine library," a Twine game, features the zine *Muffin Bones*.

While Nora enjoyed the fact that their game could create a clean visualization of what had become a large, unruly data set, the game didn't prove all that useful in thinking about zine networks. The zines in SSC contained reviews for hundreds of zines that couldn't be found in local collections—when someone clicked the link for such a zine in the Twine game, they hit a dead end, a passage with no data.

The process of developing the Twine game proved much more useful than the end result. Twine's back end is a storyboard, in which linked passages, represented by squares, are connected with arrows. This back end is where authors compose their stories and develop their games. When Nora created a passage for each zine they had cataloged, and connected them to one another via hyperlinks, the result on the front end was the game shown above. But the result on the back end was a giant, complex map that reminded Nora of Alice's chart—a way to visually map out social connections. Nora abandoned their archive simulation game, and instead focused on developing their map, inverting Twine to make the composition screen the exhibition screen. They created passages using the metadata from 150 zines, and those zines mentioned nearly 900 others. When finished, the game clocked in at 1,017 passages, all but 32 of which were connected to one another. However, there were limits to how far Twine's back end could be taken as an exhibition platform. It wasn't possible to zoom far enough out on Twine's storyboard to see all of the zines at once—the screenshot in Figure 5.3 is a small subsection of a much larger map.

Twine, in many ways, was not an ideal medium for this endeavor. First of all, network mapping really isn't Twine's intended purpose. Even though Nora was able to use the back end of Twine to make the map, because the storyboard is usually only seen by content creators, it is nearly impossible to display to the public.

Nora tried to mitigate the technical challenges Twine presented by replicating their map using applications actually designed for network mapping (Figure 5.4).

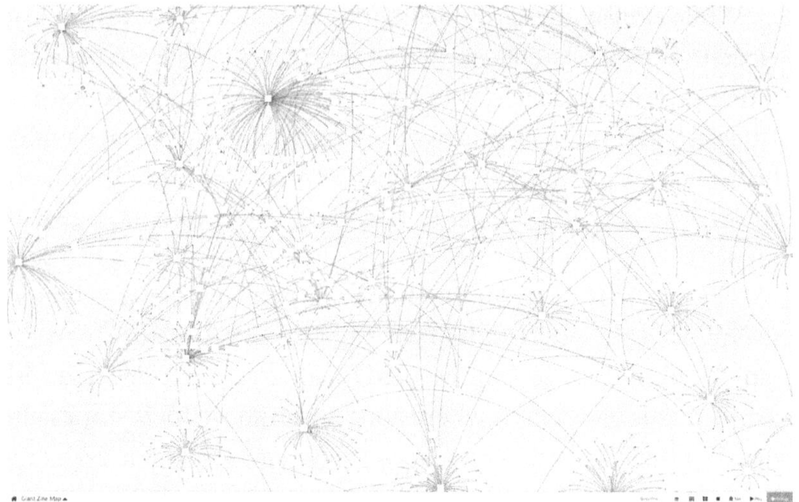

Figure 5.3. The backend view of the Twine map, partially zoomed out. Each square represents a zine.

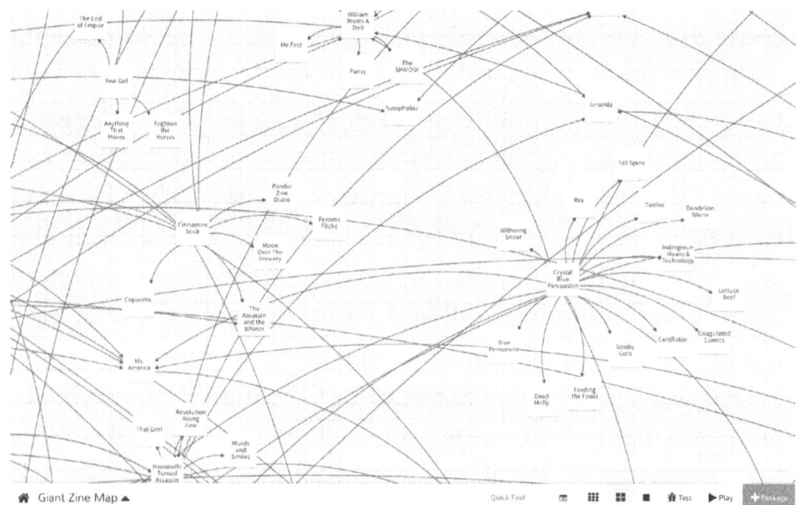

Figure 5.4. A close-up of the Twine map, zoomed in so that you can read zine titles.

Though these technologies often could produce more streamlined, shareable visualizations, Nora ultimately returned to Twine. There were many straightforward reasons that Nora preferred Twine, but perhaps the most important explanation for why Twine worked so well for mapping zines was that it actually didn't work very well at all. The clunkiness of the Twine map revealed something important about the zines themselves. In a blog post for Five College Digital Humanities, Nora wrote, "The more I tried to force zine data into neat visualizations, the more the zines themselves pushed back against them."[21] Twine, in all of its technical encumbrances, represented the DIY nature of zines better than smoother, more simplified software.

As Nora built their Twine map, they began to use it both as a visual aid for networks and a tool for further research. Many zines that became hubs on the network map—in other words, zines mentioned by many other zines—couldn't be found in any of the local zine collections. Nora was particularly interested in networks of people of color and queer people making zines in the 1990s, which riot-grrrl-centric-zine historiography often failed to acknowledge. Many zine archives reflected this lacuna in their collections—and Nora's Twine map reflected it in the zine data it lacked.

Moreover, Nora's back end Twine map itself resisted full exhibition—parts of the map would always be hidden. As members of our team moved through the "Zines Scenes" and "Locating Zines" projects and on to the preparation for the seminar "Beyond the Riot: Zines in Archives and Digital Space," we were still just learning these tools. At the same time, we were beginning to reflect on other questions: should zinesters control access to metadata about their zines, and to their social networks? Might a network visualization that obscures part of the scene represent it better than one that makes all the connections equally visible? While representation is important, how do we also foreground the ability to choose how one is represented? While these questions started to emerge before the seminar began, it was the experience of the semester itself that helped us provisionally answer them. For this reason, before turning to the seminar itself, it would be helpful to address here one of the visualization tools we decided to use in that course, which we only really tackled in detail once the course was underway: Gephi.

Getting Ready for the Class: Developing Other Tools

Wary of Twine's technical limitations in a classroom context, and interested in a network mapping software that would enable students to map out smaller networks of zine creators, we found a software called Gephi. Like Twine, Gephi allowed users to connect nodes (zines) with lines. And like Twine, Gephi was a peculiar, somewhat cumbersome software with a steep learning curve. But unlike Twine, Gephi was actually designed for the purpose of network mapping.

To explore Gephi and what it could do, Michele decided to see what would happen if, instead of mapping every single zine she could find, she searched for networks of a single zine creator, Lauren Jade Martin. Martin began writing zines in high school in the 1990s (*Boredom Sucks, Fuck You, High School!*) and continued in college and grad school (*You Might as Well Live*, *Quantify*). When she donated her collection of over 500 zines to the Barnard Zine Library in 2005, she said,

> Initially, I made zines as a way to connect with other bored and alienated teenagers! As I got older, they became a means to share my words and images on topics I felt were neglected in the mainstream as well as in feminist and punk subculture: mixed-race and queer identity, domestic violence, political action...[22]

Martin's long-running zines and her large donation to a major zine collection make her a prominent creator in multiple networks of zinesters. Michele searched our collected metadata (which now included data from collections at Smith, Hampshire, Mount Holyoke, and Flywheel) for zines by Martin, as well as mentions of the many zines she published. Because Martin wasn't well-represented in the Western Massachusetts collections, Michele also searched one digital collection, the Queer Zine Archive Project, collecting her own metadata from the zines she found there (Figure 5.5).

The visualization in Figure 5.5 shows a number of zines that Martin made, like *You Might as Well Live,* zines she contributed to, like the compilation *Evolution of a Race Riot,* or zines she was mentioned in—and then the zines that mentioned those zines. Visualizing zine networks in this way helped identify communities of creators. Further, it helped us see beyond a prominent name or major donor and the dominant frame of a given archival collection.

Figure 5.5. Visualization of Lauren Jade Martin zine networks, using Gephi and drawing on metadata from Hampshire College, Mount Holyoke College, Smith College, Flywheel Zine Library, and QZAP.

As with Twine, this Gephi map was limited by the collections it used. In the visualization, the apparent network significance of certain of Martin's zines (indicated by text size) had to do with their prevalence in local holdings. *You Might as Well Live* is large because there were multiple issues in the local collections. But *Boredom Sucks*, a zine Martin wrote in high school, is small because there were no local holdings of that zine. When, in a subsequent Gephi visualization, Michele added metadata from zines by Martin at the Barnard Zine Library, *Boredom Sucks* blew up. The network thickened with these additional titles.

In creating the network visualization assignment for the seminar, we turned to Gephi as a tool with which students could identify, and explore, other networks within predominantly white, riot grrrl-centric zine collections. At the same time, Gephi—and data visualization on the whole—did not serve to represent histories of critique and disputation among zine creators, and it also did not succinctly represent the unruliness of zines as texts and objects. Finally, digitizing, and displaying, zine data raised privacy concerns, even when zine creators had consented to having their work available in physical archives. Our approach had been influenced by the "Zine Librarian Code of Ethics," developed by the same networks that created xZINECOREx and which states that, "Whenever possible, it is important to give creators the right of refusal if they do not wish their work to be highly visible."[23] We wondered how to engage with questions of consent and reciprocity when it came to the metadata itself—and the stories that data made possible.

BEYOND THE RIOT: BRINGING THE UNDERGRADUATE CLASSROOM INTO THE ARCHIVES

The goal of the fall 2016 seminar, Beyond the Riot: Zines in Archives and Digital Space (BTR), was for students to complete original research in 1990s feminist, queer, and BIPOC zine networks, drawing on local zine collections and using DH tools. While one objective was for students to understand the dominant narratives of riot grrrl and girl zines in the 1990s, which informed what had been collected locally and were important stories in their own right, the more important objective was to move "beyond the riot," or beyond *riot grrrl,* to the other intersecting scenes, networks, and contexts in which these zines and their creators were embedded. We approached this work in two parts. In the first part, we taught students the skills they would need for doing primary research in zine collections, while also developing critical approaches to studying collections and zine libraries themselves. In the second part, we trained students in DH tools (Google My Maps, Gephi, StoryMap JS) that would help them perceive the networks in which specific zinesters operated. The seminar was led by a teaching team of five: Michele and Alana were the main co-instructors, Nora moved into the role of teaching assistant, and Leslie Fields and Mount Holyoke librarian Julie Adamo joined as additional core instructors.

When we visited the four collections in the first part of the course, students experienced the heterogeneity of our local zine collections. We created hands-on workshops that taught skills and framed critical issues appropriate to each site. At the SSC, we worked with SSC and Smith College collaborators to teach students not only how to navigate a reading room, read a finding aid, and browse through an archival box, but how to understand the Girl Zines Collection in the context of SSC's status as a collection of women's history, and next to collections of periodicals like Daughters of Bilitis's *The Ladder* and the Third World Women's Alliance's *Triple Jeopardy.*[24] At Hampshire, in contrast, we taught students how to use the Zine Collection Catablog and locate zines in the library, while also assigning texts on the politics of cataloging.[25] One of Mount Holyoke Archives and Special Collections' biggest collections of zines is located in the personal papers of alumna Margaret Rooks, also a founder of Pioneer Valley Riot Grrrl, and for that visit we taught students how to approach a personal papers collection while also having a discussion with the donor herself.[26] And for the site visit to Flywheel Zine Library, which constitutes one wall in a small side-room at this nonprofit arts space, we sat in a circle of folding chairs drinking coffee with volunteer Jeremy Smith before exploring the zine holdings and discussing K.J. Rawson's concept of "environmental accessibility" in the archives.[27]

To close the first section of the seminar, Alana and Nora facilitated students in the first project: mapping the geographical spread of zines in the local collections with Google My Maps. This short assignment accomplished three things: first, it introduced students to our collected metadata (to which they had added in these opening weeks), showed them how the metadata could be used to make meaning, and gave them a chance to try out, with an easy application and small data set that Alana had prepared, what it would be like to work on a DH project in teams. Second, it helped students to see that a collection, even if it was not geographically marked, probably would not include an even distribution of materials from all over the country or world. And third, the Google My Maps project helped students understand that the representation of zines in archives is not neutral—it is tied to what a collection prioritizes, and who donates to the collection.

Flywheel took us off campus, but mostly BTR was a multi-campus experience, both in terms of where we met and who participated in the course. The seminar enrolled students from across the Five College consortium, with relatively even numbers from Hampshire, Mount Holyoke, and Smith, and fewer from UMass-Amherst. BTR was headquartered at Hampshire, and we had an assigned classroom in Emily Dickinson Hall; however, we seldom gathered there. Students gained a sense of grounding and consistency not in a regular classroom but in their teams. We assembled student teams based on student strengths and affinities, with each one representing students from at least three different institutions.

Teams sat together in class, worked together on projects, and each developed an identity. These student teams became crucial mutual support structures for students, especially as we entered into the second part of the course.

In the second part of BTR, we focused on networks and scenes of zine creators, DH skill-building, and critical issues in data visualization and digitization. Students completed two team projects: one in network visualization and the other in digital annotation. For the network visualization project, student teams identified a scene of zine creators by first identifying a "network hub," then gathering zine metadata related to this network, and finally building a visualization of that network in Gephi. One goal of this project was to understand individual zines in terms of how they circulated in meaningful and dynamic networks of creators; another goal was to experiment with the possibilities and limits of data-driven network analysis to visibilize and understand scenes and subcultures. As we were beginning this project, former zinester Lauren Jade Martin, whose zines include *You Might as Well Live*, *Boredom Sucks*, and *Quantify*, visited the class via Skype, to talk with students about her experience in zine culture, and what it was like to donate her large collection of zines to the Barnard Zine Library in 2005.

In order for students to understand how artists, activists, and scholars had used digital tools, DH collaborators Miriam Neptune, Jack Gieseking, and Maggie Galvan spoke to the seminar about their own work, in person and via Skype. We asked them, how do these tools relate to your own commitments to racial justice, intersectional feminism, and queer practices? What are some of the limitations or dangers of tools like Gephi and Timeline JS, as you use them or as others have used them? How have your collaborations with project teams, with archives, and with research subjects worked? In the wake of these rich discussions, Gieseking and Neptune also met with students in our lab session to help them assemble their data sets.

For the digital annotation project, teams picked a single issue of a zine and then chose one page to annotate. Here, the objectives were to conduct research, to unpack the rich contexts of the chosen page, to learn Storymap JS (a mapping app that we used against the grain to "tour" a page of text), as well as to develop ethical research practices in relation to digitization and consent. To accompany this project, we welcomed Milo Miller of the Queer Zine Archive Project (QZAP) to discuss their history and their decision to fully digitize zines, grappled with Kelly Wooten's powerful statement from Sallie Bingham, "Why We Are Not Digitizing Zines," and read and discussed the POCZP's White Ally FAQ, which laid out conditions for white students and researchers who wanted to engage with digitized zines that had been created by and for zinesters of color.[28] These examples helped students understand that digitization is *publishing* and, if the end result is to make the digital copy public, it should not be done without creator permission. As paragraph 1.2 of the Zine Librarians Code of Ethics previously cited states, "Whenever possible, it is important to give creators the right of refusal if they do not wish their work to be highly visible."[29] Following the POCZP's White Ally FAQ, white students grappled with the fact that just because digitization made zines more accessible did not mean that POCZP's zines were for *them* and their research projects. While only one team was able to get permission from the creator to digitize a page of their zine, all the teams completed the assignment informed by these ethical and political questions.

We created BTR with these layered objectives to test out what was essentially an experimental methodology for researching zines as embedded in creator networks, and to find evidence for these creator networks in the zines themselves—and in the form of metadata we collected about these zines. While each student team met the seminar's objectives and completed three original research projects using DH tools, the ambition, rapid pace, and data focus of the seminar sometimes kept us from doing what many students were there to do: read and make zines. It felt good, then, to return to Emily Dickinson Hall at Hampshire College for the last class of the semester, where each team brought four cut-and-paste pages for a compilation zine. After class and with the semester over, Alana made photocopies of the class zine, stuffed them into envelopes, and sent them out to each student, thus creating the kind of correspondence networks that we had been mapping in BTR.

COLLABORATING ACROSS HIERARCHIES

In order to bring an undergraduate seminar into the archives and teach students to use these digital tools, we needed a tight core project team. Additionally, we needed to be able to collaborate across academic institutions, and beyond them. Influenced by zine and zine archiving cultures themselves, we made collaboration and collective work central to how we developed and taught the course, just as we made it central to how students learned in the course. We practiced the aspects of zine culture Todd Honma names in his essay on teaching Asian American zines as part of a praxis of community engagement and solidarity: "resource sharing, skills development, and the promotion of participatory culture," in which each team member "contribute(d) according to their own capacities towards a shared collective experience."[30] By putting horizontal collaboration and team-based work at the center, however, we also had to confront the multiple hierarchies within our academic institutions that were not set up to facilitate such work. Moreover, there were other implicit hierarchies at work between grant-funded academic projects like ours and independent, community-based projects that we supported. In response, we found ways to make sure labor was both valued and compensated. We confronted these hierarchies in ways that were often provisional and improvisational—often we did more to draw attention to an unjust system than to transform it. We do not write to explain how we transformed a system. Instead, we write to insist that experimental, transdisciplinary projects and courses like BTR are made possible only by deeply collaborative work in and out of the classroom, yet the hierarchical systems in place often prevent such collaborative work from echoing the values of the projects themselves.

We saw our horizontal, collaborative ethos as akin to the ethos of zines. When someone decides to self-publish a zine and directly share their creativity and knowledge with others, they are eschewing conventional notions of expertise, hierarchies of knowledge, and gatekeeping practices in publishing. This ethos has been carried forward by the many zinesters who have become zine librarians and archivists, including those who have developed independent and community-based collections, and those who work in conventional, institutionally-affiliated libraries and special collections, especially in the network that is linked through the zinelibraries.info hub. This network hosts a Zine Librarian (un)Conference each summer, where they model what it looks like to work horizontally across grassroots and institutional contexts. This network developed and published the "Zine Librarians Code of Ethics" in 2015, which covers issues of acquisition, access, preservation, use, and organization in a way that foregrounds archiving from *within* a community; rejecting the "myth of library/archival 'neutrality'"; and being accountable to "our users, our institutions, our authors, donors, and communities."[31] This network also propelled the creation of xZINECOREx, the shared zine metadata standard we discussed above, which is the seed for a larger project to create a zine union catalog based on linked open data. Members of this network draw on their subcultural knowledge and experiences to theorize and develop ethical archiving practices.

Also, we worked hard not to perpetuate the divide between humanities and cultural studies scholars of the "Archive" and the intellectual and professional labor of archivists, a divide that is gendered and classed and, as Michelle Caswell writes, where the archivist field "has been construed as predominantly female, professional (that is, not academic), and service-oriented, and as such, unworthy of engagement."[32] Our core teaching team, composed of one faculty member, two librarians, an archivist, and an undergraduate teaching assistant (Michele, Alana, Julie, Leslie, and Nora) worked together on course development for almost a year, with some of us coming together to build knowledge and a set of shared reference texts for even longer. By developing the course in conversation with each other over that time, and shaping the course together, we shifted the usual division of intellectual labor and authority between faculty, professional staff, and undergraduate teaching assistants.[33] We shared responsibility for all aspects of the seminar. That said, we were operating in an institutional academic hierarchy that controlled our ability to manage our own time, to receive compensation, and to gain professional recognition. While we were all team members on a Multi-Campus Collaborative Blended Learning Grant from the Teagle Foundation and administered by Five Colleges, Inc., that grant was designed to put faculty at the fore, not staff or students. Any faculty associated with our project could easily receive a substantial summer stipend for minimal work. Stipends were also available for students, allowing us to compensate Nora as a teaching assistant, as we had compensated student catalogers with our previous DH grant. Staff—even if they were members of the core project team—could not receive any direct payment at all. Likewise, when it came to teaching, Michele would be compensated as part of her regular salary, while Alana would teach on top of their librarian duties and without additional compensation. In order to mitigate this inequitable situation, we worked hard to ask supervisors for work releases and coworkers for coverage, as well as negotiating staff professional development funds in our grant, to compensate and recognize Alana, Leslie, and Julie for their labor and professional expertise. Alana, Leslie, and Julie made it clear how and when they would be available for the course, and all of us kept those boundaries in mind throughout the semester.

For the archivists and librarians in the core team, this seminar was a welcome experiment, intellectually and pedagogically. BTR gave us a rare and welcome opportunity to raise political, practical, historical, and ethical questions about collections and tools with undergraduate students—not just teach students how to use them. At the very same time, students came to understand that the zine collections we engaged were produced through the physical and intellectual labor of professional and community archivists and librarians. During our cataloging workshop, for example, when we explained that each record in the online library catalog represents the labor of a person working through a similar process, we observed some students in the class having a "lightbulb" moment.[34] What had seemed like neutral instruments—the library catalog and the Library of Congress classification system—were the work of individuals with professional guidelines and ethics, workloads, and subject expertise. In this way, the obstacles to compensation and recognition were frustrating in another sense, also: they made it hard to consider how the seminar could be a model for sustainable cross-campus and staff-faculty collaboration.

We also wanted to leverage the resources of our private liberal arts colleges and PWIs to collaborate with grassroots and independent zine projects in an accountable way. Our grant made it easy to gain approval for guest speakers' honoraria, but it was trickier to include in our budget the digital collections that we were assigning to students and using for projects—POCZP and QZAP—two projects with which Alana had a relationship. Eventually we were able to get two larger honoraria approved for these projects. Capistrano's POCZP requested an additional layer of accountability in the form of a report. She asked about the impetus for the class and how the class used POCZP resources, and she asked for a list of specific zines accessed (so she could distribute the honoraria among the zinesters) and a copy of the syllabus. Finally, she asked, "Any thoughts you have on how academic spaces can better partner and support entities like POC Zine Project moving forward?" We responded, in part:

> We'd encourage other students, librarians, archivists and faculty to have explicit conversations about what it means (financially, politically, ethically) to access resources collected, digitized and made available by a POC-run grassroots archive vs. institutional archives (which are still staffed predominantly by white archivists). Like the POC Zine Project, we also encourage student and faculty researchers to consider their positionality when using POC zines for research projects, and to be accountable to creators and collection maintainers for the ethical and just use of zines as research resources.

We were surprised at first to receive this request for a report, but completing it turned our relationship with the POCZP from something characterized by a transaction, where we congratulated ourselves for making the grant funds available, to something characterized by accountability and care. Our principle in BTR was one of horizontal collaboration. If we had found ways to highlight and confront hierarchies that stood in the way of collaboration, Capistrano's questionnaire flipped the hierarchy between our PWI liberal arts colleges and the POC Zine Archive on its head by demanding answers from *us*.

CONCLUSION

In the end, BTR pushed against hierarchies that structure learning, while also making those hierarchies palpable to students, who may have imagined archives, libraries, and catalog entries to be neutral, or imagined zines to be pure sites of liberation and not complicated artifacts themselves: problematic markers of a subculture characterized by white supremacy and riven by battles around racism, ableism, and transphobia. We collaborated widely, valued and compensated the labor of those who shared their knowledge and expertise (even if it meant working around the structure of our grant), and worked to be accountable to the networks we were building. We added to, and built projects with, our collection of metadata about 1990s and 2000s zine networks, in conversation with creators and archivists, and we ended with questions about privacy, authority, and control that made us pause before granting wide access to the data we had gathered, or pushing students to make their visualization projects public, balancing questions of access with questions of ethics and privacy.

We began this project more than six years ago, and taught the course four years ago. Much happened in these years, from Black Lives Matter, to Standing Rock, to Trump. Since we began conceptualizing the course, many projects have sprung to life, many debates have opened and closed, and initiatives that were just starting are now culminating. We celebrate the collective labor of zine librarians, archivists, catalogers, and developers who have produced a zine union catalog, ZineCat, which enables researchers to discover zines beyond local archival collections, and to access zines from community, autonomous, public, and academic libraries and archives. Working with ZineCat could dramatically widen researchers' understanding of what zines are collected where, and model a catalog that "attempts to harmonize, rather than normalize and find mutuality, rather than control of creators and descriptors."[35] The History of Domestic Work and Worker Organizing, an incredible political education tool in Timeline JS which Nora worked on as a third-year in Jennifer Guglielmo's course and which we discussed in initial stages with Miriam

Neptune at Smith in 2016, is coming to completion.[36] Cassandra Hradil's "zine net work" is a data visualization of the holdings of the Barnard Zine Library and does, in a public form, what we were attempting to do with BTR.[37] There have also been multiple projects and conversations in recent years about what it would mean to digitally link community archives and their holdings, including Diversifying the Digital Historical Record and the Community Archives Collaborative, founded and inspired by Michelle Caswell and Bergis Jules, among others.[38]

A number of projects from the past several years have been helping us continue to pursue questions as they relate to metadata privacy in relation to archiving and archival research that foregrounds one's relationship to those one is researching. These twin concerns are emphasized in Documenting the Now's 2018 white paper, authored by Bergis Jules, Ed Summers, and Dr. Vernon Mitchell, Jr.:

1. Archivists should engage and work with the communities they wish to document.
2. Documentation efforts must go beyond what can be collected without permission from the web and social media.
3. Archivists should follow social media platforms' terms of service where they are congruent with the values of the communities they are attempting to document.
4. When possible, archivists should apply traditional archival practices such as appraisal, collection development, and donor relations to social media and web materials.[39]

While Documenting the Now and other like-minded projects focus on social media, other historical digital archives model how to create user agreements that make explicit the ethical agreements expected of those who access the corpus. One excellent example is the Colored Conventions Project (CCP), which requires users to commit to these principles:

- I honor CCP's commitment to a use of data that humanizes and acknowledges the Black people whose collective organizational histories are assembled here. Although the subjects of data sets are often reduced to abstract data points, I will contextualize and narrate the conditions of the people who appear as "data" and to name them when possible.
- I will include the above language in my first citation of any data I pull/use from the CCP Corpus.
- I will be sensitive to a standard use of language that again reduces 19th-century Black people to being objects. Words like "item" and "object," standard in digital humanities and data collection, fall into this category.
- I will acknowledge that Colored Conventions were produced through collectives rather than by the work of singular figures or events.
- I will fully attribute the CCP for corpora content.

Such projects continue to instruct us as we continue teaching and working, and we see affinities between them and POCZP's "White Ally FAQ" and the "Zine Librarian Code of Ethics."

We can envision how the work of a course like BTR would be enriched by collaborating with scholars and artists who could contextualize zines in terms of other scenes of subcultural creation and resistance, including BIPOC- and queer-led music scenes, slam poetry, and activist videography. We also imagine necessary projects and courses that build with Licona's theorizations of third space zines, which "re(en)vision and represent multiply situated, nondominant subjectivities in pursuit of coalition building to address local inequities."[40] Such work would enable students and teachers a way to address historic and current strategies and experiences of coalition building for social change.

NOTES

1 Karen Green and Tristan Taormino, eds., *Girls Guide to Taking Over the World: Writings from The Girl Zine Revolution* (New York: St. Martin's Griffin, 1997), xi.

2 Tristan Taormino, "An Interview with Action Girl's Sarah Dyer," in *A Girl's Guide to Taking Over the World: Writings from the Girl Zine Revolution*, ed. Tristan Taormino and Karen Green (New York: St. Martin's Griffin, 1997), 168.

3 For examples of this narrative, see Sara Marcus, *Girls to the Front: The True Story of the Riot Grrrl Revolution* (New York: Harper Perennial, 2010); Jessica Rosenberg and Gitana Garofalo, "Riot Grrrl: Revolutions from Within," *Signs* 23, no. 3 (April 1, 1998): 809–41, https://doi.org/10.1086/495289. For an interrogation of this narrative, see Mimi Thi Nguyen, "Riot Grrrl, Race, and Revival," *Women & Performance: A Journal of Feminist Theory* 22, no. 2–3 (July 1, 2012): 173–96, https://doi.org/10.1080/0740770X.2012.721082.

4 Our understanding of archives as sites that contribute to symbolic annihilation draws on Michelle Caswell's theorization in "Seeing Yourself in History: Community Archives in the Fight Against Symbolic Annihilation," *The Public Historian* 36, no. 4 (November 2014): 26–37.

5 Mimi Thi Nguyen, "Riot Grrrl, Race, and Revival"; Mimi Thi Nguyen, "Minor Threats," *Radical History Review 2015*, no. 122 (May 1, 2015): 11–24, https://doi.org/10.1215/01636545-2849495; Janice Radway, "Girl Zine Networks, Underground Itineraries, and Riot Grrrl History: Making Sense of the Struggle for New Social Forms in the 1990s and Beyond," *Journal of American Studies* 50, no. 1 (February 2016): 1–31, https://doi.org/10.1017/S0021875815002625.

6 Nguyen, "Minor Threats," 197.

7 Nguyen, "Riot Grrrl, Race, and Revival," 17.

8 Our understanding of this timeline is directly informed by Janice Radway, "From the Underground to the Archive in Ten Years: Girl Zines, the 1990s, and the Challenge of Historical Narration" (National Humanities Center, Research Triangle, NC, 2015), https://nationalhumanitiescenter.org/radway-girl-zines-1990s-challenge-of-historical-narration/.

9 Alison Piepmeier, *Girl Zines: Making Media, Doing Feminism* (New York: NYU Press, 2009); Adela C. Licona, *Zines in Third Space: Radical Cooperation and Borderlands Rhetoric* (Albany: State University of New York Press, 2012).

10 Kate Eichhorn, *The Archival Turn in Feminism: Outrage in Order* (Philadelphia: Temple University Press, 2013).

11 Radway, "From the Underground to the Archive in Ten Years."

12 For more on the People of Color Zine Project, see: POC Zine Project, "About," Tumblr, https://poczineproject.tumblr.com/about; Daniel C. Brouwer and Adela C. Licona, "Trans(Affective)Mediation: Feeling Our Way from Paper to Digitized Zines and Back Again," *Critical Studies in Media Communication* 33, no. 1 (January 1, 2016): 70–83, https://doi.org/10.1080/15295036.2015.1129062.

13 Nguyen, "Minor Threats," 17.

14 Nguyen, "Riot Grrrl, Race, and Revival," 190.

15 We think of articulating histories with zines following Adela C. Licona's theorization of the politics of articulation in "(B)orderlands' Rhetorics and Representations: The Transformative Potential of Feminist Third-Space Scholarship and Zines," *NWSA Journal* 17, no. 2 (2005): 104–29.

16 Nguyen, "Riot Grrrl, Race, and Revival," 187.

17 Nguyen, "Riot Grrrl, Race, and Revival," 174.

18 In our research we discovered that "Girl Zines Collection" is a misnomer: the majority of the zines came not from Taormino and Green (though many did) but from Tinúviel, a cofounder of Kill Rock Stars records and founder of the label Villa Villakula. Many zines in the collection were rock and indie fanzines that did not fit at all under the genre tag of "girl zines." In the wake of our class, SSC revised the finding aid, renaming the collection the "Sophia Smith Zine Collection." It renders an accurate account of the zine collection, cross referencing it with the Tinúviel Papers, and listing the other donors to the collection, including several boxes of unprocessed zines that we examined in 2016 and which had not previously been included in the finding aid. See Sophia Smith Zine Collection, Periodicals Collection, Sophia Smith Collection, Smith College Special Collections, Northampton, Massachusetts. https://findingaids.smith.edu/repositories/2/resources/749

19 For details about xZINECOREx in zine format see Milo Miller, "ZINECORE Zine," *Zinelibraries.Info* (blog), April 12, 2013, https://www.zinelibraries.info/2013/04/12/zinecore-zine/. The Flywheel Zine Library, another key collection in Western Massachusetts, catalogs its own collection using these standards.

20 While Nora often came to these questions on their own, we later anticipated these questions by assigning Jenna Freedman and Rhonda Kauffman's key text on the topic in the seminar. Jenna Freedman and Rhonda Kauffman, "Cutter and Paste: A DIY Guide for Catalogers Who Don't Know About Zines and Zine Librarians Who Don't Know About

Cataloging," in *Informed Agitation: Library and Information Skills in Social Justice Movements and Beyond*, ed. Melissa Morrone (Sacramento: Letter Juice Press, 2014).

21 Nora Claire Miller, "Locating Zines: 5CollDH Fellowship Wrap-Up Post," *Five College Digital Humanities* (blog), August 1, 2016, https://5colldh.org/locating-zines-fellowship-wrap-up/.

22 "Donor Spotlight: Lauren Jade Martin," LiveJournal, Barnard Zine Library, May 11, 2010, https://barnardzines.livejournal.com/72317.html.

23 Zine Librarians Interest Group, "Zine Librarians Code of Ethics," October 2015, https://www.zinelibraries.info/2016/05/30/code-of-ethics-1115-web-version/.

24 *The Ladder - A Lesbian Review,* 1959-72, Periodicals Collection, Sophia Smith Collection, Smith College Special Collections, Northampton, Massachusetts; *Triple Jeopardy,* November 1971-Feb 1975, Third World Women's Alliance, Bay Area chapter records, Sophia Smith Collection, SSC-MS-00697, Smith College Special Collections, Northampton, Massachusetts.

25 The catablog has not been updated since 2016, but it is currently still available. Hampshire College Zine Collection, Hampshire College, https://sites.hampshire.edu/zines/.

26 Margaret Rooks Papers, MS-0861, Mount Holyoke College Archives and Special Collections, South Hadley, Massachusetts, https://aspace.fivecolleges.edu/repositories/2/resources/328.

27 K. J. Rawson, "Accessing Transgender // Desiring Queer(Er?) Archival Logics," *Archivaria*, no. 68 (2009): 127.

28 Kelly Wooten, "Why We're Not Digitizing Zines," *Duke Digital Collections Blog* (blog), September 21, 2009, https://blogs.library.duke.edu/digital-collections/2009/09/21/why-were-not-digitizing-zines/; POC Zine Project, "White Ally FAQ," Tumblr, https://poczineproject.tumblr.com/white-ally-faq.

29 Zine Librarians Interest Group, "Code of Ethics."

30 Todd Honma, "From Archives to Action: Zines, Participatory Culture, and Community Engagement in Asian America," *Radical Teacher* 105 (July 7, 2016): 34, https://doi.org/10.5195/rt.2016.277.

31 Zine Librarians Interest Group, "Code of Ethics."

32 Michelle Caswell, "'The Archive' Is Not an Archives: On Acknowledging the Intellectual Contributions of Archival Studies," *UCLA* (June 27, 2021), https://escholarship.org/uc/item/7bn4v1fk. For a discussion of the difference between "the Archive" and "archives," which Caswell also cites, see Alana

Kumbier, *Ephemeral Material* (Litwin Books, 2014), 10-13, https://litwinbooks.com/books/ephemeral-material/.

33 While librarians and archivists have faculty status at some colleges and universities, they do not in the private liberal arts colleges in our consortium. The only member of the Five Colleges that affords librarians and archivists that status in UMass-Amherst, which is also the only institution in the consortium where librarians and archivists are unionized.

34 This lightbulb was powered by class readings like Freedman and Kauffman, "Cutter and Paste"; and Emily Drabinski, "Queering the Catalog: Queer Theory and the Politics of Correction," *The Library Quarterly: Information, Community, Policy* 83, no. 2 (2013): 94–111, https://doi.org/10.1086/669547. In a future iteration of the course, we might add work by Jessica Tai, "Cultural Humility as a Framework for Anti-Oppressive Archival Description," in "Radical Empathy in Archival Practice," eds. Elvia Arroyo-Ramírez, Jasmine Jones, Shannon O'Neill, and Holly Smith. Special issue, *Journal of Critical Library and Information Studies* 3, no. 2 (2021). DOI: https://doi.org/10.24242/jclis.v3i2.120, and Michelle Caswell, "Dusting for Fingerprints: Introducing Feminist Standpoint Appraisal," ed. Elvia Arroyo Ramirez et al., *Journal of Critical Library and Information Studies*, Radical Empathy in Archival Practice, 3 (2019), https://journals.litwinbooks.com/index.php/jclis/article/view/113. Tai and Caswell directly address archival work (where we focused on library work), and theorize how to practice anti-oppressive description. Their articles call upon archives to center the knowledge and perspectives of archivists and collaborators from oppressed communities.

35 Jenna Freedman and Lauren Kehoe, "ZineCat at ALA 2019," *Zine Union Catalog Blog* (blog), June 23, 2019, http://blog.zinecat.org/zinecat-at-ala-2019.

36 Michelle Joffroy, Jennifer Guglielmo, and Diana Sierra Becerra, "Putting History in Domestic Workers' Hands: A Community-Based Digital Humanities Project," *The Abusable Past* (blog), September 2, 2019, https://www.radicalhistoryreview.org/abusablepast/putting-history-in-domestic-workers-hands-a-community-based-digital-humanities-project/.

37 Cassandra Hradil, "zine net work," http://zinenet.work/.

38 Michelle Caswell, Christopher Harter, and Bergis Jules, "Diversifying the Digital Historical Record: Integrating Community Archives in National Strategies for Access to Digital Cultural Heritage," *D-Lib Magazine* 23, no. 5/6 (June 2017), https://doi.org/10.1045/may2017-caswell; "Community

Archives Collaborative," South Asian American Digital Archive (SAADA), October 30, 2019, https://www.saada.org/project/community-archives-collaborative.

39 Bergis Jules, Ed Summers, and Vernon Mitchell Jr., "*Documenting the Now* White Paper: Ethical Considerations for Archiving Social Media Content Generated by Contemporary Social Movements: Challenges, Opportunities, and Recommendations," April 2018, https://www.docnow.io/docs/docnow-whitepaper-2018.pdf. Other projects we have been inspired by are Archives for Black Lives in Philadelphia and Anti-Racist Description Working Group, "Archives for Black Lives in Philadelphia: Anti-Racist Description Resources" (Archives for Black Lives, October 2019), https://archivesforblacklives.files.wordpress.com/2019/10/ardr_final.pdf and The Archivists Against Collective, "About Us," Archivists Against History Repeating Itself, http://www.archivistsagainst.org/about-us/.

40 Licona, *Zines in Third Space,* 3.

BIBLIOGRAPHY

Archives for Black Lives in Philadelphia and Anti-Racist Description Working Group. "Archives for Black Lives in Philadelphia: Anti-Racist Description Resources." Archives for Black Lives, October 2019. https://archivesforblacklives.files.wordpress.com/2019/10/ardr_final.pdf.

Brouwer, Daniel C., and Adela C. Licona. "Trans(Affective)Mediation: Feeling Our Way from Paper to Digitized Zines and Back Again." *Critical Studies in Media Communication* 33, no. 1 (January 1, 2016): 70–83. https://doi.org/10.1080/15295036.2015.1129062.

Caswell, Michelle. "'The Archive' Is Not an Archives: On Acknowledging the Intellectual Contributions of Archival Studies." *UCLA* (June 27, 2021). https://escholarship.org/uc/item/7bn4v1fk.

Caswell, Michelle. "Dusting for Fingerprints: Introducing Feminist Standpoint Appraisal." Edited by Elvia Arroyo Ramirez, Jasmine Jones, Shannon O'Neill, and Holly Smith. *Journal of Critical Library and Information Studies*, Radical Empathy in Archival Practice, 3 (2019). https://journals.litwinbooks.com/index.php/jclis/article/view/113.

Caswell, Michelle. "Seeing Yourself in History: Community Archives in the Fight Against Symbolic Annihilation." *The Public Historian* 36, no. 4 (November 2014): 26–37.

Caswell, Michelle, Christopher Harter, and Bergis Jules. "Diversifying the Digital Historical Record: Integrating Community Archives in National Strategies for Access to Digital Cultural Heritage." *D-Lib Magazine* 23, no. 5/6 (June 2017). https://doi.org/10.1045/may2017-caswell.

South Asian American Digital Archive (SAADA). "Community Archives Collaborative." October 30, 2019. https://www.saada.org/project/community-archives-collaborative.

Barnard Zine Library. "Donor Spotlight: Lauren Jade Martin." LiveJournal, May 11, 2010. https://barnardzines.livejournal.com/72317.html.

Drabinski, Emily. "Queering the Catalog: Queer Theory and the Politics of Correction." *The Library Quarterly: Information, Community, Policy* 83, no. 2 (2013): 94–111. https://doi.org/10.1086/669547.

Eichhorn, Kate. *The Archival Turn in Feminism: Outrage in Order.* Philadelphia: Temple University Press, 2013.

Freedman, Jenna, and Rhonda Kauffman. "Cutter and Paste: A DIY Guide for Catalogers Who Don't Know About Zines and Zine Librarians Who Don't Know About Cataloging." In *Informed Agitation: Library and Information Skills in Social Justice Movements and Beyond*, edited by Melissa Morrone. Sacramento: Letter Juice Press, 2014.

Freedman, Jenna, and Lauren Kehoe. "ZineCat at ALA 2019." *Zine Union Catalog Blog* (blog), June 23, 2019. http://blog.zinecat.org/zinecat-at-ala-2019.

Green, Karen, and Tristan Taormino, eds. *Girls Guide to Taking Over the World: Writings from The Girl Zine Revolution.* New York: St. Martin's Griffin, 1997.

Honma, Todd. "From Archives to Action: Zines, Participatory Culture, and Community Engagement in Asian America." *Radical Teacher* 105 (July 7, 2016): 33–43. https://doi.org/10.5195/rt.2016.277.

Hradil, Cassandra. zine net work. https://zinenet.work/

Joffroy, Michelle, Jennifer Guglielmo, and Diana Sierra Becerra. "Putting History in Domestic Workers' Hands: A Community-Based Digital Humanities Project." *The Abusable Past* (blog), September 2, 2019. https://www.radicalhistoryreview.org/abusablepast/putting-history-in-domestic-workers-hands-a-community-based-digital-humanities-project/.

Jules, Bergis, Ed Summers, and Vernon Jr. Mitchell. "*Documenting the Now* White Paper: Ethical Considerations for Archiving Social Media Content Generated by Contemporary Social Movements: Challenges, Opportunities, and Recommendations," April 2018. https://www.docnow.io/docs/docnow-whitepaper-2018.pdf.

Kumbier, Alana. *Ephemeral Material*. Litwin Books, 2014. https://litwinbooks.com/books/ephemeral-material/.

Licona, Adela C. "(B)Orderlands' Rhetorics and Representations: The Transformative Potential of Feminist Third-Space Scholarship and Zines." *NWSA Journal* 17, no. 2 (2005): 104–29.

Licona, Adela C. *Zines in Third Space: Radical Cooperation and Borderlands Rhetoric*. Albany: State University of New York Press, 2012.

Marcus, Sara. *Girls to the Front: The True Story of the Riot Grrrl Revolution*. New York: Harper Perennial, 2010.

Miller, Milo. "ZINECORE Zine." *Zinelibraries.Info* (blog), April 12, 2013. https://www.zinelibraries.info/2013/04/12/zinecore-zine/.

Miller, Nora Claire. "Locating Zines: 5CollDH Fellowship Wrap-Up Post." *Five College Digital Humanities* (blog), August 1, 2016. https://5colldh.org/locating-zines-fellowship-wrap-up/.

Nguyen, Mimi Thi. "Minor Threats." *Radical History Review 2015*, no. 122 (May 1, 2015): 11–24. https://doi.org/10.1215/01636545-2849495.

Nguyen, Mimi Thi. "Riot Grrrl, Race, and Revival." *Women & Performance: A Journal of Feminist Theory* 22, no. 2–3 (July 1, 2012): 173–96. https://doi.org/10.1080/0740770X.2012.721082.

Piepmeier, Alison. *Girl Zines: Making Media, Doing Feminism*. 0 edition. New York: NYU Press, 2009.

POC Zine Project. "White Ally FAQ." Tumblr. https://poczineproject.tumblr.com/white-ally-faq.

Radway, Janice. "*From the Underground to the Archive in Ten Years: Girl Zines, the 1990s, and the Challenge of Historical Narration.*" National Humanities Center, Research Triangle, NC, 2015. https://nationalhumanitiescenter.org/radway-girl-zines-1990s-challenge-of-historical-narration/.

Radway, Janice. "Girl Zine Networks, Underground Itineraries, and Riot Grrrl History: Making Sense of the Struggle for New Social Forms in the 1990s and Beyond." *Journal of American Studies* 50, no. 1 (February 2016): 1–31. https://doi.org/10.1017/S0021875815002625.

Rawson, K. J. "Accessing Transgender // Desiring Er?) Archival Logics." *Archivaria*, no. 68 (2009): 123–40.

Rosenberg, Jessica, and Gitana Garofalo. "Riot Grrrl: Revolutions from Within." Signs 23, no. 3 (April 1, 1998): 809–41. https://doi.org/10.1086/495289.

Sophia Smith Zine Collection. Smith College Special Collections, Northampton, Massachusetts. https://findingaids.smith.edu/repositories/2/resources/749.

Tai, Jessica. "Cultural Humility as a Framework for Anti-Oppressive Archival Description," in "Radical Empathy in Archival Practice," eds. Elvia Arroyo-Ramírez, Jasmine Jones, Shannon O'Neill, and Holly Smith. Special issue, Journal of Critical Library and Information Studies 3, no. 2 (2021). DOI: https://doi.org/10.24242/jclis.v3i2.120

Taormino, Tristan. "An Interview with Action Girl's Sarah Dyer." In *Girl's Guide to Taking Over the World: Writings from the Girl Zine Revolution*, edited by Tristan Taormino and Karen Green. New York: St. Martin's Griffin, 1997.

The Archivists Against Collective. "About Us." Archivists Against History Repeating Itself. http://www.archivistsagainst.org/about-us/.

Wooten, Kelly. "Why We're Not Digitizing Zines." *Duke Digital Collections Blog* (blog), September 21, 2009. https://blogs.library.duke.edu/digital-collections/2009/09/21/why-were-not-digitizing-zines/.

Zine Librarians Interest Group. "Zine Librarians Code of Ethics," October 2015. https://www.zinelibraries.info/2016/05/30/code-of-ethics-1115-web-version/.

ACKNOWLEDGMENTS

From the start of this project, our thinking was informed, and improved, by Jenna Freedman, Milo Miller, Mimi Thi Nguyen, Marisa Parham, and Janice Radway. Our closest collaborators, Julie Adamo and Leslie Fields, helped us dream Beyond the Riot into being and handle its complex realities. We learned from many collaborators who brought their expertise and care to our projects, including Michelle Anderer, Maureen Callahan, Daniela Capistrano, Margaret Galvan, Jack Gieseking, Jennifer Guglielmo, Lauren Jade Martin, Sylvia Moisany, Jeffrey Moro, Miriam Neptune, Hanna Pennington, José Rodriguez, Margaret Rooks, Kate Singer, Jeremy Smith, Sara Smith, and Kate Sumner. During all stages of this project, colleagues at the Hampshire College Library, especially Rachel Beckwith, Jennifer Gunter King, Anne Macon, Heather McCann, and Bonnie Vigeland, supported our work, thought with us, and covered teaching and reference duties when Alana could not. We thank Five College Digital Humanities and Blended Learning, and the Teagle and Mellon Foundations, for the grants that supported this work. For their generous comments and feedback on an earlier draft of this essay, we thank Julie Adamo, Leslie Fields, Jenna Freedman, and the Five College Women's Studies Research Center fellows' seminar. And finally, we thank the students of Beyond the Riot in fall 2016 for traveling down this road with us and giving it your all.

CHAPTER SIX

PREPARING, PRACTICING, SUSTAINING: ARCHIVES OF STUDENT PROTEST AS CRITICAL ARCHIVE PEDAGOGY

Christopher Jones, Elizabeth Rodrigues, Rachel Schnepper, and Temitayo Wolff

INTRODUCTION

> *From its abolitionist roots to the incubation of the Social Gospel movement, Grinnell has a deeply meaningful history and a legacy of activism.*[1]

Grinnell College, located in Grinnell, Iowa, identifies strongly with its history of progressive activism, from its abolitionist roots to the incubation of the Social Gospel movement to the student protests of the 1960s.[2] The Grinnell College Archives are rich with its history of activism. As the Grinnell College Special Collections and Archives detail, "these materials record the dramatic social, political, and curricular changes that have affected American culture: abolition and the civil rights movement, political unrest and anti-war activism, feminism and changing gender roles, and the value of core curriculum requirements."[3] However, amid the flurry of admissions materials and the minimal time allotted to institutional history in most curricular paths, it is most common for Grinnellians (student, faculty, and staff alike) to have a relatively abstract sense of what this history actually is. A "legacy of activism" is often referenced without mention of any specific group, action, or commitment. This deficit of institutional memory is hardly unique to Grinnell, but it can become especially problematic when the struggles of the past are monumentalized as self-evident and inevitable institutional decisions. At the very least, this loss deprives students of the chance to learn more about the process of social change. At worst, it can encourage deflection on contemporary questions of social justice by fostering a sense that Grinnell College is likely to do the right thing because it has done the right thing in the past.

In this chapter, we argue that engaging undergraduate students in the creation of digital archives of student protest at Grinnell restores the critical impact of these archives. Through this engagement, the institutional authority of the archive is transformed through its deployment as a "usable past," defined as a mode of "thinking about the past in the present"[4] through "active efforts... made [by a variety of professional and non-professional practitioners] to link experiences, documents and materials of the past with contemporary issues and experiences."[5] In this way, the college archives can serve current student activism and offer lessons for future student-centered archival projects.

In what follows, we will discuss the steps we have taken to advocate for student-centered critical archival work on campus. The first section provides an overview of scholarship on the intersection of small liberal arts college (SLAC) archives and critical archival practice. We use these critical frameworks to examine the relationship between content, authority, student engagement, and the Grinnell College archives. The second section, "Preparing," details an instructional unit introducing critical digital archives through an exercise in metadata creation. This section includes a session outline, rationales for each component, and reflection on the unit's effectiveness. The third section, "Practicing," examines two contexts (Context 1 and Context 2) in which we have attempted to go from introduction to application of critical archival practice with the explicit goal of asking students to document student dissent and thereby reconsider who has the authority to narrate college history. In Context 1, students in a digital humanities short course plan and prototype projects that link the past and present of student activism on campus. In Context 2, Temitayo Wolff reflects on the work of undergraduate digital scholarship fellows on an archival project for Grinnell's Kimbo Black Cultural Center. Both contexts demonstrate that such processes of remediation can raise student consciousness of the archive as a contested and created site. In our conclusion, "Sustaining," we reflect on the infrastructures of labor, funding, and student engagement present (or not yet present) to apply the lessons we have learned from these endeavors.

For context, our "we" is composed of four people and focuses on our collaboration at Grinnell College, where Christopher Jones is archivist of the college, Elizabeth Rodrigues is Humanities and Digital Scholarship Librarian, Rachel Schnepper was the Associate Director of Academic Technology from 2015–17, and Temitayo Wolff, alumna of Grinnell College, was a longtime student archives and special collections worker and a Vivero Digital Scholarship Fellow 2018–19. Rodrigues and Schnepper co-founded the Vivero Digital Scholarship Fellows program, discussed later, and Jones was a central collaborator in all of the pedagogical and project work described. "We" refers to this group as coauthors unless otherwise specified. The reflective sections of Context 2 employ the first-person to foreground Wolff's authority on the dynamics of being a student ostensibly centered by a critical archival pedagogy of remediation.

SLAC ARCHIVES AND CRITICAL ARCHIVAL PRACTICE

Jarrett Drake, in his 2016 keynote address to the Digital Library Forum Liberal Arts Pre-conference, argues for the critical linkage of college archives, student protest, and the structural transformation of liberal arts education.[6] Drake frames his talk with a question: "Should institutional archives of liberal arts colleges document student protests and activism that critique or otherwise implicate the college, and if so, why?" In the answer that follows, he calls on us to examine the explicit and implicit functions of a liberal arts college in a democratic society. Explicitly, the liberal arts college aims to develop critical and independent thought in preparation for responsible citizenship. It is, etymologically and aspirationally, education for freedom. Implicitly, however, the liberal arts college is structurally positioned in capitalist society to reproduce social inequality and exclusion. This implicit mission is carried out formally and informally, in policies, revenue models, and unexamined inequities in campus culture that tend to allow historical inequities to persist. Drake argues that archival practices that center student protest provide a means to call attention to how specific institutions and liberal arts education in general often fall short of their liberatory aspirations for some (or even many) students. The archive's authority would, in this scenario, provide a counterweight to official institutional history.

Grinnell College's commitment to the creation and curation of its own history is evidenced through such actions as the retention of its original foundational documents and the recreation of the minutes of the Board of Trustees after the 1882 tornado that completely razed the College campus. The archives span multiple cycles of economic boom and bust, a civil war, two world wars, and several local catastrophes, including the aforementioned tornado. Over the last twenty years, the staff of Grinnell's archives have made an especially concerted effort to include materials and perspectives that fall outside of the traditionally defined authority of the college. That is, there has been a particular push to collect documents and objects that could tell a story other than the official narrative presented by the college in documents such as admissions materials, public-facing web pages, and administrative communications.

In the specific case of Grinnell College, however, it is also possible for the documentation of dissent to become an *affirmation* of institutional authority. Grinnell's brand is protest. This brand identity is not without basis in fact, but embracing a brand is different from living a commitment to justice. The archive inevitably plays a role in this dynamic. As Mimi Thi Nguyen in the *Radical History Review* asks, "How do the politics surrounding institutional discourses of a minor threat, especially at the crash with race or gender, displace or defuse that threat through its incorporation into a politics, history, or archive?"[7] At Grinnell, the "minor threat"[8] of student protest has been incorporated into the institutional history of the college, threatening to neutralize the critical edge of dissent. A glimpse at archival photos may leave students with a sense that protest is part of being a Grinnellian, but it takes a deeper engagement to begin to understand that struggle against institutional norms is part of meaningful protest, and that this struggle is uncomfortable and demanding at a personal level.

Critical archival pedagogy is a tool for engagement that recovers the struggle, contingency, and provisionality of protest movements on campus. As Carden et al. define it, critical archival pedagogy is a "conceptualization of archives as sites where content and process are linked through continuous dialogue," where "powers collide and are resisted, and where knowledge-based collectivity is developed." Critical archival pedagogy is also profoundly student-centered in that students are made aware of "their role as co-producers of course inquiry, content, and pedagogy," and "collaborative decision-making remain[s] integral."[9] In this instructional paradigm, students produce knowledge just as much as the archives do. We draw on frameworks of critical archival pedagogy as we seek to engage students in archives of student protest.

Specifically, we have found that digitization projects focused on specific histories of campus protest present opportunities for critical engagement through a focus on digital archives as a series of acts of remediation. Grusin and Bolter introduced the term "remediation" to describe the practice of representing one medium within another medium, which they argue is the defining feature of digital media.[10] More recently, Sandra Gabriele and Hannah McGregor have called attention to how the dynamic of remediation pervades the project of digitizing print periodicals.[11] Some digital remediations aspire to a state of transparency, in which the "digital medium wants to erase itself, so that the viewer stands in the same relationship to the content as she would if she were confronting the original medium."[12] A similar statement might be made of some definitions of archives, in which the political dynamics of selection, preservation, and display are never openly acknowledged to users. Other digital remediations "seem to want to emphasize the difference rather than erase it," introducing a dynamic of self-reflexivity that opens the door to a more critical practice.[13] Recognizing remediation as a dynamic inherent to digital archive creation offers numerous angles of critical reflection, including the process of digitization itself, the creation of metadata, the selection of a platform for display and preservation, and, last but not least, the selection, arrangement, and narrativization of the archival materials themselves.

Seeing digitization as remediation foregrounds the choices of tool, format, and display that ultimately create a new representational product rather than suggesting that the result is some kind of faithful, "real" copy. By introducing students to the practice of making such choices and having them reflect on the results of their choices in their final products, we introduce them to the human dynamics that underlie the creation of all archival collections; a banker's box on a shelf is no more natural or inevitable than a database. The concept of remediation encapsulates the choices and contingencies we want to make visible to students, specifically in the context of the history of student protest. This awareness, ultimately, is what transforms the authority of our archives.

PREPARING: CRITICAL ARCHIVAL PEDAGOGY OF STUDENT PROTEST IN CLASSROOM CONTEXTS

Critical archival pedagogy requires humanizing the terms "authority" and "archives." By humanize, we mean to raise student awareness of the multiple historically-embedded and personally-enacted choices that create archives and determine their authority. The Association of College and Research Libraries' (ACRL) "Framework for Information Literacy for Higher Education"[14] emphasizes the human context of authority by defining it as communally constructed, stating, "[a]uthority is constructed in that various communities may recognize different types of authority." The authors of the Framework go on to elaborate the characteristics of an "expert" evaluator of authority: "Experts understand that authority is a type of influence recognized or exerted within a community...Experts understand the need to determine the validity of the information created by different authorities and to acknowledge biases that privilege some sources of authority over others." Grappling with authority means recognizing histories of power in collection as well as interpretation. The Rare Book and Manuscript Section of ACRL, in their "Guidelines for Primary Source Literacy," builds on ACRL's definition of "authority" by specifying that it may also refer to "the authority to preserve, collect, access, and use/reuse."[15] In the community of a liberal arts college, who has had the power to exercise authority? In turn, how authoritative is the liberal arts college archive in the context of any particular event or historical question? In this section, we discuss two types of classroom sessions that we have used to prompt critical reckoning with archival authority. The first is a more conceptual overview, which can accompany any course's visit to the archives. The second is a hands-on metadata creation activity, best suited for courses that include the creation of a digital archival collection of some kind. Through these sessions, students begin to see that there is no act of description or organization that is not also an act of remediation.

INTRODUCTION TO THE CONCEPT AND CONTENT OF THE ARCHIVE

In the context of a broad institutional push toward creating opportunities for mentored undergraduate research in all disciplines, Grinnell's archive has seen an increasing number of class visits. While many instructors do request the archivist of the college, Christopher Jones, to give an introduction to databases and other electronic resources, or an even broader introduction to the college libraries and how to find help, Jones receives more and more requests to talk about what an archive is and how it operates. He has recently begun getting frequent requests to talk about how to gain access to archives outside of Grinnell and what to do when there. Topics of discussion frequently include who is responsible for creating the college archive, who maintains it and how, and whose perspectives are included or recorded. There has also been increased interest in student protest, whether on campus or off.

During class visits, materials documenting student activity on campus are commonly pulled, and one observation that is routinely made is that most of the material has been generated by the college and not the students or student groups that are being documented. These discussions frequently turn to the gaps that exist in the archive, why they are there, and how they might be filled. Such class discussions, then, become an apt platform for Jones to stress that student perspectives and voices are integral to the history of the institution, and while the archives staff have ample access to college-created material, student-created material is much more difficult to come by and can leave gaps. These discussions frequently end with Jones explicitly asking students to be in contact with him if they would like to discuss in more detail how to archive their own materials, whether as individuals, or as members of a student group, athletic team, music group, etc. This tactic has been effective in bringing to light the need for closer collaboration between the college archives and the student population and has resulted in increasingly broad holdings of students' activities, particularly student groups and the Student Government Association. In this way, Jones is practicing the philosophy that "'radicalism' isn't unapproachable," as Schwenk argues.[16]

Thus, as students engage with the archive, they become more aware of how its content is driven by human selection. Their relationship to archival authority changes: they begin to see themselves as potentially having the authority to "collect, access, and use/reuse" archival materials, and they see how the authority of the archive that results depends on their exercising this agency. They also become more aware of the limits of what can be archived. Projects of remediation, or representing one medium within another medium, offer the opportunity to build this awareness through practice.

INTRODUCTION TO ARCHIVAL METADATA

Critical approaches to metadata provide an accessible entry point to the idea that archives do not simply exist but are actively made. Piloted first during a digital humanities course taught by Rodrigues and Schnepper in the spring 2017, we have developed a session that uses a hands-on metadata creation activity to introduce students to contingencies of archival description and provoke a more nuanced consideration of archival authority. Entitled *Social Justice and Digital Humanities: Theories and Methods*, this introduction to digital humanities course was centered around asking students to work with archival material, both digital and analog, using digital tools. Each week, students read a combination of provocative and foundational pieces to digital humanities, interrogated digital archival projects, and familiarized themselves with digital tools. During the second week of the course, students visited Grinnell's Archives and Special Collections where they were tasked to create metadata for preselected materials focused on Grinnell's history of activism, consider what communities (academic researchers, alumni) of users would be privileged by the metadata choices made, and consider how different choices in metadata would make the materials more discoverable by additional communities. Then, students were asked to grapple with the process of transferring that metadata to a system (Omeka) with options to make objects digitally accessible.

Step 1: A Brief Introduction to Metadata

The session begins in the physical space of special collections. Prior to the session, the archivist identifies a number of items related to the history of student protest. These items are laid out and numbered 1, 2, and so on. Students are asked to work in pairs and use laptops to fill out an online form (typically using Google Forms) to create basic metadata for each item.[17] Before they begin, we do an intentionally brief explanation of the metadata fields in the form, highlighting their role in eventual searches. In some contexts, it may also be appropriate to offer a high-level overview of Dublin Core, a widely used metadata schema. For the field of "Creator," for example, we simply say "this field describes who created the object." As they begin to fill out the form, students may turn to the archivist and instructors for answers to questions such as, "how do I find out the creator?", "what if the creator is more than one person?", and "do all the papers in this folder need their own metadata?" Because this exercise is designed to introduce them to metadata creation as a form of intellectual and critical labor, we decline to answer and assure them they should answer these questions on their own as best they can in the time allotted, and more importantly to note why they chose one answer or way of inputting metadata over another. In the process of filling out the form, they are challenged to come up with a basic rationale and practice.

Step 2: Compare Results

The session then moves to a space where the resulting spreadsheet of metadata form responses can be projected. We share a read-only link to this spreadsheet with the students and ask them to continue working in pairs to review the metadata they created in comparison with that created by other groups. After five minutes or so, we then pose questions for them to answer in preparation for sharing out with the full class. The questions are designed to focus their attention on what differences in metadata imply about content, conventions, and accessibility. Specifically, we ask them to 1) identify and describe a field where their answer varied from another group's; 2) verbalize the rationale that they applied to arrive at their own selection and speculate why the other group made the choice that they did; 3) reflect on what differences in audience these choices imply—for a subject term, for example, who would be likely to use each term and therefore who would be likely to find an object; and 4) propose how these differences might be resolved—for example, would it mean agreeing on a set of subject terms beforehand (controlled vocabulary) or agreeing that names should be entered as LastName, FirstName (format conventions)? These are challenging questions, and it may be useful to walk through an example first, either on the fly based on the form responses, or based on a preselected digital record for an object in an archive with a distinctive mission and audience.

After several or all pairs have shared their answers, the instructors facilitate a synthesis of the various answers to question 4 on how differences might be resolved as a set of agreed upon practices to best represent a digital collection/exhibit/archive for the history of student protest at Grinnell. Finally, we ask the students to revise the metadata for one object based on the assumptions and conventions the group agreed upon. The learning goal is to recognize that, while accurate metadata may seem self-evident after it has been created, it is not obvious or easy. Every element of metadata signifies a series of choices, each privileging certain audiences for and uses of a particular archive. In this way, our exercise shares much in common with an assignment Michelle Caswell developed following the presidential election of 2016, designed to enable her students "to identify the ways in which white privilege is embedded in archival institutions and to collectively strategize concrete steps to dismantle white supremacy in their own archival practice."[18]

The session could be complete at this point, but depending on time and context, it may be desirable to continue on to a hands-on exercise in creating an object record in an actual digital archival collection tool.

Step 3: Simulate Implementation

For this follow up activity, we have used a locally installed Omeka Classic sandbox. It could easily be conducted using a locally hosted installation or Omeka.net, Omeka's hosting service. As Omeka is web-based, we can hold this session anywhere students have Internet access, for example a computer lab or a regular classroom if enough students have access to laptops. The relevant feature is item creation based on metadata fields, so other tools, such as ArcGIS Story Maps, could be used instead. In any case, the instructor will want to clarify in advance log in or account creation procedures, private/public status of created items, and basic interface navigation.

We begin with a brief example of a finished Omeka project, discussing how the tool allows us to make materials accessible and tell a story using digital materials.[19] Using our Omeka sandbox, students are asked to create an item using their revised metadata. We have found a combination of instructor demonstration and instruction sheet to work best in introducing the steps in this process. In our exercises, we have not used born-digital or digitized objects, so the question of what will be uploaded as a file or image becomes a discussion of planning for digitization and considering creators' legal and ethical rights. Depending on the tool, students may encounter constraints that complicate their newly-formed best practices, such as character limits or English-only character sets.

After students have created at least one item, we pose an open-ended reflection question such as, "what did you notice about this process?" or "what were the most challenging and the least challenging parts of this process?" Seemingly simplistic answers such as "It was hard to remember where to click" can be unpacked with follow up questions on what the goal of a particular interface design might have been. The instructor prompts students to consider how the process they've gone through for one item would scale to an entire project: what are some ways that they could ensure consistency and quality if multiple people were working to create dozens or even hundreds of items? Depending on time, this may be an opportunity to introduce the concept of bulk upload, which puts the focus back on the metadata itself as the single most significant element of a digital humanities project because of its impact on sustainability, access, and ethical representation.

The goals of this activity are to begin to demystify a digital tool by giving them a chance to work on the production side and to show how the preparatory work of metadata creation is essential to any digital manifestation of archival materials. As in the metadata creation exercise, students should become more aware of the numerous choices that shape the seemingly objective presentation of archival materials.

REFLECTIONS ON THE SESSION

In the three iterations of this session that we have offered (one for the short course and two for the digital scholarship fellows' bootcamp), we have found it to be very effective at inducing an epistemological and attitudinal shift in students' understanding of metadata creation. Reflective blog posts written by the students after a 2017 iteration of the session included the following insights:

> In addition to looking at these physical archives I found reading about metadata, or "data about data" was very interesting as it is not something I think about often, but a term I have heard thrown around a lot in this digital age where so many people are concerned about the privacy of their personal data online. Another thing I found myself thinking about often during this week was the history of exactly who got to choose what was "important" enough to be archived. In both the cases of metadata and physical and online archives, executive decisions are made in which certain data or projects simply aren't deemed to be useful or important enough to be saved.
>
> Before this class, I had never heard of metadata before and had no idea it connected to the digital humanities at all. Now I know that it's a really important part of collecting and analyzing data.
>
> As we coded these objects and contributed to the class metadata, my partner and I was able to agree on the basic information of the objects such as the title and date of publication. However, when it came to describing the object and narrowing down the main subject of the objects, we had similar yet different perspectives. These differing perspectives were further shown through the class metadata as groups that coded the same object also coded the object differently than our group. This in-class activity showed me that interrater reliability is crucial in Digital Humanities given that data can be described in a multitude of ways, but the overall summary of the data needs to be clear and concrete so that users of the data can have a solid understanding of what the data is about.

As demonstrated by these reflections, students begin to perceive that the ability to describe is a kind of power because they are asked, briefly, to wield that power. As they do, they see not only that they must make choices, but that others make different choices, all of them consequential for future discovery of, access to, and use of materials. This new understanding is not always transferred to their project work. Additional guidance is needed to develop project-specific practices and follow them consistently.

PRACTICING

The following section examines our attempt to apply the lessons of critical archival pedagogy to critical archival practice around the history of student protest in two specific contexts: a critical digital humanities short course (Context 1) and a digital archival project connected to the Conney M. Kimbo Black Cultural Center (Context 2).

Context 1: Digital Humanities Short Course

"Social Justice and Digital Humanities: Theories and Methods," a one-credit course taught by Rodrigues and Schnepper in the spring of 2017, approached the archive of student protest at Grinnell College through the lens of digital scholarship as critical remediation. Jarrett Drake's keynote served as a key intellectual framework for our development of the course. Indeed, we had students watch it before the first day of class. We anticipated that the two subjects, social justice and digital humanities, would be a productive pairing, not just because students (at the time) had few other opportunities to explore digital humanities, but also because digital humanities is home to a strong (though imperfect and far from universally shared) tradition of scholarship that speaks to the issues that drive social justice activism, such as histories of race-, gender-, and class-based oppression. We anticipated that students would be strongly motivated to tell a story about social justice activism at Grinnell, and this would in turn fuel their motivation to engage with archives and tools for remediating them in digital form. Through course material, students would have to consider that archives represent not "institutional history" writ large but a series of choices about what evidence will be available for the formation of histories.

Building from this session's introduction to metadata toward a broader critical understanding requires building the opportunity for students to put ideas into practice. Students were asked to apply its lessons to a final project, which could be a detailed proposal or prototype of a digital archival exhibition or digital narrative about student protest at Grinnell College. One group proposed a timeline of divestment movements on campus, creating a TimelineJS exhibit about the South African Apartheid divestment campaign and outlining its extension to the then ongoing fossil fuel divestment campaign, speculating that striking parallels between the two movements would affirm the persistence of present-day student activists. Another group conducted video interviews with faculty, staff, and community members who participated in Grinnell-based protests against the Vietnam War, bringing temporal range and added depth to the photographic and print records that constitute the college archive of these protests. A third group developed a long-arc narrative of African American student organization around specific demands for recognition, resources, and support. The fourth group undertook to document incidents of harassment that took place on and near campus, which had become a focus of student activism around Title IX enforcement and a flurry of incidents following the 2016 presidential election.

The range and critical engagement of the project prototypes developed by students demonstrate that this introduction to the college archives was effective in catalyzing a more agential relationship to archival records: they saw themselves as potential creators and collectors of archival materials, and they were more attuned to the fact that there are no neutral archives, with each record representing a choice about what was valuable and how it would be named, categorized, and organized. They also saw archival work more urgently, making direct connections between histories that had been unknown to them and the potentials of contemporary student activism.

Context 2: Black Cultural Center Archives Project

Background on the Project

The Conney M. Kimbo Black Cultural Center, known on campus as the BCC, is a residence, study area, lending library, event venue, and social space for Black students on Grinnell College's campus. The BCC opened at the start of the 1969–1970 school year, two years after the Concerned Black Students (CBS) student group formed. The house was proposed as a home for the "cultural, social, and political events and activities of the CBS organization" and was secured after debate between legislative members of CBS and college administrators.[20] In early 2018, after the unexpected resignation of the student monitors who lived in the BCC, the college closed the house and suspended independent student-run activities at the BCC indefinitely. The house was reopened later in the semester after continued pushback led by Black students. As this brief overview of its history suggests, the BCC is a site where the past and present of student protest co-exist, and it is therefore a site whose history is continually revised, contested, and constructed in service of student and institutional goals.

The BCC digital archive project began in the summer of 2017. In its infancy, the project was commissioned by the Assistant Director of the College's Office of Intercultural Affairs (ICA). They noted the accumulation of physical objects—decades worth of ephemera, artifacts, and clutter—in the house. They envisioned that a student archivist would sort through, organize, and digitize the salient contents of the BCC to ultimately put together a digital archive in time for the center's fiftieth anniversary. That summer, the ICA hired a student to live in the BCC and begin the digitization process. During this time, the student scanned more than 100 pages of scrapbooks dated from the 1980s through the early 2000s. A second student, a member of the first cohort of the Vivero Digital Scholarship Fellows program, continued the project in academic year 2017–18.[21] She scanned and digitized hundreds of photographs and uploaded them to a shared folder, and she made plans to interview students, alumni, and staff. Wolff was hired as a member of the next cohort of Vivero fellows. She and another student were assigned to the project based on students' expressed preferences. To Wolff and the other newly assigned fellow, it seemed that the result of the initial digitization efforts was the spread of the BCC's archival clutter from the house itself into the digital sphere. The images had no metadata attached to them, and they often spent their coworking hours brainstorming how to make sense of the wealth of materials.

Despite these challenges, the second year of the project began with lofty goals. The initial vision for the archive was an interactive virtual reality (VR) model of the BCC. After that was determined not to be feasible (or desirable, as discussed below), the plan shifted to create an Omeka site with an embedded timeline that would highlight noteworthy moments in BCC history and the broader history of Black student life during the last fifty years. The site would also contain photo albums composed of scanned images. Wolff and her project partner created the Omeka site, but without robust metadata for the digital objects found it impossible to proceed. The project was further complicated when the staff project lead left the college to take a job at another institution in early 2019. In spring 2019, Wolff graduated from Grinnell College, as did two prior student contributors. At the present time, the project has stalled.

Reflections: Methodology and Setbacks

In attempting to determine the causes of the BCC archive project's failure up to this point, I (Wolff) have reflected on the successes I observed in Vivero fellows' digital projects. Other projects had faculty project leads rather than staff. These projects continued research into which the faculty member had already invested time, energy, and scholarship; many of the other fellows functioned like research assistants with a digital humanities focus. Our project lead, the Assistant Director of the College's ICA, had a different relationship to the project. In the scope of their professional duties, this project occupied a minor role, rather than being part of a supported research agenda as in the case of faculty. Understandably, they took a more hands-off approach than most faculty project leads. The BCC archive project was also personal and close to home for me in a way that other projects might not have been for other students. I think a degree of personal investment in a project can generate passion to drive what may be tedious and meticulous digital project work. But the self-imposed pressure I felt to do the BCC justice through the project was ever-present in my life on campus—how could it not be? The recent closure of the BCC was fresh in my memory. I had interpreted the closure as a symbolic devaluation and deprioritization of Black community on campus. The stakes of the archival project in my mind then became the potential reaffirmation of the house's—and by extension, Black students'—historical and present value at the college, a feat that was contingent upon my effective creative leadership.

When it felt like the major decisions for the project's direction were in my hands, inaction, at times, seemed less harmful than potentially unsuccessful or inadequate action. For example, an early vision for the archive was an interactive VR model of the BCC. Internally, I questioned the viability of the VR idea, for three reasons: 1) the fact that students continue to live in the BCC—it was someone's home, not a museum to explore; 2) there is a (usually) unspoken rule that non-Black students do not enter the BCC without invitation from a Black student—o offer easily accessible virtual tours of the space seemed like an invasive and unnecessary violation of this rule; 3) Four days of digital humanities bootcamp simply had not prepared us for a project as technically demanding as VR modeling. I kept my thoughts to myself and made no efforts to advance the VR model idea, but my reticence caused discomfort and hostility during coworking hours rather than discussions or solutions.

The flipside to this coin: because our project lead took such a hands-off approach, the project presented an opportunity for student-led research, creativity, and narration. I think this potential is valuable. The project does not have to be owned and managed by a single faculty or staff member at the college—rather the focus and content of the BCC archive can be community-driven. The logical next step is to ask who makes up the community in question. No one on the project actually used the BCC regularly. Our project lead was not a student or alumnus and therefore never a regular visitor to the BCC. I used the space only occasionally as a student, and my partner on the project had never been to the BCC before we started. I was frustrated that my project partner was white and that she had signed on to the project in spite of her expressed concern about the relationship between her whiteness and her selection of the project. I was unwilling, however, to bring this concern up with my partner or with the Vivero leaders until months later, and at the same time I was questioning my own qualifications for the project. I felt shoehorned into the role by my belief that the project should have Black student leadership, but there was a constant conflict between my desire to take charge and my desire to step back.

The model of the Vivero Digital Scholarship Student Fellowship Program is valuable because it equips students who are interested in digital scholarship with the tools to pursue it. Vivero enables project leads to realize ideas with a social justice focus that otherwise might remain just ideas. Furthermore, Vivero ensures that the student collaborators are paid.[22] A downside to Vivero's model is the fact that there is a limit to the pool of students who can be placed on any given project.[23] Students who might be better equipped to carry out this project will not necessarily apply for the Vivero fellowship. The first student who worked on the project was a perfect fit. He lived in the BCC at the time, was involved with the ICA throughout his time at Grinnell, and was simultaneously employed at the college Archives. (He is currently pursuing an MLIS and will be a fantastic librarian.)

At its fullest potential, the BCC digital archive can be a student-centered, student-maintained multimedia digital resource for collective memory, amended and passed down by cohorts of Black students and alumni who value the BCC. But in order for this potential to be realized, student leaders with an existing investment in the BCC must be connected with the resources and support offered by the Vivero fellowship program.

Anecdotally, students often note times that the college touts the social justice efforts of its students in promotional materials, while undermining student efforts to organize. Sometimes, the same student activism that the college discourages is endorsed years later to showcase the initiative of its students and their commitment to social justice. The BCC is a product of Black students' dissatisfaction at Grinnell College and Black students' demands that the college do better. Of course, this fact means that the BCC's existence is inextricable from the existence of Grinnell College. Nevertheless, the origin of the BCC seems at odds with institutional encouragement of the BCC's preservation.[24]

I recognize the tension that exists between my resistance to any degree of college involvement in the project and my emphasis on both the lack of guidance I received and the necessity of college funding to pay students. A fully student-driven and maintained project is not impossible, but it would mean sacrificing the possibilities of college funding, college time, institutional structure, and support. Then again, I know that students, and in particular Black students at Grinnell College, are capable of organizing independently and effectively. I also know I will not be the one to decide the future of this project, but I see potential and merit in the prospect that it might reemerge differently.

SUSTAINING

The following concluding reflections are again coauthored by the "we" of Jones, Rodrigues, Schnepper, and Wolff. As an embodiment of the critical consciousness that a Grinnell College liberal arts education seeks to inspire, the history of student protest is to be celebrated. It is also a history that should bring us up short at the recognition that every instance of protest is an instance in which, as Drake reminds us, "Young adults, mostly ages 18 to 22, have collectively looked at college professors, presidents, and practitioners and said, in unison, '*do better*.'"[25] It is not enough to archive student protest; that archive must be made a vital presence in working memory.

Our contexts of practice have shown us that sustaining our efforts at critical archival pedagogy will require imagining pedagogy and digital project work differently. Digital archival pedagogy and projects require planning time and a willingness by all parties to deliberate in the context of unequal institutional power accorded faculty, staff, and students. Creating time for critical archival pedagogy of student protest can be especially difficult given that the archivist of the college and other librarians, although in faculty positions at Grinnell, do not typically teach stand-alone, credit-bearing courses. The projects resulting from the digital humanities short course taught by Rodrigues and Schnepper suggest that building coursework around archival remediation is a promising avenue for connecting activist memory to contemporary practice, but it is not an avenue either of us could regularly open on our own. The Vivero Digital Fellows program has been, in part, an attempt at establishing a more permanent collaborative space for critical digital projects.

With respect to digital project work, Wolff's experience on the BCC project exemplifies the pitfalls on the way to realizing the potential of centering student authority in digital collections as an emerging site of institutional archival practice. As Wolff relates, projects such as this one, which work with archives of student protest and student experience relevant to ongoing struggle and experience, entail perhaps even more emotional labor than technical labor. Developing a meaningful and practical metadata schema is a big ask in itself, but balancing the goals of college administration, the desires of current students, the unknown desires of future students and alumni, and the ethical frameworks of critical digital practice is at least an order of magnitude larger. Remediation as a mode of critical digital work revolves around decision-making, and decision-making is a form of labor magnified when the decisions that need to be made are de facto entries in ongoing struggles over who owns, cares for, and narrates a group's history on campus.

These challenges in some way arise from the very aspirations of critical archival pedagogy, the Vivero Digital Scholarship Fellows program, and a liberal arts education itself. Addressing these challenges, then, should not simply be a matter of falling back on proven project models but rather holding ourselves to a more rigorous exploration of potentials. As Wolff suggests, one of these potentials is to position the BCC as a community archive within or alongside the college archives, in which the students of the BCC would be trained, paid, and supported to develop its digital archival collection. The term "community archive" refers to "grassroots, community-owned and -controlled initiatives that collect, describe, and make accessible materials of the community's own choosing on its own terms."[26] Recognizing the BCC as a distinct community within the broader college community could allow us to reconceive its relationship to the archive and bring its members closer to being "fully empowered to represent their past, construct their present and envision their futures as forms of liberation."[27] While a group of students within a college are not the primary type of community associated with such archives, the framework fits in our context. Black students at Grinnell, past and present, have expressed feeling themselves unrepresented in and even excluded from typical narratives of Grinnellian identity. As Caswell, Migoni, Geraci, and Cifor have found, a thriving community archive has the potential to impact members of that community on at least three levels: ontologically ("in which members of marginalized communities get confirmation 'I am here'"); epistemologically ("in which members of marginalized communities get confirmation 'we were here'"); and socially ("in which members of marginalized communities get confirmation 'we belong here'").[28] Caswell, Migoni, Geraci, and Cifor's use of the term "belong" is particularly striking to us, as it is precisely the word that the college uses to frame current discussions of the ways in which our broader community is falling short of full inclusivity for students from marginalized and underrepresented backgrounds.

While archival practice cannot address all of the challenges these students face, it might well serve as a concrete site of student empowerment in relationship to their own narratives of self and belonging. Such work would likely need to begin with hammering out a decision-making process that empowered student archivists to create and interpret digital objects within a clear sense of the community's goals and the project's inevitable limitations. Different constituencies might be responsible for decisions in different areas (the archivist of the college might have a final say on digitization methods, the student archivists determine the metadata schema, and the BCC student leadership group might get to decide which events are highlighted in a digital exhibit) in the context of ongoing conversation and consultation. As employees of the college tasked with creating the structures through which students experience archival learning and project work, we (Rodrigues, Jones, and Schnepper) need to continue to build a practical path between making students aware of archival decisions and preparing students to make archival decisions in order to truly claim that the authority of the college archives has been transformed.

NOTES

1 "Tradition," Grinnell College, https://www.grinnell.edu/about/at-a-glance/tradition.

2 In 1843, eleven Congregational ministers, recently graduated from Andover Theological Seminary in Andover, MA, responded to a request posted by the American Home Missionary Society for ministers to travel into the as yet untamed territory that would eventually become Iowa. Before leaving for the

Iowa territories, the group of young ministers, who began referring to themselves as the Iowa Band, decided that they would each build a church and form a ministry in the new territory, and together the eleven would establish a college. Each of the young men did indeed go on to build at least one church in what would become eastern Iowa, and in 1846, three years after first arriving in the territory, they founded Iowa College and would later be renamed Grinnell College. Throughout its history, the College has continually shown support for social justice, whether through the activities of the faculty and staff, its students, or its benefactors. For example, College faculty continued to live the commitment to social justice by seeking to keep students out of the Japanese-American internment camps during WWII. They managed to enroll two students, so the effort was not as wildly successful as had been hoped, but it did keep two students out of American prison camps. The College's educational mission has also had a direct impact on progressive social programs in the United States. For example, The College also graduated five students during the 1910s who would later go on to hold integral positions in the Works Progress Administration (WPA): Hallie Flanagan Davis '11 was the director of the Federal Theatre Project, Paul Appleby '13 was the deputy director of the U.S. Bureau of the Budget, Chester Davis '11 became the director of the Agricultural Adjustment Administration, Florence Kerr '12 was the assistant commissioner of the Works Progress Administration, and perhaps most notable of the five, Harry Hopkins '12 held the position of Chief Presidential Advisor to the President of the United States and was the architect of the New Deal.

3 "Special Collections and Archives," Grinnell College, https://www.grinnell.edu/academics/libraries/special-collections-and-archives.

4 Hilda Kean and Paul Ashton, "Introduction: People and their Pasts and Public History Today," in *People and their Pasts: Public History Today,* eds. Paul Ashton and Hilda Kean (London: Palgrave Macmillan, 2009), 4.

5 Paul Griffin, "Making Usable Pasts: Collaboration, Labour and Activism in the Archive," *Area* 50, no. 4 (2018): 502, https://doi.org/10.1111/area.12384.

6 Jarrett M. Drake, "Documenting Dissent in the Contemporary College Archive: Finding Our Function within the Liberal Arts," *Medium*, November 7, 2016, https://medium.com/on-archivy/documenting-dissent-liberal-arts-e1c69e574ff8.

7 Mimi Thi Nguyen, "Minor Threats," *Radical History Review 2015*, no. 122 (May 1, 2015): 13, https://doi.org/10.1215/01636545-2849495.

8 When referring to a minor threat, Nguyen is describing the objects of marginal groups, such as printed material, that once circulated in their communities that have now found their way into institutional archives.

9 Kailah R. Carden et al., "A Critical Archival Pedagogy: The Lesbian Herstory Archives and a Course in Radical Lesbian Thought," *Radical Teacher* 105 (July 7, 2016): 23–32, https://doi.org/10.5195/rt.2016.275.

10 Jay David Bolter and Richard Grusin, "Remediation," *Configurations* 4, no. 3 (Fall 1996): 311–58, https://doi.org/10.1353/con.1996.0018.

11 Sandra Gabriele, "Transfiguring the Newspaper: From Paper to Microfilm to Database," *Amodern*, no. 2 (October 2013), http://amodern.net/article/transfiguring-the-newspaper/#pdf; Hannah McGregor, "Remediation as Reading: Digitising *The Western Home Monthly*," *Archives and Manuscripts* 42, no. 3 (September 2, 2014): 248–57, https://doi.org/10.1080/01576895.2014.958864.

12 Bolter and Gursin, "Remediation," 340.

13 Bolter and Gursin, "Remediation," 340.

14 American Library Association, "Framework for Information Literacy for Higher Education," February 9, 2015, http://www.ala.org/acrl/standards/ilframework.

15 Association of College and Research Libraries' Rare Book and Manuscript Section-Society of American Archivists Joint Task Force on the Development of Guidelines for Primary Source Literacy, "Guidelines for Primary Source Literacy" (American Library Association, February 12, 2018), http://www.ala.org/acrl/sites/ala.org.acrl/files/content/standards/Primary%20Source%20Literacy2018.pdf.

16 Kim Schwenk, "Another World Possible: Radical Archiving in the 21st Century," *Progressive Librarian*, no. 36/37 (Fall 2011): 58.

17 This exercise is adapted from an exercise led by Dr. Miriam Posner in a 2016 faculty workshop during the Digital Bridges for Humanistic Inquiry grant.

18 Michelle Caswell, "Teaching to Dismantle White Supremacy in Archives," *The Library Quarterly* 87, no. 3 (June 8, 2017): 223, https://doi.org/10.1086/692299.

19 The Omeka site (Omeka.org) includes a useful set of exemplar projects.

20 Roxane Brown, "Cultural Center Three Years Old Now," *The Scarlet & Black*, February 18, 1972.

21 The Vivero Digital Scholarship Student Fellowship Program is a training and mentorship program that seeks to grow the diversity of the digital liberal arts community at Grinnell College and beyond. The program seeks to recruit and support students from underrepresented backgrounds to work closely with faculty and staff project leads as digital scholarship research assistants, paid for both project work and ongoing training. For more information see https://vivero.sites.grinnell.edu/.

22 When the BCC Archive project starts up again, I believe it is crucial that the students who work on the project are paid, whether through ICA, Vivero, or another channel. If the College considers the BCC a valuable space and

its documentation a valuable endeavor, then the labor and time of student archivists is also valuable.

23 For example, students were hired as Fellows before projects and project leads were identified. While this recruitment process emphasizes equal access to the opportunities the program offers, it does not guarantee that the best students for a particular job will know to apply or have their qualifications for a particular project acknowledged.

24 I (Wolff) recognize that the institution of Grinnell College is not a single entity. The staff of the Office of Intercultural Affairs, the faculty and staff members who founded Vivero, and the people who decided to close the BCC are not the same people; and, of course, the administrators who were resistant to the BCC's initial opening in 1969 are by and large not the same individuals who make decisions at the college now.

25 Jarrett Drake, "Documenting Dissent in the Contemporary College Archive: Finding our Function within the Liberal Arts," (keynote address, filmed at Digital Library Federation Liberal Arts Colleges Pre-Conference, hosted at the Pfister Hotel in Milwaukee, WI, on November 6, 2016. Text available at https://medium.com/on-archivy/documenting-dissent-liberal-arts-e1c69e574ff8. Video available at https://www.youtube.com/watch?v=4xwftPUTB5g.

26 Alex H. Poole, "The Information Work of Community Archives: A Systematic Literature Review," *Journal of Documentation* 76, no. 3 (January 1, 2020): 657-687, doi: 10.1108/JD-07-2019-0140.

27 Michelle Caswell et al., "'To Be Able to Imagine Otherwise': Community Archives and the Importance of Representation," *Archives and Records* 38, no. 1 (January 2, 2017): 6, https://doi.org/10.1080/23257962.2016.1260445.

28 Caswell et al., "'To Be Able to Imagine Otherwise,'" 6.

BIBLIOGRAPHY

Association of College and Research Libraries' Rare Book and Manuscript Section–Society of American Archivists Joint Task Force on the Development of Guidelines for Primary Source Literacy. "Guidelines for Primary Source Literacy." American Library Association, February 12, 2018. http://www.ala.org/acrl/sites/ala.org.acrl/files/content/standards/Primary%20Source%20Literacy2018.pdf.

Bolter, Jay David, and Richard Grusin. "Remediation." *Configurations* 4, no. 3 (Fall 1996): 311–58. https://doi.org/10.1353/con.1996.0018.

Brown, Roxane. "Cultural Center Three Years Old Now." *The Scarlet & Black*. February 18, 1972.

Carden, Kailah R., Sabina E. Vaught, Arturo Muñoz, Vanessa Pinto, Cecilia Vaught, and Maya Zeigler. "A Critical Archival Pedagogy: The Lesbian Herstory Archives and a Course in Radical Lesbian Thought." *Radical Teacher* 105 (July 7, 2016): 23–32. https://doi.org/10.5195/rt.2016.275.

Caswell, Michelle. "Teaching to Dismantle White Supremacy in Archives." *The Library Quarterly* 87, no. 3 (July 2017): 222–35. https://doi.org/10.1086/692299.

Caswell, Michelle, Alda Allina Migoni, Noah Geraci, and Marika Cifor. "'To Be Able to Imagine Otherwise': Community Archives and the Importance of Representation." *Archives and Records* 38, no. 1 (January 2, 2017): 5–26. https://doi.org/10.1080/23257962.2016.1260445.

Drake, Jarrett M. "Documenting Dissent in the Contemporary College Archive: Finding Our Function within the Liberal Arts." *Medium*. November 7, 2016. https://medium.com/on-archivy/documenting-dissent-liberal-arts-e1c69e574ff8.

American Library Association. "Framework for Information Literacy for Higher Education," February 9, 2015. http://www.ala.org/acrl/standards/ilframework.

Gabriele, Sandra. "Transfiguring the Newspaper: From Paper to Microfilm to Database." *Amodern*, no. 2 (October 2013). http://amodern.net/article/transfiguring-the-newspaper/#pdf.

Griffin, Paul. "Making Usable Pasts: Collaboration, Labour and Activism in the Archive." *Area* 50, no. 4 (2018): 501–8. https://doi.org/10.1111/area.12384.

Kean, Hilda, and Paul Ashton. "Introduction: People and Their Pasts and Public History Today." In *People and Their Pasts: Public History Today*, edited by Paul Ashton and Hilda Kean, 1–20. London: Palgrave Macmillan UK, 2009. https://doi.org/10.1057/9780230234468_1.

McGregor, Hannah. "Remediation as Reading: Digitising *The Western Home Monthly*." *Archives and Manuscripts* 42, no. 3 (September 2, 2014): 248–57. https://doi.org/10.1080/01576895.2014.958864.

Nguyen, Mimi Thi. "Minor Threats." *Radical History Review 2015*, no. 122 (May 1, 2015): 11–24. https://doi.org/10.1215/01636545-2849495.

Poole, Alex H. "The Information Work of Community Archives: A Systematic Literature Review." *Journal of Documentation* 76, no. 3 (January 1, 2020): 657–87. https://doi.org/10.1108/JD-07-2019-0140.

Schwenk, Kim. "Another World Possible: Radical Archiving in the 21st Century." *Progressive Librarian*, no. 36/37 (Fall 2011): 51–58.

Grinnell College. "Special Collections and Archives," https://www.grinnell.edu/academics/libraries/special-collections-and-archives.

Grinnell College. "Tradition." https://www.grinnell.edu/about/at-a-glance/tradition.

CHAPTER SEVEN

CONFRONTING ISSUES OF POWER AND PRIVILEGE WITH STUDENT-DESIGNED PUBLIC ONLINE EXHIBITS

Elise Nacca and Elon Lang

In this chapter we discuss how we—a librarian and a lecturer in the Humanities Program at the University of Texas at Austin (UT-Austin)—came to design an undergraduate class that opens up archives to student research and opens students' eyes to the ethical issues at stake in the role archives play as gatekeepers to the historical and cultural record. While archives can be dynamic places to teach primary source analysis, the research process, and information literacy to students of all levels, they can also be especially intimidating to undergraduate students and to their instructors. Some of the reasons for this intimidation are practical: archives' institutional resources and conservation or security policies can limit access to collections and prevent them from being used actively in classrooms. Instructors thus can encounter logistic problems in using archives that can impact their ability to plan for and conduct classes that fulfill their pedagogical goals.

Additionally, collections often reflect hierarchies of power and privilege so that students from diverse backgrounds cannot see themselves reflected therein and majority students run the risk of perpetuating these power structures by not confronting them. As Randall Jimerson lays out, archives can be spaces where elites cement their power through controlling the narrative and discourse.[1] When we use our power as archivists to call these deeply embedded practices into account, archives can also be spaces that "provide a forum to recognize and legitimize the role of disenfranchised groups in society."[2] When students, undergraduates in particular, encounter archives structured around white, male, and heteronormative power structures, they can get the impression that archives exclude them and the diverse voices of people who may share their own cultural backgrounds. This sense of exclusion is amplified by the perception that archival research requires a level of expertise, specialization, and permission that they don't possess or have yet to attain.

In order to address these perceptions while taking advantage of the incredible benefits of teaching with archives, we have attempted to create an undergraduate course that not only introduces undergraduates to the process of developing an original archival research project, but also introduces them to the process by which archives themselves are created. This course, called "Giving Voice to Hidden Histories" is taught in the Liberal Arts Honors and Humanities programs at the UT-Austin. The goal of this course is to lead both novice and intermediate-level undergraduate researchers to do original social-justice-themed archival research projects (on underutilized special collections on the UT-Austin campus) and to communicate the results of that humanistic research to a general audience. The course leads students through hands-on activities in archival collections, teaches students how to do original historical research with primary sources, exposes students to issues of copyright and the post-custodial responsibilities institutional collections have, and gets students to become aware of the biases we can pass along through metadata creation. The course also teaches lifelong digital literacy skills by asking students to collaboratively design an Omeka[3] digital archive and exhibit website for their capstone group projects.

We argue that this course effectively achieves our teaching objectives because we build it on a model of interdisciplinary collaboration and decentered authority and privilege. As an ongoing collaboration between a librarian and a faculty member, this course represents a pedagogy in which the librarian acts as the entry point to the broad range of expertise that librarians and archivists have in academic research communities. This course is also designed to be responsive to student feedback. Indeed, every iteration is rebuilt upon the suggestions of cohorts who share ideas and suggestions at the end of every semester. In this way, we explicitly show that (just as the students do in their capstone project that remakes a year-to-year exhibit website) the course itself is meant to be refined and our pedagogy confronted. We attempt to incorporate numerous expert voices in the information professions throughout the course in order to draw attention to how authority is constructed. We want to show how the best research and social action relies on multiple sources of authority and participants who responsibly claim their own.

Although we did not initially set out to do so, we have found that these collaborations address a central problem in the humanities that Michelle Caswell identified in 2016: "humanities scholarship is suffering from a failure of interdisciplinarity when it comes to archives." Caswell elaborates on this diagnosis with the claim that:

> the two discussions—of "the archive" by humanities scholars, and of archives by archival studies scholars (located in library and information studies departments and schools of information)—are happening on parallel tracks in which scholars in both disciplines are largely not taking part in the same conversations, not speaking the same conceptual languages, and not benefiting from each other's insights.[4]

We agree. But, while we have recognized the differences in the conventions and professional goals in each of our disciplines, we have found lots of common ground in how we think about the responsibilities and ethical considerations that all instructors and librarians alike want students to wrestle with when they are developing primary source literacies.

While we are uniquely privileged to have access to several world-class research archives on our campus at the University of Texas at Austin, we also argue that the design of our curriculum is meant to address the common experience many librarians and archivists across institutions share: that their expertise is underutilized in semester-long coursework. This underutilization is sometimes a result of institutions' resource allocation but also because instructors who incorporate engagement with archives into their lessons usually opt for one-shot instruction sessions or show-and-tell sessions with collection materials instead of more sustained engagements. What we have been able to do effectively in our collaboration is to deploy the expertise of archives professionals at key moments throughout the semester to expose students to the ways metadata and description, copyright and fair use, and post-custodialism are considered in real-world contexts. A librarian or archivist is also helpful in identifying underutilized special collections on a campus and can advocate for their inclusion in courses with goals like this one. These goals are to create a pedagogy for research, analysis, and information literacy with an instrumental, student-driven, hands-on approach that foregrounds ethics and social justice. Thus, we teach students how to use special collections to do research, while also teaching them to use a digital tool for the communication of humanities research to a general audience. Overall, this creates contexts in which students must collaborate with each other, with information professionals, and with their instructors in order to assume responsibility for conducting ethical and original humanist scholarship.

TEACHING THE ARCHIVE AS HISTORY'S DYNAMIC STARTING POINT

This class came about as a result of a serendipitous encounter we had at a UT Libraries lightning talk event. Nacca was pitching an idea she had to expand research opportunities in undergraduate coursework through closer collaborations with instructional faculty. She wanted to work with instructors who were willing to take risks and work with undergrads in archives and collections that could lead to more hands-on activities and incorporate conversations around the gaps and silences in archival research. Lang—who was in attendance—was already teaching a course in the Liberal Arts Honors program in which students did original research in performing arts collections at the Harry Ransom Center. His course was dogged by its insularity, though. While students succeeded in learning key research skills usually not taught to humanists before grad school, and produced high quality scholarship, its topic did not have broad appeal to students not interested in the history of theater. Also, even as the successful students presented publishable work within this discipline, they realized that the increased level of specialization in their work made their audience very small—and in fact fortified the privileged status of their subjects and the exclusivity of their archival research efforts. Thus, while Lang's mission for his course had been to promote the accessibility of archives for undergraduate research, the structure of the class did the opposite.

When we started collaborating, we brainstormed how to address: (1) appealing to liberal arts students who came from a wide variety of disciplinary majors; (2) giving space to students from diverse backgrounds to see themselves in the archives, and pushing white heteronormative students to acknowledge the effects of the silence and gaps in collecting practices; and (3) creating a public, generalist audience for students' work rather than an academic specialist audience.

We addressed these partly by organizing the course around a new central theme: *social justice*. Social justice is a common concern shared by liberal arts students in their academic, extracurricular, and professional interests. It is a theme that connects diverse historical records and cultural materials across collections and across archives on the UT-Austin campus. We also decided that instead of asking students to work toward a seminar-length research paper that would be submitted only to Lang, they would develop a public-facing project in which they could share their research with a general audience. Doing so would give a voice to the historical narratives about the pursuit of social justice they uncovered throughout the semester. Rather than pushing students to develop the next step in critical scholarship on the topic they selected to research, we opted instead to emphasize their making an argument to explain the significance of the collection materials they "discovered" in their archival research. As support for this work, we sought to contextualize it with readings and exercises that get students to consider central concerns in critical archival studies discourse. As they did their research, we wanted them to critique why some historical narratives and archival materials have been given a bigger voice than others over time. So, in order to make such abstract ethical elements of this discourse feel more concrete, we decided to get students to encounter these issues themselves through the process of building an archive and making exhibits out of it.

The resulting class we designed is structured as an undergraduate seminar in which students learn to write ethical and approachable historical narratives using archival materials. Students know from the beginning of the class that their grade depends on participating actively in all discussions in class, and contributing to a running set of short essay prompts with threaded responses on the online course management system in which they engage with each other's thoughts about a set of articles from critical archival studies literature.

We begin the class with a couple of weeks in which students learn about the nature of archives by connecting their own experiences to the theoretical place archives have come to occupy in humanities scholarship. For example, we get them to examine Derrida's claim that "the archive has always been a pledge, and like every pledge, a token of the future"[5] by first having them describe a time when they have chosen to save or discard memorabilia from their own lives based on their practical needs and uncertainty about what future purpose the items will have. We then ask them to compare these experiences to concerns that institutions must face when building collections—especially dwelling on how certain collecting missions might create gaps and absences in the archival record. While students are reading and reflecting (in short responses or journaling) on critical essays about the intersection between archiving and social justice,[6] we also lead them through a series of guided exercises using online and then physical archives to help them learn basic document and object analysis techniques. In this phase of the class, our goal is to introduce them to strategies of observation and the logistics of doing archival research. We also hope to get them excited about the possibilities for historical and ethical discovery by exposing them to underutilized collections at available archives on campus.

The next step is to get students to do independent analysis on a small set of archival items and to learn how to find secondary scholarship that contextualizes them. That is, to prompt them to ask questions about their items that lead them from *observations* to interpretive *suppositions* about their meaning and significance. We ask them to prepare class presentations in which they turn their interpretive *suppositions* into interpretive *claims* by finding historical and other disciplinary research to support various interpretations they could make of their materials. The assignment prompt we use, in fact, asks students to find two different scholarly disciplines in which to situate their interpretations.

For example, a treatise from the 1600s about English laws pertaining to women could be situated both in the disciplines of book history and feminist legal theory. In our experiences, the class's collaborative discussion-based ethos becomes particularly productive at this time as the students give each other constructive feedback on their presentations. Our role as instructors is to encourage *them* to suggest other disciplines and contexts for each presenter to explore. By cultivating an atmosphere that celebrates exploration and inquiry—getting each student comfortable with presenting frequently on ideas-in-progress rather than finished products—we encourage students to help each other develop their analytical and contextualization techniques together around the social justice theme that everyone shares. This fosters a class culture in which everyone learns to accept each other's ideas and perspectives, and where cooperation and helping each other develop ideas is the baseline norm for their praxis.

These initial presentations build toward a capstone project in which students turn their academic research plans into public histories. They first assemble an "all-but-the-paper" research portfolio for their midterm assignment. This includes, for example, edited research notes; document analyses and transcriptions; accurate citations; and an annotated bibliography. This gets them to produce all the background material they would need to write up a seminar paper interpreting a selected archival item and making a claim as to its scholarly significance, without actually writing up the paper. The emphasis in the assignment is on having students develop expertise on their selected archival collections that can be productively applied to communicating their research to a public audience.

After developing this expertise on their archival materials, the students then experiment with the digital content management and web-publishing platform, Omeka. Their first project is to develop a pitch for a digitized collection of their independently researched archival materials with draft metadata. After assembling their own individual collections, they then proceed to collaborate with each other to develop exhibits out of these collections on the site. Students have a lot of in-class time to do group work and to report frequently back to the class on their findings and plans. Ultimately, their final assignment is to work together to take over and promote our class's ongoing public-facing Omeka website,[7] and to work with each other to attempt to design narrative and thematic relationships between all the exhibits they create for the year. In the final few weeks of the semester, they are all deeply engaged in multimodal writing, project management, and strategizing how to call attention to their work on social media. It is heartening to watch them all apply themselves to divvying up the responsibilities of designing the appearance of the website and all its new exhibits, copyediting, regularizing metadata vocabulary and tags, and promoting their work to audiences they care about.

The course culminates in a website launch event where students present their online exhibit to a live audience that usually includes many of the librarian and archival professionals with whom they have worked throughout the class. Even in 2020, when we had to finish the second half of the course exclusively online due to our COVID-19 campus closure, students prepared a live launch event over a Zoom video conference. Along with on-campus archival stakeholders, audience members also included alumni of the class—some of whom had already graduated from the university—who wished to see how this class had used exhibits from previous years as models for new work. Since the students are partly responsible for organizing and promoting the event on top of building the site itself, they have an opportunity to experience what it feels like to take pride in and ownership of a published work product from start to finish. They also have to develop a keen sense of what it takes to make a case for why their project might matter to an audience who has invested in their success.

GOALS AND SKILLS

Our primary goal is for students to learn how to do original academic research. But perhaps of equal importance is to give students an experience in archival stewardship and curation that illustrates how underutilized archival materials can contain hidden stories that—when revealed and analyzed—can expand the understanding of history. One of the main ways that we've been able to get the support of administrators, both in our host academic program and in the libraries, for this course is by touting how this primary goal helps students cultivate "practical" real-world skills. In universities where liberal arts programs and libraries feel pressured by outside forces to demonstrate how they prepare students to compete in a variety of professional sectors when they graduate, describing learning outcomes in terms of skills and real-world experiences can open up new avenues of support. One main avenue has been to emphasize how our course offers "experiential learning" opportunities to liberal arts students, that is coursework that involves experiences that extend beyond the classroom to engage directly with the professional world.[8] The experiential learning elements of the course help students develop four integrated skill sets:

- independent inquiry;
- information literacy;
- communicating research findings;
- promoting inclusivity, social justice, and accessibility.

Independent Inquiry

In order to promote students' independence in this class, instruction requires a lot of listening so that we can guide students to become aware of the steps they're taking through their own inquiry process. We ask students to develop their own research questions by prompting them to begin making analytical observations about primary sources found in the archives. We give them a list of prompts to start from (sometimes listing them with a lot of blank space on a worksheet to encourage more writing), such as:

1. What is the item? What type of item is it? If a recognizable type (like a letter) what genre of letter is it (an appeal, a love note, a request for money, etc.)?
2. What are its material traits? (Does it look used? Are there folds, corrected typos, etc.?)
3. Who created it? (How can you be sure?)
4. When was it created? And where? (How can you be sure?)
5. Why was this item created? What was its creator's purpose? How earnest were they in their purpose?

As students present their observations to the class in informal talks and small writing assignments shared to discussion threads on the class website, we work to get presenters and their classmates to recognize when they make the leap from observations to inferences. That is to say, we try to prompt them frequently to describe the details on a document or object that address these basic analytical questions. Whenever they attempt to answer one of these questions by making an *assumption* about what their observations mean we ask them again to describe the evidence from their observations that enables them to make such an interpretation. By helping them label the parts of their analysis as observations or interpretations, they begin to see how they themselves use assumptions and inferences to build up their understanding of things in the world.

Next, we ask students to develop strategies for figuring out if their inferences could be proven to be true using research in scholarly secondary sources. When they actually track down and read this scholarship and compare it to their analysis, they realize that each answer they figure out leads them toward more questions. They start to realize that even when they find an extensive scholarly discourse on a topic, they can still have a lot of room to articulate their own interpretation of what their selected archival primary sources could mean, and to make a case for the significance of their interpretations. The main emphasis is to encourage students to practice independent inquiry as an iterative process that requires going back and forth between analysis, searching, reading, writing, presenting, getting feedback, and then more analysis, searching, reading, writing and presenting, and so on.

Information Literacy

Instructing information literacy to upper-division undergraduates involves teaching students how to find and interpret primary and secondary sources and to recognize the differences between them in the information rich environments of college campuses. Using assignments like an item contextualization exercise (prompt follows), students build upon their archival object analysis observations and questions to experiment with how individual sources can be analyzed and critiqued in multiple scholarly contexts. By using questions like these, we ask students to use their analysis to generate search terms in different disciplines to apply to specific scholarly databases. This helps students learn how information is organized for use in different academic fields—and also how that organization can reflect histories of assumptions about power and normativity that have changed over time to reflect an increased sensitivity to social justice.

ITEM CONTEXTUALIZATION PRESENTATION PROMPT

For this presentation, situate the item you're analyzing in at least **two potential research contexts**:

- For each research context, identify and *cite* a scholarly resource (e.g., a book, article, map, digital exhibit, etc.) that looks like it could help you address one or more of the questions you're collecting about this item
- While you don't have to have the research and reading *fully* done for the presentation, be ready to share what you've

found through your preliminary explorations and how and why you think each scholarly resource will help you get some answers—and label what scholarly discipline (e.g., Latin American history, book history, women and gender studies, African American and African diaspora studies) and subject field/subfield the resource seems to be a part of (e.g., civil rights and labor movements of 1960s–70s in the United States, 19th-century binding practices, women's suffrage, punk influences in early hip-hop music).

- Conclude with a hypothesis about how your archival item and your analysis of it **could matter** to a scholarly reader in this field (even in a small way e.g., contributing a new piece of evidence to advance the understanding of ____, etc.)

The point of this prompt is to get students to expand beyond searching Google and JSTOR to learn how effective it is for their research interests to practice the idiosyncratic searching methods for finding materials in archives, libraries, and in scholarly databases for their projects throughout the semester. Through a workshop at the libraries, we offer training on how to search for archival items at local archives using a finding aid aggregating database.[9] They also learn techniques for analyzing different types of media (visual, audio, material, textual) and about the nature of copyright and how to engage in practices of "fair use" when they publish information on the internet. Also, with the help of library experts, they learn about the nature of metadata and the way ethical issues have been intertwined with the history of metadata creation.

Communicating Research Findings

Instruction in communication strategies is integrated into the class's daily activities in order to give students lots of practice speaking about their work in low-stakes, collegial environments before moving them into more challenging contexts where their audiences are unknown. Students practice explaining their findings and their interpretations of their sources to a real audience of non-specialists every time they share their work with each other. By asking them to "report back" about their work fairly frequently throughout the semester, students receive a lot of affirmation and a lot of constructive questions from their peers and instructors that help them become comfortable talking about their ideas while these ideas are still forming. This frequent feedback also allows students to begin realizing early in the semester that some of the themes of their independent

Figure 7.1. *Community Narratives: Uncovering Hidden Perspectives*, 2020 Class Omeka website landing page.

Top row: Figure 7.1 and Figure 7.2: Two sample title pages from our class's exhibit website (2019 and 2020). Bottom row: Figure 7.3 and Figure 7.4: Exhibit landing page and a detail page from same exhibit that shows how the students synthesize their project themes across their whole collaborative exhibit design.[10]

Figure 7.2. *Highlighting Inequity and Identity in History*, 2019 Class Omeka website landing page.

research projects "speak" to each other. This lays the groundwork for them to seek to collaborate with each other to tell bigger stories when they have to set up their capstone online exhibits.

When the students are ready to take over the course Omeka website and start redesigning it around their own exhibits, establishing team-based project management strategies occurs fairly organically. We assign them a brainstorming exercise to settle on a set of definitions for their website's shared goals and they learn each other's strengths and disciplines so as to more effectively distribute the creative responsibilities of the project. In exhibit design teams, they also learn how to best take advantage of the Omeka multimedia platform for presenting a balance of writing and audiovisual media to communicate their content using the most effective designs. They also learn about features of universal design in order to ensure that their work is accessible to a wide audience.

COMMUNITY NARRATIVES: UNCOVERING HIDDEN PERSPECTIVES

About | Browse Exhibits | Browse Collections | Browse Items | Map | Exhibits Archive | Acknowledgements

Snapshots: Community Networks and Media Ephemerality

Introduction

Non-Majority Visibility in Print Media

Media of Protest, Advocacy and Activism

Visual Art Networks

Content Availability Map

Conclusion

Works Cited

Introduction

This exhibit displays a variety of media, including but not limited to newsletters, magazines, murals, and comics. Despite the variation in presentation, all of these works share a commonality in that they were intended to be dispersed to a relatively small and often local audience, meaning that there is a sort of collective ownership of them by a small community--via these temporary mediums. We hope to create a snapshot of non majority networks of people throughout the 20th century, covering topics and groups not typically represented in mainstream media and literature. One of the most compelling aspects of this exhibit is that many of these pieces were not meant to last, or were intentionally covered up and/or destroyed, mirroring the erasure and ephemerality of many of the topics they intended to bring awareness to. Some of these pieces convey information in ways that come off as insensitive or tone deaf to the issues presented; however these narratives are still important, as they add another dimension to how we typically think about the past, and highlight how people communicated about sensitive or controversial subjects through media.

We could not have found many of the items featured in this exhibit without access to archival collections at the University of Texas campus, including the LLILAS Benson Latin American Collection, the Dolph Briscoe Center for American History, and the Harry Ransom Center, which specializes in literature and cultural artifacts from the Americas and Europe. Despite the different focuses of these archives, our exhibit illustrates connections between the three centers, as all of our objects are indicative of mechanisms of activism, spread across various groups, places, and periods of time, connected by their medium of activism, and the ephemerality of the works created, as well as being a hidden voice in history.

Our exhibit is broken into subsections highlighting non-majority visibility in print media, media of protest, advocacy and activism, and visual art networks. Through these sections, various pieces are explored and analyzed in regards to media ephemerality and how non-majority communities communicate both with themselves and with others through creative outlets.

Credits: Sarah Brownson, Jenohn Euland, Zoe Roden, Vega Shah, Lucian Smith, Courtney Thomas

Figure 7.3. Details page from the 2020 collaborative student-created Omeka exhibit, *Snapshots: Community Networks and Media Ephemerality.*

What makes this project an effective model for experiential learning is the way the exhibit and website design process builds upon a series of peer-driven collaborations. Whether or not the students ever do digital exhibit design or work with Omeka in the future, they will have had a rigorous experience in team-based

communal black pride through art visibility.

"Off Our Backs:" A Woman's News-Journal Volume 1 no. 5: This is a feminist news journal that focuses on women's liberation across racial and socioeconomic backgrounds. This issue of the journal focuses on the Vietnam War and women's role in activism against the war. This news journal talks briefly on the antiwar movement, and describes how despite the fact that a significant amount of American women were against the war, the movement was dominated by males and the narrative was not inclusive of women.

Quote: "...Well, they haven't given any power to us, sisters, and we're half the people. Telling the people when to move, where to move, how to move...listening at the rallies- never any women's voices coming over the sound system."

A Chile-Texas Connection: Alice Embree published "A Chile-Texas Connection" in the Texas Observer in 1984. Acutely connected to Austin and the University of Texas, Embree recounts a reunion with many participants of an exchange program between UT students and Chileansnyears after its end. With 1984 situated in the middle of a repressive dictatorship endured by Chile between the years of 1973 and 1990, she points out the silence regarding Chile's political situation at the time, despite the University, and the country's large role in the events that had unfolded. Federico Willoughby, a member of Pinochet's junta, had been a participant of this exchange program and attended the reunion along with other participants who had been greatly impacted by the military junta's violent control over the country. Though she is writing about international events, the niche group that she describes gives the article a very personal feeling, making the silence the group experienced seem all the more deafening.

An Interview with Allende: This interview published by the North American Congress on Latin America (NACLA) details Chilean president Salvador Allende's attitudes surrounding democracy, socialism, and legacies of imperialism faced by Chile. With the United States working to undermine Allende's presidency, the NACLA provides a contrasting view of Allende and his presidency, highlighting his commitment to equality, democracy, and self determination. The NACLA is a non-profit organization that works to provide information policies between the U.S.

Figure 7.4. Landing page of the 2020 collaborative student-created Omeka exhibit, *Snapshots: Community Networks and Media Ephemerality.*

project management. Not only that but they will be able to present the product published from this collaboration when they describe their experience to others (see Figures 7.1–7.4). An end-of-semester presentation to invited guests—many collection stakeholders and experts—emphasizes the investments involved in creating a public-facing site. The audience they have had in mind all semester is now present and asking questions and reacting to their work. This helps them realize the responsibility they have as creators to represent their ideas clearly so that the greatest number of people can benefit from their work. This also helps to illustrate the responsibility they have as academics to engage directly with other published work to show how their ideas participate in an integrated network of expert historical scholarship and social justice advocacy.

Promoting Inclusivity, Social Justice, and Accessibility

Social justice themes are the glue that holds this class together. From students' selection of archival materials to their metadata creation practice to their exhibit copywriting, we sustain conversations about the ethical impact of their choices as they conduct and present their research through every step of the course. We try to expose students to a wide variety of collections early in the semester as we introduce them to each of the archive reading rooms. When we demonstrate analytical practices and research examples, we take care to feature underutilized collections that contain materials from diverse creators, organizations that have pursued civil rights, or that are illustrative of historical and ongoing struggles for social justice. Doing this allows us to help students imagine ways to engage with collections that may be minimally processed, described and organized. While the reasons for minimal processing could be explained by staffing shortages, we discuss as a class how collections stewards and institutions make decisions around which collections to prioritize and highlight and why.

All this recenters these under-studied voices by virtue of the attention the class and archive staff pay to them. While students ultimately choose their own collections to study for their final projects—using finding aids to search collections that they think would productively extend our existing Omeka site—we ask students to approve each other's choices by hearing each other's project pitches. Each student contributes their work to a friendly evaluation by their peers to collaboratively figure out how best to frame each student's project so as to adhere to the course website's mission to give voice to hidden histories.

We also emphasize that social justice includes discussions of accessibility. We have the students learn about accessibility standards and universal design, reading and discussing articles about how physical museums and archives can take specific steps to make their reading rooms and exhibits more universally accessible to people with different abilities. With physical museum galleries and study spaces as reference points, they also read about accessibility standards for web design and do an exercise in which they critique existing online exhibits on their designs. The intent of these exercises is to help them realize that design accessibility is an extension of a creator's rhetoric—and marketability. Doing these critiques as they are working on their own web designs for social justice archival exhibits has helped them see that increasing accessibility can be a practical method by which their design choices can do real work toward promoting social justice. One example of this (see Figure 7.5) can be seen in a group of students from the 2020 class who realized that most web reading tools for the visually impaired would not be able to process the images they had available to include in their exhibit. As a result, they elected to make audio transcriptions of the text in their images and include them along with the images on their site.

Students in this course make discoveries in the materials that are surprising, upsetting and run contrary to their expectations. The role that the instructor and collections experts play is

Defeat in Victory

The Price of Haitian Independence

As evident in Pierre Force's *Wealth and Disaster*, although Haiti won the Haitian Revolution in 1804, it had not won recognized independence from France. Rather, the Haitian government was required to pay the French government an indemnity "in exchange for diplomatic recognition" (111). This reparations agreement, made in 1825 and later "reduced from 150 million to 90 million francs...in 1838" (112), was largely debated by politicians in both countries, but the Haitians were especially incensed by their new president's decision to pay the indemnity "for the recognition of an independence that had already been earned with their blood" (114). Furthermore, they angrily realized that the indemnity was "'a sum that was beyond [their] means,'" and one that would become the burden of their future generations.

Regardless of the Haitian's general feelings, the reparations had already been agreed upon by leaders in both France and Haiti. In time, French citizens who had been forced out of Haiti during the revolution and who were living in various places across the globe began to receive these payments for the plantation lands and property – including slaves – that they had lost. While the United States government had refused to provide an indemnity to British loyalists – who then received some compensation from Britain – after the American Revolution, the Haitian government assented to the terms, allowing French families to get "relief from the government they had ruined themselves to prevent coming into existence" (116).

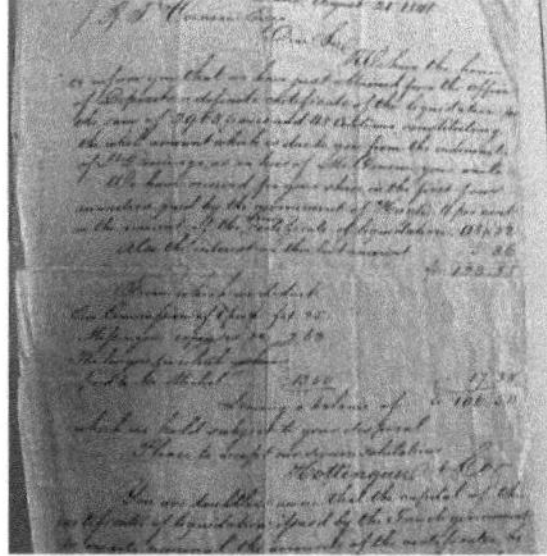

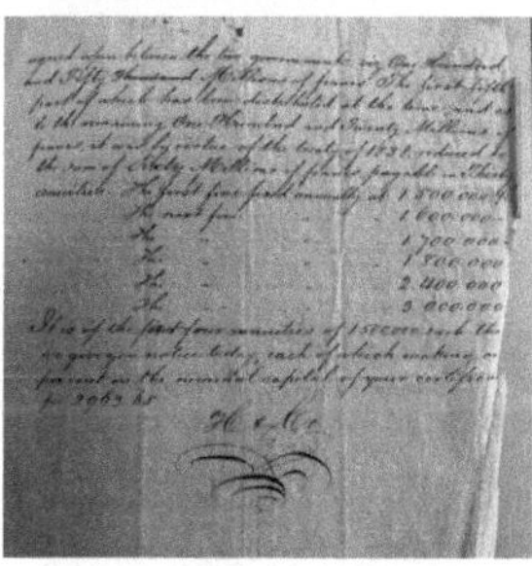

A two-page letter of reparation to the family of John Baptist Toussant Corneau from the French Banque Hottinguer.

Audio Recording of the Letter from Banque Hottinguer to the Corneau Family.

The letter displayed to the left is an example of a notice of incoming payments to a French family. In this case, it was sent to the family of John Baptist Toussant Corneau, the same man who fled the French Revolution to Haiti, the Haitian Revolution to Cuba, and eventually settled in the United States. In this letter, one can see that the French government's assessment of Corneau's incurred damages was 2,963 francs and 48 centimes, of which 4% would be paid out over the course of four years. Each year for the first four years (after the deduction of the necessary processing fees) the family would receive 106.50 francs from the French Banque Hottinguer via the Haitian government.

Finally, on the second page one can witness just how extensive the total indemnities were, scheduled to be paid at increasing rates for several decades. One may also imagine the strain that this amount of debt put on the already struggling economy of young Haiti; indeed, it was a debt so large that it altered the Haitian way of life and led to the poverty and struggle from which many of its inhabitants never fully recovered.

An audio recording of this document has been provided for increased accessibility.

Figure 7.5. Johann Rossbach, "Defeat in Victory," in *Tracking Relocations and Adaptations Throughout History*. Ed. Johann Rossbach, Divya Jagadeesh, and Grace Bumpus (members of the 2020 class cohort).[11]

to turn these difficult encounters into transformative learning moments where students shift from the typical perspective of *information consumers* to that of *knowledge creators* and become aware of all the profound responsibilities that come with that work. Furthermore, this is a moment to acknowledge the privilege those who steward our collections wield and the points at which those stewards can create space for the communities represented in collections to shape practices of collecting, preserving, describing and accessing. In this course, students are made to understand that they are stepping into this role in a real and public-facing manner that carries all the weight of responsibility and consequence.

In one recent in-class presentation, for example, a young woman who was researching Islamic American community groups expressed astonishment at such a stark contrast in the amount of racism that a set of newsletters revealed American Muslims were experiencing before and after 9/11. In another presentation, a young man showed the class an official report about Mexican Americans in public universities in the 1940s and '50s that he discovered in a collection about university policy. Throughout the presentation he used the term 'wetback' to refer to Mexican Americans, echoing the language he found in the document he was analyzing. He earnestly didn't realize that the term was considered an ethnic slur today since it was incorporated into an official bureaucratic document from the past. In both of these instances, our job as instructors was to draw attention to these moments of tension and empower the class to see them as evidence of structural racism. The authority that collections and institutions wield can obscure racism, homophobia, and other forms of discrimination under a veneer of legitimacy. When students are called on to confront these structures, they themselves wield the authority. These moments enable us to discuss with a whole class how such assumptions and terms as these carry with them the weight of unjust treatment of whole populations over time. When students make personal discoveries that push into uncomfortable territory, we can help them understand first hand the responsibility that historians—such as themselves—have to account for the past honestly while also taking care not to participate in and legitimize past histories of violence and injustice.

METADATA

In addition to the other experiential learning goals and skills in our capstone assignment, we integrate the promotion of social justice into our teaching of more granular discipline-specific skills by asking students to consider the ways in which the history of information can relate to ethics through sustained engagement with metadata. This is why we chose to use Omeka rather than other online publication platforms (like WordPress). As discussed in the section on digital literacy below, Omeka is a tool that facilitates both digital exhibits and metadata creation. The convergence of presentational and organizational tasks that students are asked to complete in the process of building a full Omeka site creates a rich space for faculty and information professionals to develop partnerships. It is also beneficial to students to realize how academia relies on the expertise that librarians and archivists have in metadata creation and how they are at the forefront of efforts to teach others how to understand the ethical responsibilities involved in representing artifacts in searchable data. For, as Michelle Caswell argues, "how archivists represent records determines how researchers may access them, and subsequently, which records they use to write histories, make legal decisions, and shape society's views of the past."[12]

In our experience in this class, teaching metadata as part of conversations about power and privilege in collecting practices can be a moment of transformative learning for students. Metadata enables discovery, identification, and selection of resources, but it is likely an aspect of a person's everyday experience with search tools that goes unnoticed. Hence, we strive to show how information professionals are trained to do the work of creating and managing metadata while balancing considerations of user needs, with applications of current and emerging standards and best practices, and with practical human investments of judgment, time and money. This is an important lesson in case students are under the impression that the process is automated or done by a machine. We chose to make lessons in metadata analysis and creation central to this course because students, through their capstone projects, begin to realize that an active difference between consuming and creating knowledge occurs in the process of labeling and describing information.

In these lessons we draw on the fact that the current university student population is already having conversations about how the language we use to describe identities and communities carries with it implications for power and privilege. Engaging students in assessing existing descriptions for artifacts as well as having them build upon, rethink, and create new metadata for the objects they are working with is a natural extension of conversations around describing identities. Above all, we encourage them to recognize the power that words have and the role those in power have to relinquish space for communities to represent themselves with language.

Creating metadata is also an opportunity for students to recognize their role in advocating for or oppressing communities, and to decide whether they have the authority to play this role at all. Often when educators teach students about metadata, we teach students that metadata is what helps people find things. However, we do not often teach them that the biases, prejudices, motives, and experiences they bring to the metadata creation process have consequences for the communities they are representing.[13] That is why, for this course, we are explicit with the students in establishing our shared goals from the beginning. To illustrate how the process of creating metadata is not neutral or benign, we introduce them to writing by metadata professionals, where there is conversation around making the metadata creation process one of collaboration and dialogue with object creators rather than a solo judgment of a cataloger, in order to bring to the surface issues around self-determination and representation.[14]

In this course, the instructor and the librarian worked together to decide upon goals for the metadata lessons, utilizing the Omeka platform's dialogue entry fields to make Dublin Core terminology more accessible (see Figure 7.6 and Figure 7.7). They then drew examples from the students' own active projects to make the lessons immediately applicable to their experience. Through a web page guide hosted by the library, the librarian created practical

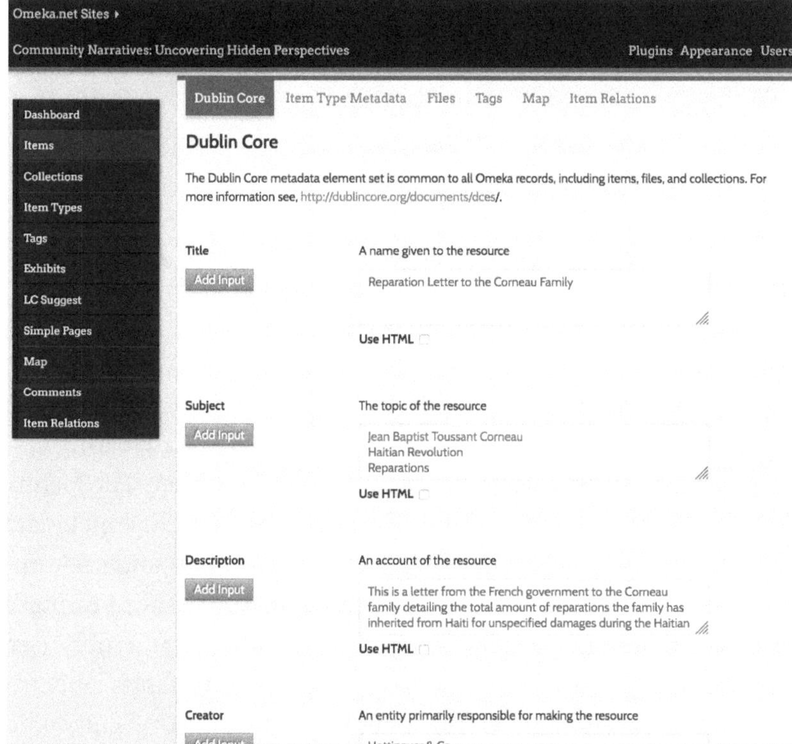

Figure 7.6. *Reparation Letter to the Corneau Family*–Example Omeka Item from 2020 class project, back end.

Reparation Letter to the Corneau Family

Dublin Core

Title Reparation Letter to the Corneau Family

Subject Jean Baptist Toussant Corneau
Haitian Revolution

Figure 7.7. *Reparation Letter to the Corneau Family*–Example Omeka Item from 2020 class project, front end.[15]

definitions and wrote-up guidance for the students to use when writing their metadata and invited expert metadata-creating colleagues to give the class a presentation on the subject. The faculty member took the lead on how to assess the students' metadata based on their goals for their students' achievement and their initial assessment of student capability. While we still need to make assessment more rigorous and systematic in this course, a rubric (see section headed Assessment later in the chapter) to assess student-generated metadata is helpful support for students or faculty who will be new to this process. Because best practices and standards are moving targets in the field of metadata, a librarian is best situated to advise on these matters and work with the faculty member to support students as they wade into this unfamiliar territory.

Over the course of our collaboration, the testimonials from students about this particular aspect of the project have described transformative learning moments:

> *In creating metadata I'm struggling with a lot of the dated language used in the 1950s, and how to make the clippings [from civil rights era news articles] searchable for an audience today, while staying true to their content.*

> *[I valued the lessons devoted to] how to allow communities control [of] the presentation of their own material. In being a student at The University of Texas this is the history of my community, although my community wasn't the one targeted. Working up my presentation involves balancing those two truths in the clippings I select and the viewpoints I present.*[16]

> *For me, metadata was a hard thing to comprehend at first but once the concept was explained by people who had worked with it before [...], it was easier to use. Metadata did end up influencing our exhibit, because tags were the way we [...] connected our exhibit to [another classmate we didn't think of], which did not seem possible at first. When working through the metadata-creation process, it became easier to visualize our exhibit and make decisions about what would be said.*

> *One of the stumbling blocks we encountered was how to avoid simply replicating histories of pain through our exhibit...The most rewarding thing about the process was understanding that the way we choose to present these items affects how history is remembered...it was interesting and weighty to be directly involved in that process. It was a struggle to consider what someone who found our exhibit through a Google search would understand as our intent and main points, and if they would understand the context. I was surprised at the responsibility this project placed on us individually.*

That students felt the weight of these decisions, that it is perhaps fair to say they had not felt this weight before when creating similar online content (like Twitter hashtags) is validation of the time we spent devoted to these lessons, the experts we brought in, and the scholarship to which students were exposed.

COPYRIGHT, FAIR USE, AND PRIVACY

We also found it immensely helpful to bring expert information professionals into the class when we sought to get students to understand their responsibilities and rights as a publisher of archival material created by others. Although students in the born-digital age often take for granted the ability to share and reproduce images they find and create online—no matter the subject of their photography—public-facing digital projects like the ones they develop in the class can pose problems for archives and special collections. When a donor agreement exists that clearly restricts digitization or making images available online, those collections can be off-limits to projects of this type unless a compromise is reached with the donor, which often requires a communication process that can take more time than a semester-long project might allow. Additionally, many collections do not have clearly stated terms of use for research and publication attached to them, so determining copyright and fair use becomes a gray area.

To address these concerns, we invite into the classroom our scholarly communications librarian, Colleen Lyon, to discuss copyright, fair use, and privacy. Although copyright law is complex and librarians rarely have the credentials to dispense legal advice on this matter, a communications specialist like Colleen may need to develop a functional expertise on the subject as part of their work for a library. Thus, they may be able to teach students about the practical aspects of copyright law that would directly apply to their work. By grounding her presentation in a risk-assessment exercise around students' own archival selections (a fair use checklist or four-factor test[17]), Colleen illustrates what it means for students creating content for the Web to think about their responsibilities as publishers. This risk-assessment is important ground to lay before discussing the fair use exception to copyright law. Information professionals regard fair use a "safety valve" for the First Amendment, a right that is vital to exercise in order for it to persist and to stay vibrant. Fair use, however, is an area in which the users must exercise their own judgment and this judgment brings with it anxiety not just for the student content creator in the class, but also for the professor and archival collection stewards because of legal ramifications if a case was brought to court.

While these potential legal issues can often cause instructors, archive professionals, and administrators to balk at plans to use public-facing digital projects in their pedagogy, we see the fair use exception that protects the use of copyrighted material in educational contexts as offering our students important real-world stakes for their work. Describing fair use to students as one of their own *conditionally* protected rights in practical terms, avoiding legalese and acknowledging the complexities in using it, conveys to them the responsibility they are undertaking. Unlike in an assignment like a seminar paper that has a lifespan that typically ends in a professor's inbox, our public-facing exhibit project carries with it a bit of "productive anxiety" about how authentic audiences will encounter the work online for an unknown time into the future. In this manner, concerns about copyright and fair use give students an experience with thinking about the implications and consequences of their own work that they likely have not had to wrestle with in their coursework heretofore.

Overall, exercises like a fair use checklist that students can apply to their public-facing objects valuably guide students through a process that not only addresses their role as ethical stewards of information but as transformers of works into new knowledge. Another beneficial outcome of these conversations that highlights the intersection of information stewardship and social justice is a discussion of Creative Commons.[18] Creative Commons licenses contrast with the ways in which we traditionally provide access to information through systems historically built on privilege. Making students aware of Creative Commons licenses and what they mean for intellectual property can encourage them to participate in the community of Creative Commons producers even beyond their work in the class, promoting the progressive move toward more open and equitable models of information sharing.

Privilege also needs to be acknowledged in teaching the capstone project by discussing the right to privacy. Privacy concerns for posting an individual's likeness on the Web are hard to address comprehensively since laws for internet privacy vary state by state, country by country. The consideration to post images of artifacts that bring someone's likeness or personal materials into public view is one that students have to manage without strong guidelines. In some cases, even, individuals represented by items in these collections may still be living. Many of these individuals may have been included without their knowledge in the physical archives from which the students select their items for digitization, since relevant materials may have been donated by other individuals. Anytime someone makes public images or information that could conceivably compromise an individual's safety or reputation they should wrestle with the profound and consequential decision to publish. As educators, we impress upon our students the significance of the privilege they have to access materials and we try to give them tools to manage the responsibility they have to treat their subjects' privacy with respect.

In this course, we chose to address considerations about this privilege and responsibility in part through a boilerplate copyright statement in the metadata for each item in our digital collection. A takedown notice that is formulated with careful consideration by the faculty member in collaboration with the participating archival institutions can serve as a notice to the public that issues of fair use and privacy have been weighed and that concerned parties may contact collection creators if they disagree with the decision to publish. While it does not absolve creators of the responsibilities inherent to their decisions made within the exhibits, nor does it guarantee that raised concerns would result in rescinding publication of an item, takedown notices do allow any unknown stakeholders an easy way to dispute work that the students make public digitally as part of their projects.

Another dimension of privacy that intersects with this project-and is a pressing concern for educators in all contexts on college campuses—is the Family Educational Rights and Privacy Act (FERPA).[19] FERPA requires that software used in the classroom is used under contract with one's educational institution or that students' parents give consent for their school work to be posted online. FERPA does not cover every real-world scenario and it is typically recommended that educators use common sense after consulting appropriate documentation. We offered students the opportunity to use aliases in this public-facing project and allowed students to opt out of making their work public at any point in the project. Because students contribute important research and insights into the collections they are analyzing, they have all found it desirable to take the option of claiming credit for their scholarly work on the class exhibits website. One consequence of students' desire to maintain a connection to their work after the class concludes—and in some cases to even include it in portfolios and resumes for job or grad school applications, is that we have just begun to realize that we need to do more work in clearly communicating how long students' work will remain online. The time frame for this is uncertain and depends not only on the continued interest in the course by its host academic program, but also in practical issues with software subscriptions. Since our primary web-publishing and online archiving tool, Omeka, currently exists in a subscription model and our funding for this subscription is contingent on unpredictable budgets for our academic program, we don't have solid answers to this question. We thus encourage anyone who wishes to build upon our pedagogical model to consider how students could expect to download or create a permanent record of their work. Many tools exist—such as the Internet Archive's Wayback Machine[20]—but some of these require password protection or isolate the dynamic connectivity of their product from the rest of the internet, diminishing long-term learning outcomes related to creating public-facing scholarship.

DIGITAL LITERACY

The digital literacy skills addressed in digital project creation are cultivated mainly through content creation and management. While we used Omeka to teach content creation for our capstone project, many tools exist. When selecting such a content management and publishing tool for your students, it is important to consider pedagogical goals. Most tools that result in a public-facing digital project offer an environment that facilitates creativity, participation, collaboration and risk-taking. These are not the usual skills taught in college classes. Students are well-acquainted with prose-writing projects with an audience perhaps limited to their immediate classmates or even just one professor, with a lifespan that ends with the semester. As you select a tool, then, keep in mind that students are, for perhaps the first time, being asked to present what they have learned and what they think in a multimodal format to an unknown and possibly infinite audience for an indeterminate amount of time. Additionally, it should never be assumed that students, even when they are digital natives, are technologically fluent in the ways that are versatile and relevant to this project.

When the project is public-facing, it is essential for the professor of the class to clarify its intended audience, or to come to agreement with the class on this. Writing for the web is a skill that can only be taught and assessed when students know whom they are meant to inform, persuade and with which existing conversations they are meant to participate. Asking students to present their research and ideas in public-facing projects is asking them to participate in civic society, to insert themselves thoughtfully and responsibly in pre-existing discourses within engaged communities and to wrestle meaningfully with the role they may play in how those communities are both uplifted and oppressed.

For the capstone project in the course discussed in this article, the authors chose Omeka mainly because of the way it allows content creators to engage with the process of writing metadata. Because Dublin Core is a metadata standard built to solve the problem of making objects findable on the Web, the builders of Omeka decided to participate in this movement, requiring that all objects be described with this schema. As discussed in the metadata section, choosing Omeka means choosing to devote instructional and project time, as well as assessment considerations, to creating metadata and to supporting students' acquisition and execution of these skills. When setting up the site, it is possible to choose which components of Dublin Core students must address. Selecting (and limiting) components with intention before students begin to process their archival materials allows instructors to focus on key lessons of description and avoid some components which may be irrelevant to projects their students are likely to develop in the class.

Regardless of the tool chosen, supporting students' use of a digital tool for their projects requires an amount of time that is often disruptive to the semester-long course. Many tools are open source and include vibrant user communities and online forums of which students may avail themselves. This is a key consideration: most of the how-to learning for a tool will be on the students' shoulders by design. We have chosen to treat this as one of the experiential learning goals of the class. Rather than hand-holding, offering students recommendations on support material is helpful so that they can take survivable risks, try things and sometimes fail so that they gather new information in order to reconfigure. What is most helpful is devoting several class periods to open lab time where students can work with one another to solve problems and get feedback on design decisions.

These design review and exhibit planning sessions are important in creating a collaborative class culture, in identifying stumbling blocks and pain points, and for fostering creativity and risk-taking as students try out ideas in the tool with advice and support from colleagues. Combined with class time devoted to exhibit design, students will have space to build the site collaboratively with intentionality and thoughtfulness. So often with complex collaborative projects, students silo themselves and feel isolated and frustrated. They tend to complete the assignment in the eleventh hour and have plenty of regrets and missed opportunities. Hence, the course schedule should reflect the time and considerations that must take place to be successful in the assignment. Doing so, and adjusting the schedule each year in response to student performance and feedback to allow for as much project development time as possible, has resulted in students in each iteration of this capstone group project consistently reflecting on how effectively they worked with their groups in collaborative exhibit design. They remarked on how surprised they were that they felt they shared a sense of responsibility with their group members and with the whole class. The source of this shared responsibility seems to be in how the public-facing nature of the digital project inspired them to feel accountable not only to their unknown potential audiences and to each other to produce polished work, but also to the subjects of their exhibits. These subjects were chosen to promote social justice awareness because they deserved to be given a voice. In the most recent iteration of the course, students also felt a duty to the course exhibit website itself as a sort of institution: they were extending and carrying on the work of students who had come before them.

POST-CUSTODIAL THEORY OF ARCHIVES

One other way we attempt to confront issues of power and privilege in archives and academic institutions more generally is by situating our class's work in relation to the post-custodial theory of archives. For this we draw on the incredible resources of the LLILAS Benson Latin American Collection on the UT campus, which has established itself as a leader in the discipline of post-custodial archiving. The Society of American Archivists defines the post-custodial theory of archives as "the idea that archivists will no longer physically acquire and maintain records, but that they will provide management oversight for records that will remain in the custody of the record creators."[21] The Human Rights Document Initiative, the Guatemalan National Police Historical Archive and international collaborations that make up the Latin American Digital Initiative are important examples of this work that showcase the ethical considerations librarians and archivists at UT Libraries are making in the field today.

Because we have expertise in this area in staff in the libraries, we invite the professionals who are doing this work to the classroom for a conversation, timing the visit after students have engaged with relevant readings.[22] Theresa Polk, our Head of Digital Initiatives at LLILAS Benson, speaks about the considerations she and her team make around archiving human rights documents. Relinquishing custody of these documents would interrupt important work for the holders of these materials. There are also privacy considerations for the individuals represented in these materials so that archivists' decisions, in the case of preserving and making accessible human rights documents, have life or death consequences. Traditional archival acquisition practices remove materials from communities and place them out of context and out of reach. These communities are then portrayed without their input or consent.[23] David Bliss, our Digital Processing Archivist, discusses LLILAS Benson's work to preserve web pages from human rights organizations, highlighting the challenges of archiving online materials and the importance of doing so for the communities who rely on these pages for their work. His discussion dovetails well with considerations students are making as they create web content and pathways for accessing it. These discussions build off course readings by Michelle Caswell and others who write about community-based archives and the underrepresented groups that own them.[24]

End-of-semester reflections from students reveal the tensions students confronted in their exhibits:

> I learned *so much about the importance of giving the archives and their authors a rightful and fair voice when presenting their materials in an archive of our creation. After all of the readings and presentations from the archivists helping with our class, I felt way more confident and prepared to create an exhibit and a collection that gave a true voice to [the individual I represented in my project].*

> *Theresa Polk's presentation and the articles on post-custodial archiving highlighted for me just how powerful archivists actually are. In Caswell's article on handling human rights, she uses the word "survivor" and eschews the definitive victim-perpetrator language because of the complexity of human rights abuse situations. It reminded me of the power of language and how we can so quickly create a narrative generalizing entire populations with just a few words. Asking a community that has been traumatized to trust us, an outside institution with the power to define them in history for the rest of the world and future generations, seems presumptuous.*

> *Having worked in archives a couple of times before this class, I have learned to appreciate listening to archivists talk about items because of how passionate they are about research and how much they know about some of these items. One of my favorite days was with Theresa Polk, who opened up the world of post-custodial archiving. She took the idea of "social justice in the archives," which we have been reading about all semester, and put [it] into context. Her talk changed the way*

I thought about creating my exhibit and made me more mindful about the way we discussed our items and themes.

Wrestling with the implications of representing these artifacts is the learning outcome of the course. That students ended the semester not with answers, but with more questions and curiosity, is exactly where we wanted them to land.

ASSESSMENT

While it is clear in our solicitation of feedback from students that the class has an impact on the way that they think about social justice and the way they relate to information, it is a unique challenge to assess their work within the framework of a college class. With a large semester-long collaborative project such as this, it is difficult to assess all aspects of the project. Focusing on key areas where the majority of instruction and emphasis lies can help. Assessing the quality of writing and research in the site is essential, but since this is a public-facing site, the responsibilities of the student creator go beyond traditional assignment goals. Deciding which criteria to focus on in a rubric that is shared with students helps them gather toward common goals for the site and for the class. The following are some of the criteria we use to assess student work with some of the prompting language we use to communicate clearly with students about what is expected of them in their capstone exhibit website:

Audience

From the beginning of the semester, we emphasize choosing and writing for a specified audience. Choosing an audience can be a collaborative aspect of the project, but students must be on the same page as to what it means to write and organize a site with its intended readers in mind.

Potential questions to ask:

- Is the audience made up of peers, students who are studying the same topics who have access to and familiarity with the same collections and scholarship?
- Is it the students' intention to make the audience those from the communities they are representing in their choices and analyses of objects?
- Could the site be geared more toward a general, non-expert audience for which it is assumed there is not much knowledge on the subjects represented?
- Additionally, what is the intention of the site? Is it to persuade, inform, advocate for, or to build upon existing knowledge in a particular topic area? Are there students who wish to reframe existing scholarship on the objects they have chosen?

Settling on these aspects as a group will help to keep students' messaging consistent throughout the site, a more challenging task than students and instructors will expect. Emphasizing and messaging around these decisions, however, is the difference between a site made up of disparate voices and intentions, each exhibit a site unto itself, and one that flows more cohesively around clear goals with clear pathways between objects and exhibits.

Metadata and Tags

Devising the criteria for assessing metadata and tags should be done in partnership with an information professional. In the case of Omeka, Dublin Core is the required schema for the site and the guidelines for that schema are helpful in creating assessments. Omeka uses tags as well, and those tags serve the unique function of creating connections and cohesiveness within a site. In addition, it is typically desirable to assess how students wrestled with the responsibilities of description.

Potential framing of a rubric for tags and metadata:

- In most cases, do the tags assigned unite objects within the site, or are they overly specific to the objects or exhibits of the author?
- Does the author consult existing tags or collaborate on the creation of tags with classmates in order to avoid unnecessary redundancy in the site (e.g., Quaker / Quakers / Quakerism)?
- Has the author chosen tags and metadata with community representation in mind, choosing—through thoughtful deliberation and research—terms agreed upon within a community as empowering and representative?
- Has the author chosen tags and metadata which perpetuate white supremacism or oppression or are otherwise derogatory toward the represented community? If so, how does the author justify these decisions with thoughtful deliberation, contextualization and/or evidence?

Formative Assessment

As stated previously, incorporating a digital tool into a collaborative semester-long project is extremely disruptive. The common friction experienced among collaborators can amplify writing and research challenges when learning a new tool is brought into the assignment. We suggest scaffolding deliverables over the course of the semester with opportunities for feedback in order to provide obstacles to procrastination and give students essential chances for reflection and recalibration. Giving students opportunities to address pain points and stumbling blocks in their process with limited consequences staves off the frustrations that could snowball and become overwhelming. For example, grading a single item's metadata before proceeding to the whole project will give the student confidence as they build upon previous knowledge to become familiar with this new skill. It can also energize them to tackle gaps and deepen their description practice as they continually hone their language. Another important moment for reflection comes during an exhibit debugging or design review session. This is when students showcase works in progress to the class and get feedback as well as advice on solving glitches in the tool and design conundrums. Open sessions such as these reinforce the collaborative and iterative nature of digital projects and discourage self-isolation.

End-of-semester surveys

Finding out what students think at the end of the semester is not only a tool for instructors who may want to use feedback for future iterations of the course, but also as a structured moment of reflection for students. Reflection is a key component of experiential learning pedagogy because many lessons taught throughout the semester may not be put into practice rigorously until the final project is finished—and they may only become clear in hindsight. A final feedback survey with directed questions can gauge how students wrestled with lessons and challenges in the course. Some of the supplemental questions we asked students to use for a final reflective writing response assignment from which the responses included in earlier sections of this chapter were drawn—are set out following this paragraph. We prefaced these questions with a prompt in which we made sure to frame the activity as an opportunity to give us feedback on how the course is designed, and how students perceived their own confidence in the essential skills they were learning throughout the semester. In order to show that we take the class culture of collaboration and cooperation seriously, we also make sure to take time at the last class meeting to let the students share reflections with each other and with the course instructors if they wish. This all helps the students feel that their experiences were important and that any difficulties they encountered were "worth it"—that they were able to contribute to institutional knowledge that can help future students in the class.

Sample prompt and questions:

Please respond to at least three of the questions below in about 250–400 words. All the facilitators of the course will be very interested in reading your constructive feedback about the assignments and training sessions we built into the course so that we can make adjustments and revisions for the next time we run it.

1. In forming your final projects, what was helpful about the support we were able to offer you on using Omeka? What was missing?
2. In forming your final projects, what was helpful about the support we were able to offer you for developing metadata for your items in your exhibits? What was missing? In what ways did the metadata creation component of the project affect your choices and decisions as you assembled the project?
3. What did you learn while working in the archives and consulting with archives staff that informed your practice of creating an archive and exhibit as you developed your digital projects?
4. What did you find most rewarding about the process of choosing a collection to research and beginning to form your digital exhibit around items you discovered? What were some stumbling blocks or "pain points" you encountered in the process?

FUTURE DIRECTIONS

Our enthusiasm for teaching this course and our ongoing collaboration is as strong as ever—and we are ever grateful for the expert information from professionals who share their time with us. Placing their experience and involvement at the center of the course helps us model for our students how their own work can be supported by and help build a community. We also find it especially rewarding to keep working to tweak the pedagogy of the class in response to our students' feedback. One common suggestion we have received over the course of several years, for example, is to allow students greater freedom to go "off book" and select their own materials to work on throughout the semester rather than to guide them with initial parameters and preselected archival starting points. In the fourth iteration of the course in Spring 2020, we implemented changes in the course structure in order to enable this: we provided longer training sessions in the first month of the course to teach students how to use online finding aids and we gave students more time in classroom sessions to work with their chosen materials while we could be present to provide assistance and feedback. As guidance, we used the work of the students' predecessors in the class: one of their preparatory assignments before we even taught a lesson on finding aids was to analyze existing content on the course Omeka website. Students were assigned to look for interesting gaps in the extant social justice collections featured on the site along with particular strengths in materials that they were interested in extending through new investigations. By doing this early in the semester, they began to think of all their work in the class as being part of an authentic scholarly discourse about what communities and what voices get included in the telling of history.

One other 'future direction' we hope to venture toward in the near future is to expand some of the basic pedagogy we have put into practice in "Giving Voice to Hidden Histories" into the realm of community archiving. In a new class, we hope to reach out to organizations and institutions in the community around UT-Austin to see if they have informal records that they would like to have preserved and promoted in an online Omeka exhibit. We are exploring partnerships with communities in Austin who are experiencing upheaval and erasure as consequences of rapid and unchecked gentrification in our city, specifically in East Austin. This neighborhood underwent similar transformations as San Francisco's Mission District did in the Dot-Com years. As discussed in Nancy Raquel Mirabel's article about the role oral histories and archives play in tracing gentrification in the Mission District, we are interested in exploring how the displacement of our East Side's Latina/o populations redefined "communities and neighborhoods on the basis of whiteness." And how policies led to "creating spaces where white bodies and desires and, most importantly, consumption, dominate and shape the neighborhood."[25]

As in previous iterations of the course, we are addressing the power and privilege students bring to the relationship as they represent these communities in online exhibits, but we are able to do so in collaboration with the community, something not possible in previous iterations of the course where the artifacts had already been collected and organized and often described by collection stewards. In this way, we are inspired by Marika Cifor et al., who in their research on community archives reveal the opportunities for these collections in "putting histories to work in service of communities and urgent social and political concerns" and to use community archives "as a means to challenge injustice, discrimination, and oppression."[26]

Throughout this experiential learning, students apply what happens in the classroom directly to the client relationship. As we seek to branch out into the community, however, we will need to be sure to prepare our students to responsibly engage with partners who may have different expectations for research products than university institutions who deal with students and scholars all the time. We also will need to incorporate new lessons on rudimentary archival processing and digitization into the course, while also making sure that these often labor-intensive activities will be productive experiential learning experiences for our students and not exploitative busy-work. Fortunately, we are lucky to have a community of archivists and librarians on our campus that has welcomed us and our students to participate in their own efforts to recenter received authorities in the telling of history. We hope to continue our collaborations with them as we experiment with new pedagogy and continue to introduce undergraduates to how information professionals view the world.

NOTES

1 Randall C. Jimerson, "Archives for All: Professional Responsibility and Social Justice," *The American Archivist* 70, no. 2 (2007): 252–281.

2 Jimerson, "Archives for All," 268.

3 Omeka is an open-source platform for publishing digital collections and curated exhibits to the Web: https://www.omeka.net/.

4 Michelle Caswell, "'The Archive' Is Not an Archives: On Acknowledging the Intellectual Contributions of Archival Studies," *UCLA* (June 27, 2021): 2, https://escholarship.org/uc/item/7bn4v1fk.

5 Jacques Derrida, *Archive Fever: A Freudian Impression*, trans. Eric Prenowitz (Chicago: University of Chicago Press, 1996), 18.

6 Kathryn Michaelis and Nicole Milano, eds., "Social Justice Sampler" (Society of American Archivists, 2017), is one collection of case studies we use as course readings. See also the SAA's Diversity and Inclusion Toolkits: https://www2.archivists.org/advocacy/diversity-and-inclusion-toolkits.

7 https://hiddenhistoriesut.org.

8 Hillary Hart et al., "Experiential Learning Working Group Final Report" (University of Texas at Austin, 2018), 4–5, provides an operating definition of "Experiential Learning" for our campus. Based on input from many faculty and staff, we developed the following structural definition of Experiential Learning:

> "Experiential learning opportunities offer students assignments and activities based on real-life situations or primary research that engages them in reflective problem-solving with multiple potential avenues of inquiry. High-quality experiential learning at UT has these hallmarks: 1) The instructor prepares students for the experience, using relevant scholarship, concepts, and frameworks, 2) Students have some agency in defining and pursuing their own questions or activities or approaches, 3) Students reflect on the experience and on why they did what they did."

We have also found UT's Faculty Innovation Center's materials helpful: https://ctl.utexas.edu/instructional-strategies/experiential-learning.

9 In Texas we have Texas Archival Resources Online (TARO) for this purpose: https://txarchives.org/home. The National Archives is structured similarly, aggregating archival finding aids and catalogs from throughout the United Kingdom, to allow inter-institutional searches: https://www.nationalarchives.gov.uk/.

10 Sarah Brownson et al., "Introduction · Snapshots: Community Networks and Media Ephemerality," Community Narratives: Uncovering

Hidden Perspectives, https://hiddenhistoriesut.org/exhibits/show/community-networks-and-media-e/introduction.

11 Johann Rossbach's audio transcription of: Hottinguer & Co., "Reparation Letter to the Corneau Family," *Community Narratives: Uncovering Hidden Perspectives*, https://hiddenhistoriesut.org/items/show/201.

12 Caswell, "'The Archive' is Not an Archives," 8.

13 Safiya Umoja Noble, *Algorithms of Oppression: How Search Engines Reinforce Racism* (New York: NYU Press, 2018).

14 Jane Sandberg, ed., *Ethical Questions in Name Authority Control* (Sacramento: Library Juice Press, 2019); Anne J. Gilliland, "Contemplating Co-Creator Rights in Archival Description," *Knowledge Organization* 39, no. 5 (2012): 340–46, https://doi.org/10.5771/0943-7444-2012-5-340; Emily Drabinski, "Teaching the Radical Catalog," in *Radical Cataloging: Essays at the Front*, ed. K. R. Roberto (Jefferson: McFarland & Company, 2008).

15 Johann Rossbach's metadata for Hottinguer & Co., "Reparation Letter to the Corneau Family," *Community Narratives: Uncovering Hidden Perspectives*, https://hiddenhistoriesut.org/items/show/201.

16 For context, this is from a student who worked with university records and clippings from the school's newspaper.

17 Resources recommended include: Copyright Advisory Services, "Fair Use Checklist," https://copyright.columbia.edu/basics/fair-use/fair-use-checklist.html; Colleen Lyon, "Copyright Crash Course," University of Texas Libraries, https://guides.lib.utexas.edu/copyright; Center for Media and Social Impact, "Fair Use, Free Speech & Intellectual Property," Center for Media and Social Impact. https://cmsimpact.org/program/fair-use/

18 Creative Commons, "Share Your Work," https://creativecommons.org/share-your-work/.

19 Student Privacy Compass, "Educators," Student Privacy Compass, https://studentprivacycompass.org/audiences/educators/.

20 The Internet Archive's Wayback Machine: https://archive.org/web/.

21 Richard Pearce-Moses, "Postarchival Theory of Archives," A Glossary of Archival and Records Terminology, Society of American Archivists, 2005, www2.archivists.org/glossary.

22 For example: Michelle Caswell, "Toward a Survivor-Centered Approach to Records Documenting Human Rights Abuse: Lessons from Community Archives," *Archival Science* 14, no. 3 (October 1, 2014): 307–22, https://doi.org/10.1007/s10502-014-9220-6; Lae'l Hughes-Watkins, "Moving Toward a Reparative Archive: A Roadmap for a Holistic Approach to Disrupting Homogenous Histories in Academic Repositories and Creating Inclusive

Spaces for Marginalized Voices," *Journal of Contemporary Archival Studies* 5, no. 1 (May 16, 2018), https://elischolar.library.yale.edu/jcas/vol5/iss1/6; Kirsten Weld, *Paper Cadavers: The Archives of Dictatorship in Guatemala* (Durham: Duke University Press, 2014), https://www.dukeupress.edu/paper-cadavers.

23 Theresa E. Polk, "Archiving Human Rights Documentation: The Promise of the Post-Custodial Approach in Latin America," *Portal: Web Magazine of LLILAS Benson Latin American Studies and Collections*, August 5, 2016, 37-39, https://repositories.lib.utexas.edu/bitstream/handle/2152/62751/12Portal_issue11_2016_Polk.pdf?sequence=3.

24 Michelle Caswell, Christopher Harter, and Bergis Jules, "Diversifying the Digital Historical Record: Integrating Community Archives in National Strategies for Access to Digital Cultural Heritage," *D-Lib Magazine* 23, no. 5/6 (June 2017), https://doi.org/10.1045/may2017-caswell.

25 Nancy Raquel Mirabal, "Geographies of Displacement: Latina/Os, Oral History, and The Politics of Gentrification in San Francisco's Mission District," *The Public Historian* 31, no. 2 (2009): 17, https://doi.org/10.1525/tph.2009.31.2.7.

26 Marika Cifor et al., "'What We Do Crosses over to Activism': The Politics and Practice of Community Archives," *The Public Historian* 40 (2018): 92, https://doi.org/10.1525/TPH.2018.40.2.69.

BIBLIOGRAPHY

Brownson, Sarah, Jenohn Euland, Zoe Roden, Vega Shah, Lucian Smith, and Courtney Thomas. "Introduction· Snapshots: Community Networks and Media Ephemerality." Community Narratives: Uncovering Hidden Perspectives, n.d. https://hiddenhistoriesut.org/exhibits/show/community-networks-and-media-e/introduction.

Caswell, Michelle. "'The Archive' Is Not an Archives: On Acknowledging the Intellectual Contributions of Archival Studies." *UCLA*, n.d., 2.

Caswell, Michelle. "Toward a Survivor-Centered Approach to Records Documenting Human Rights Abuse: Lessons from Community Archives." *Archival Science* 14, no. 3 (October 1, 2014): 307–22. https://doi.org/10.1007/s10502-014-9220-6.

Caswell, Michelle, Christopher Harter, and Bergis Jules. "Diversifying the Digital Historical Record: Integrating Community Archives in National Strategies for Access to Digital Cultural Heritage." *D-Lib Magazine* 23, no. 5/6 (June 2017). https://doi.org/10.1045/may2017-caswell.

Cifor, Marika, Michelle Caswell, Alda Allina Migoni, and Noah Geraci. "'What We Do Crosses over to Activism': The Politics and Practice of Community Archives" *The Public Historian* 40 (2018): 69–95. https://doi.org/10.1525/TPH.2018.40.2.69.

Creative Commons. "Share Your Work." https://creativecommons.org/share-your-work/.

Derrida, Jacques. *Archive Fever: A Freudian Impression.* Translated by Eric Prenowitz. Chicago: University of Chicago Press, 1996.

Drabinski, Emily. "Teaching the Radical Catalog." In *Radical Cataloging: Essays at the Front*, edited by K. R. Roberto, 8. Jefferson: McFarland & Company, 2008.

Gilliland, Anne J. "Contemplating Co-Creator Rights in Archival Description." *Knowledge Organization* 39, no. 5 (2012): 340–46. https://doi.org/10.5771/0943-7444-2012-5-340.

Hughes-Watkins, Lae'l. "Moving Toward a Reparative Archive: A Roadmap for a Holistic Approach to Disrupting Homogenous Histories in Academic Repositories and Creating Inclusive Spaces for Marginalized Voices." *Journal of Contemporary Archival Studies* 5, no. 1 (May 16, 2018). https://elischolar.library.yale.edu/jcas/vol5/iss1/6.

Michaelis, Kathryn, and Nicole Milano, eds. "Social Justice Sampler." Society of American Archivists, 2017. http://files.archivists.org/pubs/SamplerSeries/SocialJusticeSampler.pdf.

Mirabal, Nancy Raquel. "Geographies of Displacement: Latina/os, Oral History, and The Politics of Gentrification in San Francisco's Mission District." *The Public Historian* 31, no. 2 (2009): 7–31. https://doi.org/10.1525/tph.2009.31.2.7.

Pearce-Moses, Richard. "Postarchival Theory of Archives." A Glossary of Archival and Records Terminology, Society of American Archivists, 2005. www2.archivists.org/glossary.

Polk, Theresa E. "Archiving Human Rights Documentation: The Promise of the Post-Custodial Approach in Latin America." *Portal: Web Magazine of LLILAS Benson Latin American Studies and Collections*, August 5, 2016. https://repositories.lib.utexas.edu/bitstream/handle/2152/62751/12Portal_issue11_2016_Polk.pdf?sequence=3.

Sandberg, Jane, ed. *Ethical Questions in Name Authority Control.* Sacramento: Library Juice Press, 2019.

Student Privacy Compass. "Educators." Student Privacy Compass. https://studentprivacycompass.org/audiences/educators/.

Weld, Kirsten. *Paper Cadavers: The Archives of Dictatorship in Guatemala.* Durham: Duke University Press, 2014.

PART III

BEYOND THE CAMPUS

CHAPTER EIGHT

NO FONDS, NO MASTERS! FROM EMBRACING TO DISMANTLING THE POWER OF ARCHIVES

aems emswiler

INTRODUCTION

In the fall of 2012, I began organizing with the Inside Books Project (IBP), a books-to-prisons collective based in Austin, Texas. First attending weekly sessions responding to incarcerated patrons' letters, I later joined the collective and took on roles of volunteer coordination, fundraising, event-planning, library development, and, finally, project archivist. In the summer of 2020, I transitioned into an advisory role for the IBP Archive as I began doctoral studies at the University of Arizona School of Information. Through my doctoral research, I hope to facilitate wider engagement with anti-authoritarian praxes in archives, as I believe that any pedagogies or practices espousing a liberatory politics must necessarily be grounded in these principles; that is, those that reject authorial power relations characterized by hierarchical domination, social control, dehumanization, and the monopolization of life-sustaining resources. Given these aims, this chapter has served as a fruitful source of reflection on the ways academia has at varying times encouraged, inhibited, facilitated, and disrupted my capacity to engage in these anti-authoritarian practices.

I have increasingly struggled with contradictions regarding how and to what extent I can actually subvert hegemonic power in academia when it seems fundamentally opposed to dismantling the systems undergirding its authority. I specifically feel at odds with the notion we must "embrace the power of archives and use it for the good of humankind."[1] Jimerson likens this power to that of the temple, prison, and restaurant; respectfully symbolizing "control over social (collective) memory; control over preservation and security of records [and] the archivist's role as interpreter and mediator between records and users."[2] These appendages of power extend to the core functions and logics of archival practice; for example, the fundamental frameworks of provenance and *respect du fonds* asserts a hierarchical and authorial organizing principle ("fonds" being the uppermost facet of this hierarchy) founded on the "sanctity of original order, the maintenance of which focused on preserving the logical structure and internal arrangement of the records of each creator."[3]

In the wake of postmodernist critiques of these principles, many conversations on archival authority and power asserted that purportedly non-oppressive archival authorities (i.e., diverse, non-neutral, progressive, and liberal) should appropriate and re-work the pre-existing power dynamics (i.e., carceral, controlling, disciplinary, elitist, politically hegemonic) so that we may "*make* society more knowledgeable, more tolerant, more diverse, and more just"[4] (emphasis mine). These ideas echo Paulo Freire's critique of "humanitarian generosity" as a means of achieving a "liberating pedagogy."[5] Freire warns against paternalism on the part of progressive authorities who believe "they must be the executors of transformation," saying these dynamics deprive minoritized groups of agency and humanity, and do nothing to achieve radical change.[6] Freire posits that "those who authentically commit themselves to the people must re-examine themselves constantly."[7] In other words, a pedagogy of the oppressed must be a "praxis: reflection and action upon the world in order to transform it."[8]

Freire's text has a particular relevance for "participatory" and "community-engaged" archival pedagogies given the negotiations of power, resources, and authority inherent to them. For example, many arguments about embracing archival power rely on the notion of a "counter-archival" impulse that is inherently radical, and "community-based" practices as an alternative to institutional and statist hegemony. This reduction is enabled by the reliance on binaristic thinking critiqued by Jarrett Drake, who says:

> Dichotomies of local/global and community/state...enable us to think of power and dominion vertically...This view carries damning effects. It further masks and thus entrenches power, rather than revealing and redistributing it...[This] does require that we as a group of 'community archive' practitioners and scholars begin to name the stakes of our work more candidly and clearly by transitioning to a language of precise political claims and a liberatory lens to accompany it.[9]

Freire and Drake's analyses inform my view that "community-based" has increasingly become a catch-all signifier of liberation that over-resourced groups may deploy while obscuring and sustaining status quo power. This is particularly true for those that embrace legitimation bestowed by neoliberal, capitalist, and statist entities seeking to envelop more diverse, minority markets.[10] The outcome of these trends to assimilate radical individuals, groups, and cultures into the profession is not, I argue, a more liberatory profession, but the de-radicalization of these cultures. As purportedly radical and "community-based" archives face the impetus of professionalism, the subversive praxes contained therein are neutralized via appropriation, de-contextualization, and gatekeeping.[11] In this way radical culture is leveraged to evince a liberatory politics, consequently dispossessing the communities these cultural resources are extracted from and de-mobilizing social movements.[12]

Educators play an integral role in either intervening or sustaining these dynamics, as they mediate relations of power and resources between over-resourced (e.g., academia) and under-resourced groups (e.g., grassroots collectives). These resources include labor from student volunteers, time that is afforded to academics more so than working class activists outside of academia, skill sets developed from accumulated scholarship, and technology like server space, web-publishing platforms, scanners, and audio-visual tools. In their work, *Information Activism: A Queer History of Lesbian Media Technologies,* Cait McKinney describes how educators have facilitated mutually beneficial, participatory pedagogies with the Lesbian Herstory Archives, encouraging students to engage with radical queer thought, challenge fraught notions of professionalism, and re-examine the ideological underpinnings of core archival principles.[13] McKinney's work illustrates how undergraduate pedagogy can facilitate a praxis that challenges dominant ideologies and instead facilitates solidaric collaboration with under-resourced groups. I posit that this praxis is not enabled by "embracing the power of archives," but disassembling it.

What is the role of educators mediating the uneven relationships perpetuated by over-resourced institutions? How do these hegemonic institutions function on an administrative and systemic level, in comparison to the labor of radical accomplices embedded within them (e.g., educators, archivists, and others building toward transformative change)?[14] Can these accomplices teach to examine, disrupt, and rebuild the world as we have known it through the use of their power?

I argue that teaching to appropriate power does not enable students to challenge entrenched domination within the information studies field and beyond it; instead, "participatory" and "community-engaged" pedagogies must be rooted in principles of anti-authoritarianism that reject all appendages of authorial control, hierarchy, and paternalism.[15] Other anti-authoritarian principles include:

> A shared repertoire of political action based on direct action, building grassroots alternatives, community outreach and confrontation; Shared forms of organising—decentralised, horizontal and consensus-seeking; Broader cultural expression in areas as diverse as art, music, dress and diet, often associated with prominent western subcultures; Shared political language that emphasises resistance to capitalism, the state, patriarchy and more generally to hierarchy and domination.[16]

A radical archival praxis is one that embraces these tenets as an alternative to hegemonic power, and instead centers the redistribution of resources enabling sustainability, autonomy, and survival for minoritized groups.[17] How can we apply this praxis to identify and disassemble power disparities and hegemonic ideology across the social and cultural institutions we navigate? I will explore how my undergraduate experiences challenged these dynamics and cultivated a radical praxis that helped me trace competing ideologies across academic, activist, and carceral spaces.

BACKGROUND ON THE IBP

The Inside Books Project (IBP) is a books-to-prisons collective based out of Austin, Texas, where students, educators, activists, family and friends of incarcerated people, and other volunteers come together at weekly sessions to respond to incarcerated patrons' requests. Their letters, of which IBP receives over 2,000 a month, primarily ask for educational resources spanning all levels and subject areas, dictionaries (the top request), Black studies and African American history, LGBTQIA literature, legal aid, trade and how-to manuals (e.g., welding; heating, ventilation, and air conditioning (HVAC); automotive repair), health information, and Spanish-language resources.[18] The comprehensive "resource guide" developed by IBP over the years, with updates and suggestions provided by patrons, is also a top request and available free online.[19] This guide is a compiled list of addresses and information on other projects that provide services to people in prison, such as pen-pal groups, spiritual and religious organizations, and legal support.

IBP was founded in 1998 by a small group of activists who, without a unified label, shared anti-authoritarian and anarchist values, including those of mutual aid, collective decision-making, and solidarity with incarcerated communities rather than charity-based models of volunteerism.[20] They also were more aligned with prison abolitionist thought as opposed to reformist policy interventions that ultimately enable prisons to continue functioning by making them more palatable, affordable, or otherwise socially acceptable. In sum, the fundamental values informing IBP's founding were opposed to hierarchical authority leveraged to civilize or educate incarcerated people, instead centering reciprocal exchanges of dialogue, resources, and relationship building.

This is not to claim that hierarchical or oppressive power dynamics have not existed within the collective, particularly in regard to gender, race, and disability. Rather, the project could be described as prefigurative, meaning an experiment in the types of principles one hopes to see in the world; for many involved with IBP, particularly the founding group, those principles were of non-hierarchicalism, prison abolition, mutual aid, and solidarity.[21] While many volunteers still identify as anti-authoritarian, anarchist, and anti-fascist, significant growth of the project and the process of seeking 501(c)3 or non-profit status have de-centered some of these identifications. In other words, as more volunteers become involved with IBP, the work is more easily understood as charity, philanthropy, or prison reform. However, anti-authoritarian principles continue to undergird many aspects of the project; IBP remains collectively run and constituent funded, rather than relying on foundation grants or individual philanthropists, and is focused on mobilizing and redistributing resources autonomously rather than in collaboration with status institutions. As is the case from its founding, volunteers are guided to address the stated needs of patrons (i.e., reading the letters, choosing books, and writing a response), rather than imposing any ideological, spiritual, or political agendas. Oftentimes, volunteers do come in with these goals: religious, radical, and conservative alike. However, collective members take action to challenge these impulses through training and "quality control" of packages, to assure patron requests have been met as accurately as possible.

In this way, IBP prefigures anti-authoritarian social relations rather than leveraging power to enact agendas like top-down education, civilizing and reforming "criminals," and religious indoctrination. Instead, IBP's goals are to mobilize and redistribute resources while facilitating solidaric encounters between volunteers and patrons. This is especially significant considering many of IBP's patrons do not receive mail or have contact with friends or family, so the correspondence with volunteers is often as meaningful as the books themselves, and for some, even more so. In sum, access to reading and information resources is not only a way to pass time; it is a means of building community and understanding, and developing identity (both individual and collective, personal and political). It is also a crucial means of improving life-chances, imagining and moving toward a future of survival outside of prison; this is no small endeavor, particularly for those who have been incarcerated for more years than they have lived on the outside. Access to these resources decreases a person's chances of recidivism, meaning people with more access to books and information resources are less likely to be re-incarcerated.[22]

One way that patrons convey the impact of IBP's work is by sending contributions such as art, poetry, prose, essays, grievances, photographs, and crafts. These materials serve as a means of expression, personal connection with individuals, and identifications with social movements and grassroots activism. After volunteers respond to the request, the patron's work is saved to include in art shows, events, social media, and for volunteers to take home. The process of reading and responding to incarcerated people's letters and engaging with these creative works is often a pedagogical and even radicalizing process for many volunteers, who often share with collective members how their assumptions are challenged through the work. For example, such assumptions have included ideas about what incarcerated people want to read and why, patrons' range of creative expression, and how criminal punishment systems actually operate on a systemic and interpersonal level. This intervention in status quo ideologies is critical for many students coming in for classes or service hours who may consider their contributions as a one-way act of charity, disconnected from the entrenched structural violence prisons sustain. Furthermore, the individual and often intimate correspondences between those requesting books and those answering them often evolve into more sustained connection with patrons through pen-pal correspondences, visitation, and even post-release friendships.

Witnessing these generative disruptions of volunteers' expectations informed my understanding of incarcerated patrons' art and writing as a "counter-archive" to that of the state. By "counter-archive," I do not mean that the narratives of incarcerated people are a homogenous voice speaking up against statist power, as this would be an essentializing and simplistic assertion.[23] Rather, I began to see their contributions as a counter-archive *because* they provided such an expansive, multi-faceted representation of experience, in contrast to the monolithic portrayals dominant in mass media, social institutions, public policy, and popular culture. This understanding led me to found the IBP Archive (IBPA) in 2015, beginning with a massive backlog of incarcerated people's creative works accumulated haphazardly in recycled boxes, storage sheds, and collective members' closets.

My own apartment was soon filled with these boxes, until the Texas After Violence Project (TAVP) offered to share space and resources with the IBPA. This collaboration enabled me to digitize thousands of documents for preservation and, given consent, web publishing on Omeka. As an Archival Fellow with TAVP, I contributed to other projects documenting carceral state violence in Texas, primarily oral histories, while continuing to develop the IBPA with students and community members who wanted to participate in the work. Most of these volunteers came to the work with no archival knowledge; indeed, up until 2017, when I enrolled in the University of Texas at Austin School of Information, I was relying on the knowledge gained from the one undergraduate course I will describe below, mentorship from TAVP's archivist, Jane Field, and guidance from incarcerated creators. As I progressed in my archival studies, I was able to siphon resources, skills, and knowledge pertinent to aspects of the project; however, I continued to center the guidance and specific needs of incarcerated creators, and anti-authoritarian, abolitionist, and critical trans politics. These epistemologies, and the ways my introduction to archives was intimately bound up in them, were often more useful than the standards of the field for addressing issues that arose regarding archival access, preservation, and description.

What about these pedagogies supported a radical analysis of archival power and authority? How did the narrative materials forming the basis of the IBPA further cultivate my understandings of carceral power and ideological hegemony across prisons, archives, and social movements?

UNDERGRADUATE PEDAGOGY AND THE IBPA

I was introduced to IBP's work in 2012 through my undergraduate program at Southwestern University in Georgetown, Texas. Feminist and disability studies scholar, Alison Kafer, scheduled volunteer sessions at IBP as a component of her Introduction to Feminist Studies course. These visits were supplemented with readings on the intersections of carcerality, gender, sexuality, disability, and racial-capitalism.[24] Kafer's pairing of these texts with work at IBP—reading incarcerated people's letters—provided a space where I was able to recognize and disrupt the same disciplinary, cis-heteronormative, and ableist ideologies that had steeped my own educational experiences. As a queer, nonbinary, and neurodivergent person subjected to "alternative" disciplinary educational institutions in Texas, I internalized the logics ingrained in me about what counts as deviant and disposable. The first years in my undergraduate program, and particularly my work with IBP, made space for me to process these logics through narrative exchanges between incarcerated patrons, prison mailrooms, and volunteers. Responding to book requests and later building long-term, mutually supportive relationships with incarcerated queer and trans people was healing and radicalizing. This work also connected me with other grassroots organizing in solidarity with incarcerated people.

I was able to further engage with this organizing in my last semester of undergraduate work, in a course taught by Charlotte Nunes, "Freedom and Imprisonment in the American Literary Tradition." In the course, Nunes utilized "oral history stewardship as a mode of digital archival praxis" to facilitate student engagement with critical theory in the humanities.[25] This course was my first experience with digital humanities work, oral history, and archives; I was particularly impacted by transcription work with the TAVP and American Prison Writing Archive.

I was also compelled by the "grassroots methods" of oral history that could "counter the elitism of the academy [and] create rich archives of community generated memory."[26] In a reflection on teaching this class, Nunes says:

> Digital archiving thus sharpened students' abilities to compare how course texts narrate shifting ideologies with regard to US criminal justice; to detail the stories these texts tell about how

> criminal justice policies and practices impact people and communities inside prisons and beyond; and to articulate the power of narrative to establish, sustain, overturn, or transform widely held assumptions about prisons and the imprisoned.[27]

This pedagogical analysis of narrative power spoke to my understanding of the censorship records as an archive of carceral ideology used to constrain, criminalize, and take hold of our imagination (see Figures 8.1–8.3). It also contributed to my understanding of incarcerated people's narratives as a "counter-archive" that has the potential to transgress hegemonic ideology. This carceral counter-archive encompasses a spectrum of experience, asserting the humanity of imprisoned people despite state subjection, and challenges understandings of guilt, innocence, and justice that volunteers (or others interacting with the archive) may hold.

This capacity to challenge, and transform, status quo belief systems demonstrates how essential it is for imprisoned people to access outlets of expression and narrative exchange. Driven by this, I hoped a digital archive could expand the potential of transformative and pedagogical encounters for students, activists, formerly incarcerated people, their friends and family, researchers, and educators. As Nunes says of her course, "for students in the class, participating in the nuts and bolts of history and memory-making revealed how vulnerable archival records description is to bias, but also how productively narratives can be analyzed to reveal…'the ideologies that surround us.'"[28]

In the following section I will explore this ideological power through two sets of archival materials. The frameworks and practical skill sets learned in Nunes's course, such as how to use web-publishing platforms best suited for digital humanities work, facilitated the beginning of the IBPA as a digital collection on Omeka. The first collection I curated was derived from my feminist studies capstone work on carceral ideologies within censorship records. The Texas Department of Criminal Justice (TDCJ)

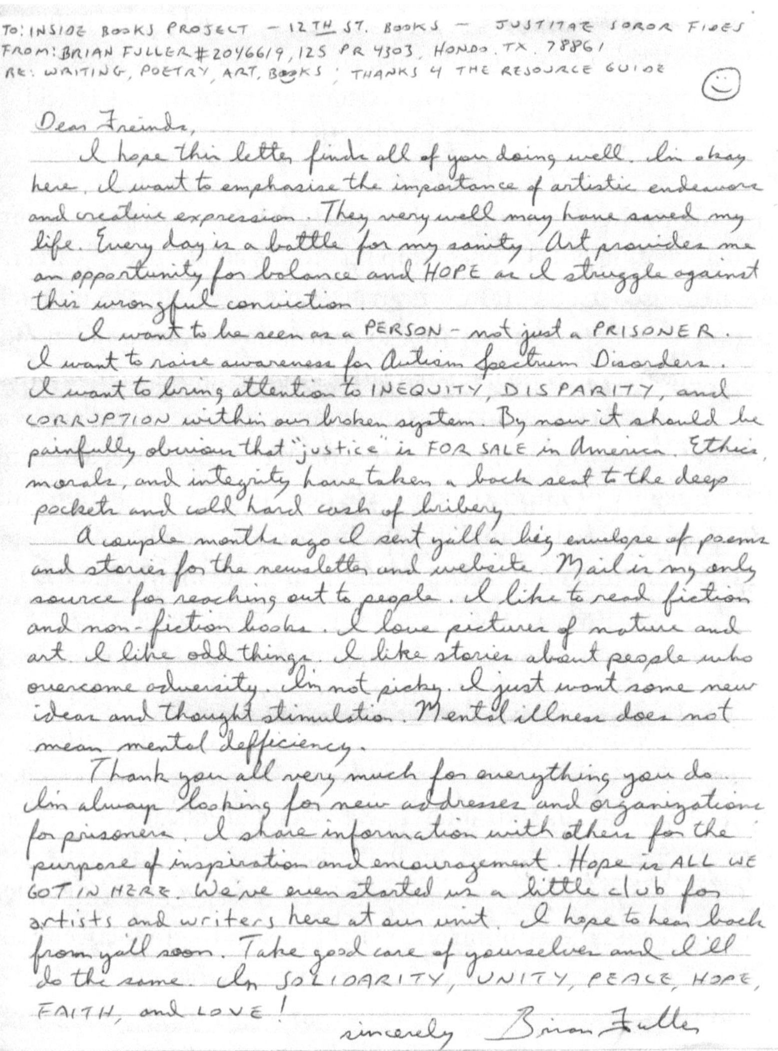

TO: INSIDE BOOKS PROJECT – 12TH ST. BOOKS – JUSTITAE SOROR FIDES
FROM: BRIAN FULLER #2046619, 125 PR 4303, HONDO, TX. 78861
RE: WRITING, POETRY, ART, BOOKS ; THANKS 4 THE RESOURCE GUIDE

Dear Freinds,

I hope this letter finds all of you doing well. Im okay here. I want to emphasise the importance of artistic endeavors and creative expression. They very well may have saved my life. Every day is a battle for my sanity. Art provides me an opportunity for balance and HOPE as I struggle against this wrongful conviction.

I want to be seen as a PERSON – not just a PRISONER. I want to raise awareness for Autism Spectrum Disorders. I want to bring attention to INEQUITY, DISPARITY, and CORRUPTION within our broken system. By now it should be painfully obvious that "justice" is FOR SALE in America. Ethics, morals, and integrity have taken a back seat to the deep pockets and cold hard cash of bribery.

A couple months ago I sent y'all a big envelope of poems and stories for the newsletter and website. Mail is my only source for reaching out to people. I like to read fiction and non-fiction books. I love pictures of nature and art. I like odd things. I like stories about people who overcome adversity. Im not picky. I just want some new ideas and thought stimulation. Mental illness does not mean mental defficiency.

Thank you all very much for everything you do. Im always looking for new addresses and organizations for prisoners. I share information with others for the purpose of inspiration and encouragement. Hope is ALL WE GOT IN HERE. We've even started us a little club for artists and writers here at our unit. I hope to hear back from y'all soon. Take good care of yourselves and I'll do the same. In SOLIDARITY, UNITY, PEACE, HOPE, FAITH, and LOVE!

sincerely Brian Fuller

Figure 8.1. Letter from Inside Books Project patron, Brian Fuller, describing the power of creative expression to generate hope and to assert the humanity of incarcerated people.

Figure 8.2. Water-color by Brian Fuller.

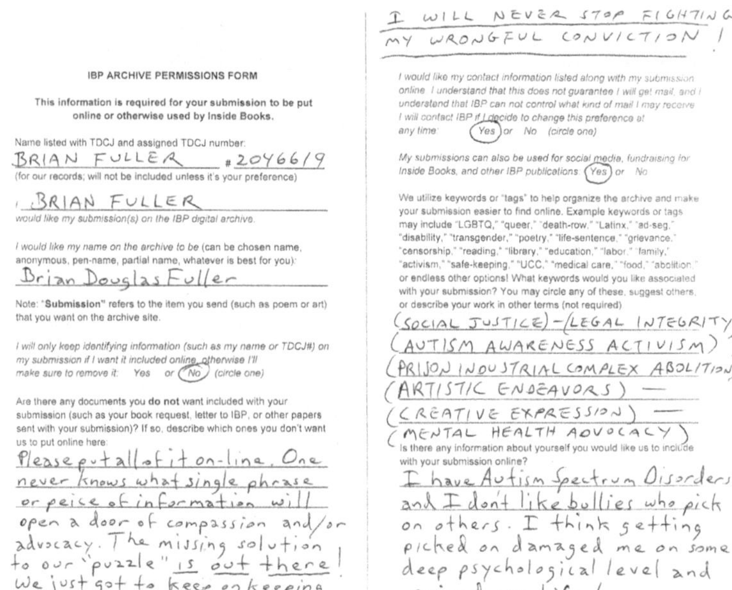

IBP ARCHIVE PERMISSIONS FORM

This information is required for your submission to be put online or otherwise used by Inside Books.

Name listed with TDCJ and assigned TDCJ number:
BRIAN FULLER #2046619
(for our records; will not be included unless it's your preference)

I BRIAN FULLER
would like my submission(s) on the IBP digital archive.

I would like my name on the archive to be (can be chosen name, anonymous, pen-name, partial name, whatever is best for you):
Brian Douglas Fuller

Note: "**Submission**" refers to the item you send (such as poem or art) that you want on the archive site.

I will only keep identifying information (such as my name or TDCJ#) on my submission if I want it included online, otherwise I'll make sure to remove it: Yes or (No) (circle one)

Are there any documents you **do not** want included with your submission (such as your book request, letter to IBP, or other papers sent with your submission)? If so, describe which ones you don't want us to put online here:
Please put all of it on-line. One never knows what single phrase or peice of information will open a door of compassion and/or advocacy. The missing solution to our "puzzle" is out there! We just got to keep on keeping on until we find it.

I WILL NEVER STOP FIGHTING MY WRONGFUL CONVICTION!

I would like my contact information listed along with my submission online. I understand that this does not guarantee I will get mail, and I understand that IBP can not control what kind of mail I may receive. I will contact IBP if I decide to change this preference at any time: (Yes) or No (circle one)

My submissions can also be used for social media, fundraising for Inside Books, and other IBP publications: (Yes) or No

We utilize keywords or "tags" to help organize the archive and make your submission easier to find online. Example keywords or tags may include "LGBTQ," "queer," "death-row," "Latinx," "ad-seg," "disability," "transgender," "poetry," "life-sentence," "grievance," "censorship," "reading," "library," "education," "labor," "family," "activism," "safe-keeping," "UCC," "medical care," "food," "abolition," or endless other options! What keywords would you like associated with your submission? You may circle any of these, suggest others, or describe your work in other terms (not required)
(SOCIAL JUSTICE) – (LEGAL INTEGRITY)
(AUTISM AWARENESS ACTIVISM)
(PRISON INDUSTRIAL COMPLEX ABOLITION)
(ARTISTIC ENDEAVORS) —
(CREATIVE EXPRESSION) —
(MENTAL HEALTH ADVOCACY)

Is there any information about yourself you would like us to include with your submission online?
I have Autism Spectrum Disorders and I don't like bullies who pick on others. I think getting picked on damaged me on some deep psychological level and ruined my life!

Figure 8.3. Early draft of an IBPA Permissions Form, filled out by incarcerated contributor, Brian Fuller. The form requests information on naming and citation, permissions to share specific documents, contact information, tags and supplemental information the artist can provide that is used for Dublin Core metadata fields in Omeka. Almost all patrons ask to share their contact information and most provide free-text description.

Censorship Documentation Collection demonstrates how the state forms discursive terrains of "criminal deviancy," Black insurrection, and sexual abnormality. I will then explore how people marked as "deviant" navigate and disrupt this terrain, focusing on the narratives of incarcerated trans women. In doing so I hope to present how engaging with incarcerated creators' narratives can be a transformative, pedagogical, and even radicalizing act by revealing and contesting ideological hegemony.

TDCJ CENSORSHIP COLLECTION: CARCERAL LOGICS AT WORK

In many ways the prison functions as an archive. Gatekeepers categorize and house individuals, deciding who has access to visitation and under what conditions. The prison ingests, labels, classifies, categorizes, segregates, surveils, deaccessions, and destroys people who have been reduced to records. It utilizes these records and their public access to produce a knowledge on the imprisoned that reifies its technologies of detainment, both within the prison and our society at large. For example, on the TDCJ website, there is a public database of every person who is or has been on death row, including their photograph, education level, race, gender, a narrative of their crime, and their final statement before their execution.[29] There is a whole series of books featuring page-by-page profiles of executed people including their physical characteristics, prior occupation(s), how old they were when executed, and what they chose for their last meal.[30] By producing these dehumanizing portraits of the imprisoned, the state construes, regulates, and reifies who falls under notions of normalcy and belonging, and who does not. These ideologies take hold of our public imagination through media, education systems, popular culture, and public policy.

While data on the imprisoned is publicly available, data on the administrative behaviors of TDCJ is hidden behind layers of arbitrary processes, legal circumvention (such as putting up barriers to information requests), and bureaucratic equivocation. Processes of censorship, for example, are nebulous. Public records of denial forms are not made available by TDCJ; they are created in the prison mailrooms and sent to approved vendors (such as IBP) when books or information is denied. The mailroom employees closely surveil all exchanges between IBP and patrons, searching for any packages that could "contain material that a reasonable person would construe as written solely for the purpose of communicating information designed to achieve the breakdown of prisons."[31] Employees are "encouraged to 'err on the side of caution' and deny books they believe might be problematic."[32] These vague guidelines allow subjective and arbitrary practices of censorship, where mailroom employees leverage their power through discipline, hierarchy, and authority.

The censorship collection includes book denial forms on trade manuals, such as HVAC repair, automotive repair, and information on plumbing or electrical wiring, which have been banned as a "security risk."[33] This is particularly harmful for incarcerated people trying to develop practical job skills for a successful post-release. Even more insidiously, works such as *Narrative of the Life of Frederick Douglass*, *Autobiography of Malcolm X*, texts on radical politics, critiques of the prison system, and discussions of white supremacy or of race in general are also often identified as security threats because, as previously cited, they could be perceived as including content advocating the abolition of prisons.

Note under "disposition" that the result of these bans is to "destroy" the books, unless the "offender" can pay to have it returned, which they almost never can.[34]

Other books or information identified as radical, counter-cultural, or anti-authoritarian are similarly banned because "it could contain information that could be used to facilitate prison disruption."

The last categories of "threat" I will mention here are texts deemed "detrimental to offenders' rehabilitation, because it would encourage deviant criminal sexual behavior."[35] This is applied to works like Alice Walker's *The Color Purple*, Toni Morrison's *The Bluest Eye*, and Anne Moody's *Coming of Age in Mississippi* (Figure 8.6). In the document under "remarks," where employees are supposed to explain the reasoning behind a ban, they often just write "racial," indicating the ways that intersections of gender, race, and sexuality are more often targeted as "deviant" and "criminal."

The TDCJ Censorship Documentation Collection of the *IBPA* exposes both carceral logics and the tangible impacts of those logics on incarcerated people. It takes hold of our public imagination, and this ideological power seeps into broader understandings of

12E-26
12 8 27

TEXAS DEPARTMENT OF CRIMINAL JUSTICE
PUBLICATION REVIEW / DENIAL NOTIFICATION

NAME ______ TDCJ# ______ UNIT Cy

TITLE OF PUBLICATION Narrative of the Life of Frederick Douglass, an American slave MSCP IOC DATE 8-24-12 DATE OFFENDER NOTIFIED 8-27-12

AUTHOR Robert. O'meally DRC DATE ______

The above listed publication has been reviewed and denied in accordance with Board Policy 03.91, Uniform Offender Correspondence Rules and Regulations. This decision may be appealed to the Director's Review Committee (DRC), PO Box 99, Huntsville, Texas 77342-0099 **WITHIN TWO (2) WEEKS** of the date of offender notification.

Check one or more reasons for denial and cite page number of objectionable material.

- ☐ (a) It contains contraband that cannot be removed;
- ☐ (b) It contains information regarding the manufacture of explosives, weapons or drugs;
- ☑ (c) It contains material that a reasonable person would construe as written solely for the purpose of communicating information designed to achieve the breakdown of prisons through offender disruption such as strikes, riots or security threat group activity;
- ☐ (d) A specific determination has been made that the publication is detrimental to offenders' rehabilitation, because it would encourage deviant criminal sexual behavior;
- ☐ (e) It contains material on the setting up and operation of criminal schemes or how to avoid detection of criminal schemes by lawful authorities charged with the responsibility for detecting such illegal activity; or
- ☐ (f) It contains sexually explicit images.

Remarks: page 35, 41, 87 racial remarks.

Does offender wish to appeal the denial? Appealable ☑ **Yes** ☐ **No** ______ 8-29-12
Offender Signature Date

Disposition: Offender should check the desired disposition.

☒ Destroy

☐ Send to the following person at the offender's expense: ______
Name and Address

______ 8-29-12 M ______ 8-29-12
Offender Signature & Date Mailroom Representative Signature & Date

IF A DISPOSITION CHOICE IS NOT EXPRESSED AND EXECUTED, OR LITIGATION HAS NOT BEGUN ON THE PUBLICATION BEING HELD FOR LITIGATION, WITHIN SIXTY (60) DAYS OF THE INITIAL DENIAL, THE PUBLICATION WILL BE DESTROYED.

UNIT DISPOSITION: ______
Date Employee's Signature

Publisher / Sender Inside Books Project.

Address 827 W. 12th Str. Austin 78701

DISTRIBUTION:
Original - Unit Copy or **SEND WITH AUTHORED BOOK OR MAGAZINE IF APPEALED TO THE DRC.**
Gold - Unit Copy
Yellow - Offender Copy
Pink - Sender of Authored Book (Previously I-193)
I-154

Figure 8.4. Texas Department of Criminal Justice denial form for *Narrative of the Life of Frederick Douglass, An American Slave* by Frederick Douglass. Reason for ban: a) "contains material that a reasonable person would construe as written solely for the purpose of communicating information designed to achieve the breakdown of prisons through offender disruption such as strikes, riots or security threat group activity;" Mailroom employee remarks: "page 35, 41, 87, racial remarks." Disposition: Destroy.

Hello. Please be mindfull of This List. Thank you

TEXAS DEPARTMENT OF CRIMINAL JUSTICE
PUBLICATION REVIEW / DENIAL NOTIFICATION

NAME ______ TDCJ# ______ UNIT RV 19

TITLE OF PUBLICATION Cultural Resistance Reader ______ MSCP LOG DATE ______ UNIT RECEIVED OR DATE 3/13/17

AUTHOR Stephen Duncombe ______ MSCP IOC DATE ______

The above listed publication has been reviewed and denied in accordance with Board Policy 03.91, Uniform Offender Correspondence Rules and Regulations. This decision may be appealed to the Director's Review Committee (DRC), PO Box 99, Huntsville, Texas 77342-0099 **WITHIN TWO (2) WEEKS** of the date of offender notification.

Check one or more reasons for denial and cite page number of objectionable material.

(a) It contains contraband that cannot be removed; (metal binding, etc)

(b) It contains information regarding the manufacture of explosives, weapons or drugs;

X (c) It contains material that a reasonable person would construe as written solely for the purpose of communicating information designed to achieve the breakdown of prisons through offender disruption such as strikes, riots or security threat group activity;

(d) A specific determination has been made that the publication is detrimental to offenders' rehabilitation, because it would encourage deviant criminal sexual behavior;

(e) It contains material on the setting up and operation of criminal schemes or how to avoid detection of criminal schemes by lawful authorities charged with the responsibility for detecting such illegal activity; or

(f) It contains sexually explicit images. (mutually exclusive)

Remarks: Pgs 56–60 contains information that could be used to facilitate prison disruption

Does offender wish to appeal the denial? ☐ Non-Appealable ☒ Yes ☐ No ______ 4/14/17
Offender Signature Date

Disposition: Offender must check the desired disposition at time denial is presented.

☒ Destroy

○ Send to the following person at the offender's expense: ______
Name and Address

______ 4/14/17 ______ C Anderson 4/14/17
Offender Signature & Date ______ Mailroom Representative Signature & Date

IF A DISPOSITION CHOICE IS NOT EXPRESSED AND EXECUTED, OR LITIGATION HAS NOT BEGUN ON THE PUBLICATION BEING HELD FOR LITIGATION, WITHIN SIXTY (60) DAYS OF THE INITIAL DENIAL OR THE DRC DECISION DATE IF APPEALED, THE PUBLICATION WILL BE DESTROYED.

DRC APPROVED/UPHELD THE DENIAL ON ______.

UNIT DISPOSITION: ______
Date ______ Employee's Signature

Publisher / Sender Inside Books Project

Address 827 West 12th St., Austin, TX 78701

DISTRIBUTION: Original - Unit Copy or **SEND WITH AUTHORED BOOK OR MAGAZINE IF APPEALED TO THE DRC.**
Yellow- Offender Copy of Denial **Pink**- Sender of Authored Book (Previously I-193) **Gold**- Offender Copy of DRC Decision

I-154 (Rev 03/12)

Figure 8.5. Texas Department of Criminal Justice denial form for *Cultural Resistance Reader* by Stephen Duncombe because it (c) contains material that a reasonable person would construe as written solely for the purpose of communicating information to achieve the breakdown of prisons through offender disruption such as strikes, riot, or security threat group activity. Mail-room remarks: "contains information that could be used to facilitate prison disruption." Appealable: Yes. Disposition: Destroy. Annotations on the document done by the incarcerated person who had requested the resource.

C2-103

TEXAS DEPARTMENT OF CRIMINAL JUSTICE
PUBLICATION REVIEW / DENIAL NOTIFICATION

NAME ______ TDCJ# ______ UNIT E2

TITLE OF PUBLICATION Coming of Age in Mississippi MSCP LOG DATE ______ OR UNIT RECEIVED DATE 3/ /13

AUTHOR Anne Moody MSCP IOC DATE ______

The above listed publication has been reviewed and denied in accordance with Board Policy 03.91, Uniform Offender Correspondence Rules and Regulations. This decision may be appealed to the Director's Review Committee (DRC), PO Box 99, Huntsville, Texas 77342-0099 **WITHIN TWO (2) WEEKS** of the date of offender notification.

Check one or more reasons for denial and cite page number of objectionable material.

- (a) It contains contraband that cannot be removed;
- (b) It contains information regarding the manufacture of explosives, weapons or drugs;
- (c) It contains material that a reasonable person would construe as written solely for the purpose of communicating information designed to achieve the breakdown of prisons through offender disruption such as strikes, riots or security threat group activity;
- ✓ (d) A specific determination has been made that the publication is detrimental to offenders' rehabilitation, because it would encourage deviant criminal sexual behavior;
- (e) It contains material on the setting up and operation of criminal schemes or how to avoid detection of criminal schemes by lawful authorities charged with the responsibility for detecting such illegal activity; or
- (f) It contains sexually explicit images.

Remarks: Page; 372 Racial

Does offender wish to appeal the denial? ☑ **Non-Appealable** ☐ **Yes** ☐ **No** ______ Offender Signature 3/29/13 Date

Disposition: Offender must check the desired disposition at the time denial is presented.

- Destroy
- Send to the following person at the offender's expense: To Sender (Name and Address)

______ 3/29/13 Offender Signature & Date ______ 3/29/13 Mailroom Representative Signature & Date

IF A DISPOSITION CHOICE IS NOT EXPRESSED AND EXECUTED, OR LITIGATION HAS NOT BEGUN ON THE PUBLICATION BEING HELD FOR LITIGATION, WITHIN SIXTY (60) DAYS OF THE INITIAL DENIAL OR THE DRC DECISION DATE IF APPEALED, THE PUBLICATION WILL BE DESTROYED.

DRC APPROVED/UPHELD THE DENIAL ON 3/26/2001.

UNIT DISPOSITION: ______ Date ______ Employee's Signature

Publisher / Sender Inside Books Project

Address 12th Street Books 827 W. 12th Street Austin, TX 78701

DISTRIBUTION: Original - Unit Copy or **SEND WITH AUTHORED BOOK OR MAGAZINE IF APPEALED TO THE DRC.**
Yellow - Offender Copy of Denial **Pink** - Sender of Authored Book (Previously I-193) **Gold** - Offender Copy of DRC Decision

I-154 (Rev 03/12)

Figure 8.6. Texas Department of Criminal Justice denial form for Anne Moody's *Coming of Age in Mississippi.* (d) "A specific determination has been made that the publication is detrimental to offenders' rehabilitation because it would encourage deviant criminal sexual behavior." Remarks by prison mailroom employee: "Page; 372 Racial." Non-Appealable.

criminality and deviancy which then manifest in dominant social institutions (such as art, journalism, media, public policy, and administration). Providing access to these ideologies allow us to challenge the functioning of them, within institutions and within ourselves. Even more importantly, providing access to the "counter talk" of imprisoned people allows for a dialectical challenge to its hegemony. Engaging with these narrative transgressions can enable students and others to challenge deeply ingrained notions of what, and whom, count as criminal, deviant, and disposable.

NARRATIVES OF TRANSGRESSION, TRANSFORMATION, AND LIBERATORY IMAGINATION

We will not read this book
unless you drive by
and hurl it over the fence
And we run under the red eye of the cameras
unseen by the guards asleep in their towers
dreaming of the arc of bullets tumbling through the air
as inmates flee
into the bleeding horizon.

We will not read this book
because the censors squatting in the mailroom
their thighs chafed
by the stench of their suspicion
will chew and spit the pages into the trash
to mourn with other slashed seditionary lies
all lies
unfit for our rehabilitation.

We will not read this book
because it will very likely speak of possibilities
beyond the borders of bricks

of probabilities
without accounting for iron
and of impossibilities
outside the shrinking circle of hope.

We will not read this book
it will not whisper its histories to us
we will not listen to its secrets
be seduced by its sweet mysteries
compelled to arise
revoke, question, accuse,
desire, confess, dream,
love and die.

We will not read this book.[36]

The collection of incarcerated people's narrative works in the IBPA includes art, fiction and non-fiction writing, crafts, photographs, and poems like the one above. This piece was read by the narrator, Jorge, in the oral history interview I transcribed for TAVP as part of my undergraduate digital humanities course. In the blog reflections I wrote as a student while transcribing Jorge's poems, I noted that "the lines 'it will not whisper its histories to us,' and the repetition of 'we will not read this book' high-light[s] the epistemological gaps rendered by censorship."[37] By this time, I was an IBP collective member, and was informally collecting censorship records that would form the basis of the first collection in the IBPA Omeka. Works like Jorge's contextualized the violence of the censorship documents I was processing, and spoke to the necessity for collections centering incarcerated creators.

Here, I examine how the narrative works of incarcerated queer and trans people reveal the epistemological control of the prison, specifically examining the ascription of "criminal sexual deviancy" that is sustained institutionally through gender oppression and sexual violence. For example, state defined gender categories are institutionalized in the site of the prison. Trans women are placed in men's units, where access to safe housing, gender-affirming care products, and appropriate health care are denied to them. This points to the ways in which these administrative procedures of classification, categorization, description, data collection, and standardization are all employed as mechanisms of surveillance and control.

One incarcerated friend and IBP patron, Edee Allynna Davis, elucidates the impacts of these mechanisms in a conversation on prison abolition work:

> Trans women's liberation and experiences and prison rights are a project of prison liberation/abolition. We (trans women) are probably the most oppressed group of people behind the prison walls. We are not afforded or granted any rights to items intended for female gender identity...I should be afforded and granted the rights to access and availabilities of all that cisgender females are on the women's units. I'm housed on a section where there are 47 men here in the 24 cells that there are. 2 people to a cell I'm #48...can you imagine what that's like?[38]

Here Edee situates trans women's lives as central to a project of abolition. She provokes the reader: "can you imagine?" and describes an existence steeped in nullification. However, while exposing this violence, Edee also moves toward a radical futurity, rooting trans women's survival in a larger project of prison abolition grounded in day-to-day survival. Edee frequently sends art to the ABC and to the pen pal group, Black and Pink, which focuses on the needs of incarcerated queer and trans people (Figure 8.7). Edee's words and art participate in movement activism outside the prison, asserting the resiliency and survival of incarcerated trans women despite day-to-day violence.

Figure 8.7. "Pride," colored pencil drawing by Edee Allynna Davis.

Content note: brief mention of sexual violence.

Lilly Anne also writes to me describing abuse she experiences from guards and other inmates in the men's unit she is assigned to. Here she is checking in with me after an assault from a cellmate. She not only speaks to the sexual violence entrenched in the site of the prison, but describes the workings of carceral epistemology outside its gates:

> The AntiRetroViral (ARV) therapy for HIV is for 28 days. I get the first dose at the Hospital and the 2nd this morning at my cell. We were at the Hospital till 4am. Highlight, they let me touch a tree for a few seconds by the van. I was handcuffed and shackled for the trip. I thanked God for allowing me to touch the tree. There are no trees in my world.[39]

In this small note, Lilly Anne illustrates how carceral logics structure how and what we are able to know, feel, and experience—including the seemingly mundane shuffling from hospital to cell, and the quotidian disruption of touching a tree in the midst of these dehumanizing transferals. Attending to these experiences is integral to supporting queer and trans world-making in the face of violence.

Since 2013 I have also written to C. Castaneda, "Inker C^2," who has been incarcerated since 1994. The art and letters Inker has sent to me over the years speak to transgression of carceral ideologies through visions of liberatory futurity. Using basic ink pens and paper, Inker C^2's detailed and multi-faceted portraits of trans people include depictions of resources that enable personal agency over one's body, gender identity, and cultural affinities. These resources include access to hormones, feminine clothing and make-up, goth and kink community, safe drug use, educational resources, friendships, romances, and dreams of an existence beyond a maximum-security prison unit (Figure 8.8). Inker C^2 asserts these transgressive futures through art and writing based on past and present experiences, despite TDCJ censorship and confinement:

> I don't think that you can tell people 'look at this it was done by an inmate in t.d.c.j. who wants to transition from male to female' and expect them to perceive the meaning of the drawing. let me

Figure 8.8. "From the Heart," pen drawing by C. Castaneda, "Inker C^2."

take that back, they would get the meaning but not the emotions that I was trying to express out of my darkest moments. for me a drawing can be like a window into the soul or the light at the end of the tunnel. it can also represent a journey, like a blue-print into

> somebody's life or like a particular incident...In this particular case books represent the help that you and every other person in Inside Books offer to people like me and the benefits of learning and searching for knowledge. hormones and money represent tools to accomplish something in this....I was thinking about the journey of transition I was thinking about transsexuals and transgender kink and drugs—things that are part of some of these people. This I know by my own experience. As for the LOOK of my models, that is what I consider extremely beautiful, erotic and alluring.[40]

Inker C^2 names the limitations of what we can know, feel, or truly understand, grappling throughout this letter with what can be shared with me or others through viewing the art. Despite the impossibilities, Inker C^2's art and writing convey much that is vital to a collective vision of liberatory futures, and I hope that access to it can facilitate movement toward these futures. For example, like Edee and Lilly, Inker C^2's writing emphasizes the importance of solidaric mutual aid and direct-action tactics like sending free books and information, providing legal support, or adding money to people's commissary funds so they can buy basic necessities. They also powerfully demonstrate what "building a shared imagination of transformative change" could look like; sharing writing and art that assert a liberatory futurity, or what Inker C^2describes as the "light at the end of the tunnel."[41] This may reflect a projected release date of 2023, and simultaneously a future without prisons and other institutions that maintain carceral violence.

In *Cruising Utopia: The Then and There of Queer Futurity,* José Esteban Muñoz reflects on the nature of temporality, futurity, and utopia in queer archives:

> Queer cultural production is both an acknowledgment of the lack that is endemic to any heteronormative rendering of the world and a building, a "world making," in the face of that lack...Queer utopian practice is about "building" and "doing" in response to that status of nothing assigned to us by the heteronormative world.[42]

Queer and trans people's art and writing points to this utopian world-making that transgresses time and space. For example, Inker C^2's work shows a wrist-watch tearing in half next to letters from IBP that are coming forward from a dark background (Figure 8.9). Transfemme people bask in their bodies and gaze upon each other in

Figure 8.9. "Thanks to a Friend," pen drawing by C. Castaneda, "Inker C^2."

adoration, surrounded by hormones used in transgender-affirming therapy, recreational drugs, and books titled "Happiness and Hope," "LGBTQ," and "Thanks to a Friend." This piece represents multiple modes of transformation, agency and expression that should be engaged with as we collectively organize toward liberatory futures.

CONCLUSION

In 2017, the IBPA was invited to share space and resources with the TAVP, which enabled me to move dozens of boxes from my small apartment and begin a sustained relationship where resources, labor, and organizing work took place in a shared office space. Over the years, community members, and undergraduate and graduate volunteers all participated in building the IBPA by processing physical materials, digitizing items, describing content, and collaborating on community events. Furthermore, the collections have been accessed by activists, educators, students, researchers, and formerly incarcerated people. For example, in February 2017 the IBPA collaborated with the Texas Advocates for Justice and Anarchist Black Cross to curate an exhibit on TDCJ censorship forms and incarcerated people's poetry in the Texas State Capitol during a state-wide gathering in support of incarcerated and undocumented communities (Figure 8.10).[43] This exhibit ruptured the space by drawing attention to the violence of statist, carceral logics in the censorship documents. Furthermore, the IBPA has also been a part of community art shows at the independent anarchist book-store MonkeyWrench Books and other grassroots organizations in Austin to fundraise for the incarcerated contributors. Utilizing the collections to garner direct support for creators is a main goal for the project, above any other pedagogical or research purposes. For example, it can provide an opportunity for creators to be compensated for work; recently Inker C²'s artwork was featured on the cover of a literary journal, *Feminist Formations*, "Teaching the feminist 'classics' now" (Figure 8.11).[44]

Figure 8.10. Photograph of a collaborative installation by Austin Anarchist Black Cross (ABC) and the Inside Books Project (IBP) Archive at the Texas State Capitol for a day-long event in support of incarcerated and undocumented communities. The installation featured censorship forms for an IBP newsletter that was banned for mentioning a prison strike. Another panel features incarcerated people's writing.

Figure 8.11. Inker C^2's artwork is featured on the cover of the literary journal, *Feminist Formations*, an issue on "Teaching the feminist 'classics' now."

The materials have also been used to build educational exhibits on impacts of incarceration, the death penalty, and censorship practices within academic spaces, such as an exhibit at the Perry-Castañeda Library (PCL) research library at the University of Texas at Austin in the fall of 2019 (Figures 8.12 and 8.13). One curriculum for a web-based American Studies course for undergraduates at the University of Texas, Austin called "Prison Art, Literature, and Protest" included IBPA materials as part of its course readings.[45] On why she included the archive in this course, Holly Genovese says:

> I wanted the students to see local/Texas connections to carceral writing and art as well as introduce them to the idea of 'vernacular' prison art and writing...We are reading a lot of well-known writers and scholars and activists but I wanted them to have access to cultural production outside of that.[46]

Figure 8.12. IBPA exhibit at the Perry-Castañeda Library (PCL) featuring censorship documentation.

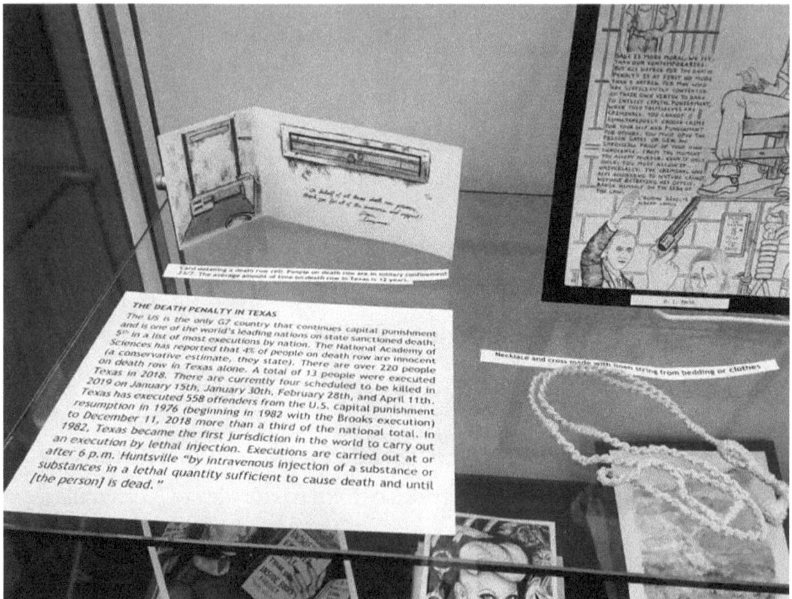

Figure 8.13. IBPA exhibit at the Perry-Castañeda Library (PCL) featuring crafts and art made by people on death row. There is also a small information page on "The death penalty in Texas."

It is rewarding to see this project come full circle, from first being developed in an undergraduate course on prison narratives, to being included in the curriculum for one! In a time when so much learning, organizing, and labor has moved online, it is even more pivotal to facilitate access to primary source narratives of incarcerated people. When Genovese's students accessed the archive, for example, they saw the most recent digital collection, a collaboration with the TAVP called "Sheltering Justice: Stories from the Intersection of COVID-19 and Mass Incarceration."[47] The Sheltering Justice project "aims to document, archive, and share stories about the real time impacts of the COVID-19 pandemic on the lives, health, and well-being of our communities and the compounding impact of incarceration."[48] As students and others feel the sense of isolation this pandemic has induced, it is critical to encourage engagement with individuals who are doubly impacted by the COVID-19 pandemic, so that educators, activists, and family members of imprisoned people can activate awareness and solidarity with this often forgotten population.

One poem featured in the IBPA, "Now you Know World," by Sten Elysium, drives home the necessity of conveying to the public the day-to-day lives of the hundreds of thousands of people that are contained in cages for months, years, and, for many, decades:

> Now you know world
>
> Our pain
> You know the sting
> Of quarantine
> Which is our everyday
> Shut Away
> From the rest of the world
> Now you know World
> The deadliness
> Of silences
> The monotony
> Of confinement to a bed
> The fear of being stuck
> In your own head
> The dread of another day
> With nothing to say
> Now you know world
> Our desolation
> Our frustration
> Our exasperation
> Our desperation
> And our isolation
> Now you know world
> What it's like
> To not see

Your family
To not hold
So dear
To be socially distanced
From those you miss
And just wish
To hug
Now you know world
Our plight
And the fright
Of searching for oneself
And discovering how close
You are
To Hell
Or searching your soul
And hating the story
That is told
Now you know World
Our story
Trying to fix yourself
Piece by broken piece
And being met with struggle
And the feelings of futility
Now you know world
What it's like
To hope
To pray
For the day
That your exile
Would end
Now you know world
What it's like to have no choice
To have to be strong
To carry on

And to move along
To have to endure
Or give up and ensure
Your death
Now you know world
What it's like
To not be
Free
And to be like
Me
Now you know world.[49]

Despite these generative and transformative outcomes, some fundamental barriers remain in place, speaking to my central argument regarding power and authority in archives. In the last months of 2020, I moved from Austin to Tucson to begin my PhD; concurrently, in light of the pandemic, my undergraduate institution revoked the IBPA Omeka account to provide more server space for its current students. Given the archive was developed in collaboration with the individual educators named here, who had moved onto jobs at different universities, and the lack of any agreement between myself and the school about the terms of the project, there was nothing to be done besides scramble to migrate the collections to a new domain with the support of TAVP's archivist, Jane Field. This abrupt transition emphasized the precarity of grassroots archival projects developed outside the purview of institutional legitimation. While these collaborations between individuals or small groups enable mutually supportive and solidaric relationships, the IBPA and similar grassroots projects experience barriers to sustainability because they are not granted legitimacy by authorities in positions of power (within universities and the nonprofit sector alike). For example, the IBPA is often ineligible for grants due to requirements like high annual budgets, even for grants specific to "community-based archives." Instead, a small amount of Patreon donations fund supplies and a few hours of monthly labor are taken on by organizers contributing unpaid labor to multiple projects outside of the IBPA. This again demonstrates how the sustainability of the archive relies on the labor of individual volunteers or academic accomplices while fundamental disparities regarding the distribution of resources and power remain in place. This is not to say that these relationships are futile by any means; they play a pivotal role in moving toward broader transformative change. However, I posit, this transformative change necessitates new approaches to power and authority in archives. This is particularly true for grassroots, anti-authoritarian projects, as they pose a particular threat to status quo power relations. The authorities who benefit from these power relations continue to gatekeep resources while appropriating radical culture and praxis to evince liberatory aims.

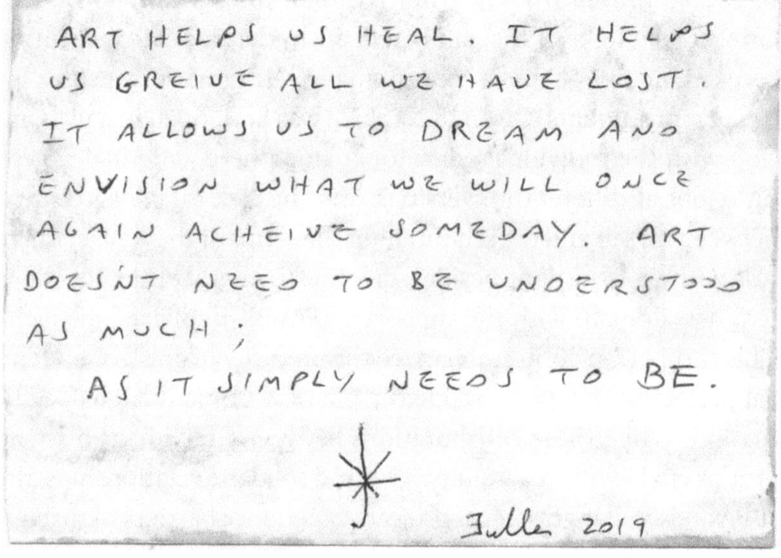

ART HELPS US HEAL. IT HELPS
US GREIVE ALL WE HAVE LOST.
IT ALLOWS US TO DREAM AND
ENVISION WHAT WE WILL ONCE
AGAIN ACHEIVE SOMEDAY. ART
DOESN'T NEED TO BE UNDERSTOOD
AS MUCH ;
AS IT SIMPLY NEEDS TO BE.

Fuller 2019

Figure 8.14. Small note with handwritten text, "Art helps us heal. It helps us greive [*sic*] all we have lost. It allows us to dream and envision what we will once again acheive [*sic*] someday. Art doesn't need to be understood as much; as it simply needs to be." Signed Fuller, 2019.

In sum, I posit that for educators, academic accomplices, and archivists to move toward revolutionary change, we must re-examine predominant notions around power in archives, and adopt more explicitly anti-authoritarian praxes. In this way, we can collectively build shared imaginations of liberatory futures, centering the narratives of those most impacted by carceral state violence. Incarcerated people's "counter-archives" can subvert these hegemonic logics, facilitating a more transparent and accurate understanding of how criminal punishment systems operate in the site of the prison and beyond it. In this way we can, on a structural, ideological, and interpersonal level, "achieve the breakdown of prisons."

NOTES

1 Randall C. Jimerson, "Embracing the Power of Archives," *The American Archivist* 69, no. 1 (2006): 24; Ketelaar, "Archival Temples, Archival Prisons"; Rodney G. S. Carter, "Of Things Said and Unsaid: Power, Archival Silences, and Power in Silence," *Archivaria*, September 25, 2006, 215–33; Joan M. Schwartz and Terry Cook, "Archives, Records, and Power: The Making of Modern Memory," *Archival Science* 2, no. 1 (March 2002): 1–19, https://doi.org/10.1007/BF02435628.

2 Jimerson, "Embracing the Power of Archives," 24.

3 Terry Cook, "The Concept of the Archival Fonds in the Post-Custodial Era: Theory, Problems and Solutions," *Archivaria* 35, no. 35 (1993); Jarrett M. Drake, "RadTech Meets RadArch: Towards A New Principle for Archives and Archival Description," *On Archivy*, *Medium*, April 7, 2016, https://medium.com/on-archivy/radtech-meets-radarch-towards-a-new-principle-for-archives-and-archival-description-568f133e4325.

4 Jimerson, "Embracing the Power of Archives," 28.

5 Paulo Freire, *Pedagogy of the Oppressed*, trans. Myra Bergman Ramos, New rev., 20th Anniversary (New York: Continuum, 1993), 30-32.

6 Freire, *Pedagogy of the Oppressed, 42.*

7 Freire, *Pedagogy of the Oppressed, 42.*

8 Freire, *Pedagogy of the Oppressed, 33.*

9 Jarrett M. Drake, "Seismic Shifts: On Archival Fact and Fictions," *Medium*, August 20, 2018, https://medium.com/community-archives/seismic-shifts-on-archival-fact-and-fictions-6db4d5c655ae.

10 Yusef Omowale, "We Already Are," *Sustainable Futures, Medium*, September 3, 2018, https://medium.com/community-archives/we-already-are-52438b863e31; Zakiya Collier, "Call to Action: Archiving State-Sanctioned Violence Against Black People," *Sustainable Futures, Medium*, June 6, 2020, https://medium.com/community-archives/call-to-action-archiving-state-sanctioned-violence-against-black-people-d629c956689a; W. Richard Scott, "Institutional Carriers: Reviewing Modes of Transporting Ideas over Time and Space and Considering Their Consequences," *Industrial and Corporate Change* 12, no. 4 (August 1, 2003): 879–94, https://doi.org/10.1093/icc/12.4.879; Jonathan H. Turner, *The Institutional Order: Economy, Kinship, Religion, Polity, Law, and Education in Evolutionary and Comparative Perspective*, 1st edition (New York: Longman Pub Group, 1997).

11 Benjamin Hutchens, "Techniques of Forgetting? Hypo-Amnesic History and the An-Archive," *Substance* 36, no. 2 (2007): 37–55.

12 Jan Descartes et al., "Anti-Fascism in the Archive: Interference Archive's Collaboration with No. NOT EVER.," *Radical History Review* 2020, no. 138 (October 1, 2020): 179–91, https://doi.org/10.1215/01636545-8359580; Alycia Sellie et al., "Interference Archive: A Free Space for Social Movement Culture," *Archival Science* 15, no. 4 (December 1, 2015): 453–72, https://doi.org/10.1007/s10502-015-9245-5.

13 Cait McKinney, "Feminist Digitization Practices at the Lesbian Herstory Archives," in *Information Activism: A Queer History of Lesbian Media Technologies* (Durham: Duke University Press, 2020).

14 On what I mean by "accomplices," see "Accomplices Not Allies: Abolishing the Ally Industrial Complex," *Indigenous Action Media* (blog), May 4, 2014, http://www.indigenousaction.org/accomplices-not-allies-abolishing-the-ally-industrial-complex/.

15 Benjamin Franks, Nathan Jun, and Leonard Williams, eds., *Anarchism: A Conceptual Approach*, 1st edition (New York: Routledge, 2018); Uri Gordon, *Anarchy Alive! Anti-Authoritarian Politics from Practice to Theory* (London: Pluto Press, 2008).

16 Gordon, *Anarchy Alive!*, 4. See also 17–18, 29–46.

17 I have expanded on these principles in more detail here: aems emswiler, "'Conditions of Possibility': Towards an Archival Praxis Informed by Black Feminist Anarchism and a Critical Trans Politics" (Thesis, 2020), https://doi.org/10.26153/tsw/14268; aems emswiler, "Exceeding Survival: Militant Memory and Insurrectionary Archivism in the Fight for Futurity," in *Fitting in, Sticking Out: Queer (In)Visibilities and the Perils of Inclusion* (Oakland: PM Press, 2022).

18 List based on experience processing and prepping book requests. For a more extensive list, see "Donate Used Books in Austin," Inside Books Project, https://insidebooksproject.org/donate-books.

19 "IBP Resource Guide," Inside Books Project, https://insidebooksproject.org/resource-guide.

20 Skot Oh and Dani King, personal correspondences, March 2, 2021.

21 Dan Swain, "Not Not but Not yet: Present and Future in Prefigurative Politics," *Political Studies* 67, no. 1 (2019): 47–62, https://doi.org/10.1177/0032321717741233.

22 aems emswiler, "The Literacy Needs of Incarcerated People," LibGuides: The University of Texas Austin School of Information LIS, March 27, 2019, https://ischool-utexas.libguides.com/c.php?g=922086; Megan Sweeney, *The Story Within Us: Women Prisoners Reflect on Reading* (Champaign: University of Illinois Press, 2012).

23 There are many different notions of the "counter archive." Here, I am directly drawing on my undergraduate capstone, which represents the organic conception derived from my work with IBP, prior to any engagement with scholarship I have encountered since then. aems emswiler, "'To Achieve the Breakdown of Prisons:' Narrative Hegemonies and Transgressions in the Prison Industrial Complex" (Feminist Studies MA Capstone, overseen by Dr. Alison Kafer, Georgetown, Texas., Southwestern University, 2014).

24 Angela Y. Davis, *Are Prisons Obsolete?*, Open Media Book (New York: Seven Stories Press, 2003); Dean Spade, *Normal Life: Administrative Violence, Critical Trans Politics, and the Limits of Law*, Revised and expanded edition (Durham: Duke University Press, 2015); Eric A. Stanley and Nat Smith, eds., *Captive Genders: Trans Embodiment and the Prison Industrial Complex* (Oakland: AK Press, 2011); Liat Ben-Moshe, Chris Chapman, and Allison C. Carey, eds., *Disability Incarcerated: Imprisonment and Disability in the United States and Canada*, First edition (New York: Palgrave Macmillan, 2014).

25 Charlotte Nunes, "'Connecting to the Ideologies That Surround Us': Oral History Stewardship as an Entry Point to Critical Theory in the Undergraduate Classroom," *Oral History Review* 44, no. 2 (September 13, 2017): 348–62.

26 Nunes, "'Connecting to the Ideologies That Surround Us,'" 2.

27 Nunes, "'Connecting to the Ideologies That Surround Us,'" 13.

28 Nunes, "'Connecting to the Ideologies That Surround Us,'" 12.

29 Texas Department of Criminal Justice, "Death Row Information," https://www.tdcj.texas.gov/death_row/dr_offenders_on_dr.html.

30 Bill Crawford, *Texas Death Row: Executions in the Modern Era* (New York: Penguin, 2008).

31 Texas Department of Criminal Justice, "Uniform Inmate Correspondence Rules," February 25, 2020, https://www.tdcj.texas.gov/documents/policy/BP0391.pdf.

32 United States Court of Appeals, Fifth Circuit, "Prison Legal News v. Livingston No. 11–40128.," FindLaw, June 1, 2012, https://caselaw.findlaw.com/us-5th-circuit/1602416.html.

33 Texas Department of Criminal Justice, "Denial Form for *Auto Repair for Dummies* by Deanna Sclar," Inside Books Project Archive, May 1, 2013, http://ibparchive.texasafterviolence.org/items/show/292.

34 Texas Department of Criminal Justice, "Denial Form for Narrative of the Life of Frederick Douglass, An American Slave," Inside Books Project Archive, August 29, 2012, http://ibparchive.texasafterviolence.org/items/show/342.

35 Texas Department of Criminal Justice, "Uniform Inmate Correspondence Rules."

36 Jorge Antonio Renaud, "Lamentation for Literature," in aems emswiler, "Jorge Antonio Renaud Poetry Transcriptions," *Freedom and Imprisonment in American Literature* (blog), April 17, 2015, https://freedomandimprisonment.wordpress.com/2015/04/17/jorge-antonio-renaud-poetry-transcriptions/.

37 aems emswiler, "Jorge Antonio Renaud Poetry Transcriptions."

38 Edee Allynna Davis, letter to author, May 13, 2017.

39 Lilly Anne, letter to author, January 4 2018.

40 C. Castaneda, "Inker C^2," letter to author, July 7 2017.

41 C. Castaneda, "Inker C^2," letter to author, July 7 2017.

42 José Esteban Muñoz, *Cruising Utopia: The Then and There of Queer Futurity*, 10th Anniversary (New York: New York University Press, 2009), 130.

43 Jorge Renaud, "WATCH: Texas Advocates for Justice #kNOwMORE2017 highlight video and recap," Grassroots Leadership, March 31, 2017 https://grassrootsleadership.org/blog/2017/03/watch-texas-advocates-justice-knowmore2017-highlight-video-and-recap.

44 Nora Castaneda, "'Thank You IBP' (Cover Art)," *Feminist Formations* 32, no. 1 (Spring 2020), https://muse.jhu.edu/issue/42437/print.

45 https://liberalarts.utexas.edu/ams/graduate/gradstudents/profile.php?id=heg562#courses.

46 Holly Genovese, e-mail message to author, October 1, 2020.

47 "Sheltering Justice," Inside Books Project Archive, http://ibparchive.texasafterviolence.org/collections/show/15.

48 "Sheltering Justice," Texas After Violence Project, 2020, https://shelteringjustice.texasafterviolence.org/.

49 Sten Elysium, "Now You Know World," Inside Books Project Archive, http://ibparchive.texasafterviolence.org/items/show/156.

BIBLIOGRAPHY

Carter, Rodney G. S. "Of Things Said and Unsaid: Power, Archival Silences, and Power in Silence." *Archivaria*, September 25, 2006, 215–33.

Castaneda, C. ("Inker C²"). "'Thank You IBP' (Cover Art)." *Feminist Formations* 32, no. 1 (Spring 2020). https://muse.jhu.edu/issue/42437/print.

Descartes, Jan, Michele Hardesty, Jen Hoyer, Maggie Schreiner, and Brooke Shuman. "Anti-Fascism in the Archive: Interference Archive's Collaboration with No. NOT EVER." *Radical History Review* 2020, no. 138 (October 1, 2020): 179–91. https://doi.org/10.1215/01636545-8359580.

Drake, Jarrett M. "RadTech Meets RadArch: Towards A New Principle for Archives and Archival Description." *On Archivy. Medium*, April 7, 2016. https://medium.com/on-archivy/radtech-meets-radarch-towards-a-new-principle-for-archives-and-archival-description-568f133e4325.

Drake, Jarrett M. "Seismic Shifts: On Archival Fact and Fictions." *Medium*, August 20, 2018. https://medium.com/community-archives/seismic-shifts-on-archival-fact-and-fictions-6db4d5c655ae.

emswiler, aems. "'Conditions of Possibility': Towards an Archival Praxis Informed by Black Feminist Anarchism and a Critical Trans Politics," 2020. https://doi.org/10.26153/tsw/14268.

emswiler, aems. "Exceeding Survival: Militant Memory and Insurrectionary Archivism in the Fight for Futurity." In *Fitting in, Sticking Out: Queer (In) Visibilities and the Perils of Inclusion*. Oakland: PM Press, 2022.

emswiler, aems. "The Literacy Needs of Incarcerated People," LibGuides: The University of Texas Austin School of Information LIS, March 27, 2019, https://ischool-utexas.libguides.com/c.php?g=922086&p=6645837.

Franks, Benjamin, Nathan Jun, and Leonard Williams, eds. *Anarchism: A Conceptual Approach*. 1st edition. New York: Routledge, 2018.

Freire, Paulo. *Pedagogy of the oppressed*. Translated by Myra Bergman Ramos. New rev.,20th Anniversary. New York: Continuum, 1993.

McKinney, Cait. "Feminist Digitization Practices at the Lesbian Herstory Archives." In *Information Activism: A Queer History of Lesbian Media Technologies*. Durham: Duke University Press, 2020.

Schwartz, Joan M., and Terry Cook. "Archives, Records, and Power: The Making of Modern Memory." *Archival Science* 2, no. 1 (March 2002): 1–19. https://doi.org/10.1007/BF02435628.

Scott, W. Richard. "Institutional Carriers: Reviewing Modes of Transporting Ideas over Time and Space and Considering Their Consequences." *Industrial and Corporate Change* 12, no. 4 (August 1, 2003): 879–94. https://doi.org/10.1093/icc/12.4.879.

Sellie, Alycia, Jesse Goldstein, Molly Fair, and Jennifer Hoyer. "Interference Archive: A Free Space for Social Movement Culture." *Archival Science* 15, no. 4 (December 1, 2015): 453–72. https://doi.org/10.1007/s10502-015-9245-5.

Swain, Dan. "Not Not but Not Yet: Present and Future in Prefigurative Politics." *Political Studies* 67, no. 1 (2019): 47–62. https://doi.org/10.1177/0032321717741233.

Turner, Jonathan H. *The Institutional Order: Economy, Kinship, Religion, Polity, Law, and Education in Evolutionary and Comparative Perspective*. 1st edition. New York: Longman Pub Group, 1997.

CHAPTER NINE

BUILDING SUSTAINABLE COLLABORATIONS AT AN HISTORICALLY BLACK COLLEGE OR UNIVERSITY: REFLECTIONS ON CONNECTING CLASSROOMS, ARCHIVES, AND COMMUNITY PARTNERS

Marco Robinson, Phyllis Earles, and Daren White

One way that people approach the past is through local and lived experience.[1] This approach is particularly effective when researching and archiving the experiences of residents in rural towns such as Prairie View located on the northwest outskirts of Houston, Texas in Waller County. To access the documented lived experiences of people in the past, historians, archivists, and librarians work collaboratively recording, collecting, and organizing a wide range of historical materials from communities. Due to technological innovations in digitization, the increase of public interest in online exhibits created from archival items, and the growth in public consumption of online archival materials, the idea of what constitutes records of permanent value has changed.[2]

The configurations and functions associated with the archival profession have changed accordingly. But Blais and Enn's conclusion stands: "archivists, as keepers and communicators of information, must interact with all of the many groups that make up their constituency, whether they be creators or users."[3] Most important to this process is "building sustainable collaborations" on and off campus. As it relates to historically Black colleges and universities (HBCUs), this task is rewarding and challenging at the same time.

At many HBCUs, archival professionals and researchers are building bridges from the classroom to the archive and then to the community in an effort to transform the authority of the archive, including at Prairie View A&M University (PVAMU). In the context of HBCUs, these transformations at Prairie View include prioritizing archiving, formulating work schemes that center the work of the archive with the mission of the university, and focusing on preserving the local Black lived experience. In many instances, this is essential to preserving and documenting the institution's history, but also the stories of the marginalized communities which HBCUs serve. PVAMU was established in 1876 for the express purpose of providing an educational avenue to a segment of American society with no scholastic outlet or institutional conservator of their experiences in Texas. The first publicly supported HBCU in the state, PVAMU played a significant role in the lives of Black Texans and continues to be a beacon of hope by leading a robust archival effort to document and preserve the Black experience on the local, state, and national levels. This effort is concentrated on providing dynamic undergraduate training in aspects of archiving and historic preservation, forming interdisciplinary teams of archivists and scholars to be active researchers and writers, and building relationships with communities near and far to document the experiences of people of African descent and other ethnic minority groups currently or formerly residing in Texas.

As I established above, there is a growing awareness of the role of the archive and the archivist in the construction of local and national narratives, and of the necessary duty for archives to more faithfully reflect diverse communities and "to collaborate more fully with those outside of the profession."[4] To explore how HBCUs can transform the authority of the archive to account for the local Black lived experience in order to better document the African American experience in Texas, in this chapter I address innovative approaches in undergraduate pedagogy, effective strategies for project sustainability beyond the semester, best practices for experiential learning, and best practices for establishing partnerships with minority communities. More specifically, "building sustainable collaborations" on multiple levels is explored through highlighting the experiences of PVAMU archivists, professors, students, and local community members. The exploration of these project stakeholders' involvement reveals a potential model for other HBCUs to follow and illustrates the ways that minority-serving institutions play an active role in transforming the authority of the archive to stem from collaborative archival teams documenting the Black experience.

PRESERVING THE BLACK PAST IS THE FUTURE: ARCHIVING AT HBCUS AND PVAMU'S ARCHIVE IN TRANSITION

As it relates to transforming the authority of the archive, HBCU's archives can play an important role in revolutionizing and expanding their reach within the larger profession just by engaging in the favorable prospect of vigorously preserving and fully documenting their respective institutional/community histories. The historical circumstances from which HBCUs were born, namely out of slavery and segregation, are an intrinsic part of the American educational, social, and political narrative.[5] The collective history is about a race of people who continually have to claim their rightful citizenship in this great nation through the overcoming of racial violence and oppression while being enslaved.[6] Moreover, historically Black institutions were at the center of civil rights protests and societal changes in the nation during social upheavals of the 1950s and 1960s. Thus, charting the future of archives at HBCUs involves a careful refocusing on preserving and documenting the rich cultural heritage of these extraordinary institutions and the communities which they serve. Traditionally, HBCU archives have not been able to fully pursue these endeavors with the full endorsement of their institutions behind them along with the committed funding. The current shift requires HBCU archives to successfully meet this challenge and will center Black institutions of higher education among the new vanguard of university and college archives/special collections across the country, transforming the archival landscape. This vanguard is composed of archival professionals working in tandem with interdisciplinary teams of scholars to promote more cross-disciplinary collaboration and to support innovative initiatives in historic preservation and the digital humanities.

In light of this task, several HBCUs across the country have engaged in major collaborative projects with other universities to fulfill the goal. In 2018, Princeton University partnered with five HBCUs to provide training to students through the Archives Research and Collaborative History Program. Anne Jarvis, a librarian at Princeton, stated, "Archives play a crucial role in our understanding of history, which includes the importance of diversity within that history...[w]orking together with colleagues from historically black colleges and universities on this program has meant that we are providing students with practical ways in which they can work on their archives back at their home institutions."[7] This transformative work embodies the tangible ways in which college and university archives across the nation are collaborating, and, most importantly, taking the banner forward in new ways prevented by discriminatory archival practices of the past. Larger traditionally white universities and HBCU archival departments have an opportunity to change the landscape in the profession by pursuing such partnerships and collaborations. Likewise, the trajectory of these collaborations has the potential to profoundly impact undergraduate instruction at HBCUs and the capabilities of HBCU archives to effectively document the past.

For over 150 years, HBCUs have focused on education as a vehicle for addressing racial and other inequities in society by using their resources to improve the quality of life for African Americans and other marginalized groups.[8] In addition to improving quality of life for the communities they serve, HBCUs also operate as the primary—and in some cases, the only—publicly accessible repositories for the Black experience in the local communities and regions in which they exist. Unfortunately, they often do not have the funding to devote to promoting their archives, and in most cases HBCU archives are understaffed or lack staff with expertise in a wide range of digital humanities skills.[9] Whether private or public, these institutions face the same dilemmas. This workplace conundrum limits department productivity and the types of innovative approaches taken by archiving staff at HBCUs. Like other HBCUs, PVAMU is not exempt and is currently experiencing these deficits. However, PVAMU's history faculty and archival staff are working vigorously to address these challenges and issues by engaging in various types of collaboration.

PLANNING FOR THE FUTURE BY PRESERVING THE PAST: ARCHIVAL PLANNING, IMPLEMENTATION, AND COLLABORATIONS AT PVAMU SINCE 2016

The Special Collections and Archives Department (SCAD) at PVAMU provides a prime case study to explore these dynamics and to glean a model from which to chart directions for the future of archives at HBCUs. PVAMU has a rich history and is a longstanding pillar in the Black community in Texas. Similar to many HBCUs, PVAMU's archival staff and faculty face challenges documenting and preserving this storied past. SCAD staff and members of the history faculty met during the summer of 2016 to discuss potential approaches and challenges to the work they were currently engaged in within their respective areas. At this point, both departments agreed it was important to collaborate and develop an ongoing project together dealing with the impact of PVAMU and the university's historical connection to the local community.

PVAMU's story is a fundamental part of the Black experience in Texas, Texas educational history, and US educational history. PVAMU administrators, faculty, and staff played a significant role in the fight for racial justice in Texas, the American South, and the country, working alongside organizations on the national stage. SCAD, housed in the fifth floor of the main campus library, is home to more than 1,000 rare books, more than 20 manuscript collections, over 5,000 rare artifacts, and more than 25,000 photographs. SCAD has two full-time staff members, including the lead archivist,

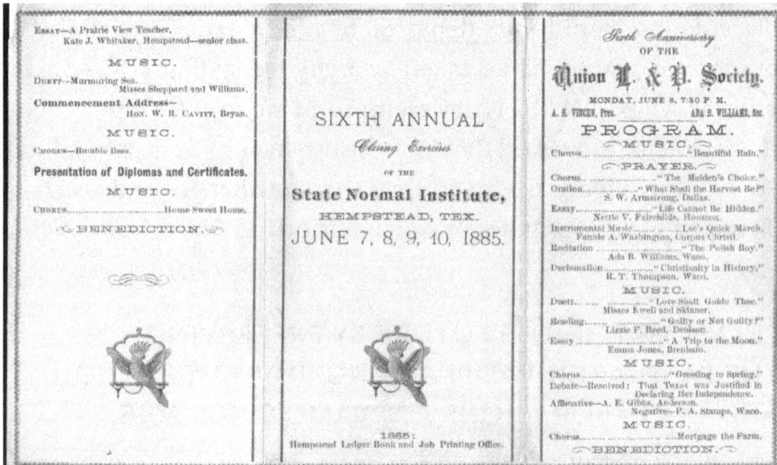
Essay—A Prairie View Teacher,
Kate J. Whitaker, Hempstead—senior class.
MUSIC.
Duett—Murmuring Sea.
Misses Sheppard and Williams.
Commencement Address—
Hon. W. R. Cavitt, Bryan.
MUSIC.
Chorus—Bumble Bees.
Presentation of Diplomas and Certificates.
MUSIC.
Chorus.......................................Home Sweet Home.
BENEDICTION.

SIXTH ANNUAL
Closing Exercises
OF THE
State Normal Institute,
HEMPSTEAD, TEX.
JUNE 7, 8, 9, 10, 1885.
1885:
Hempstead Ledger Book and Job Printing Office.

Sixth Anniversary
OF THE
Union L. & P. Society.
MONDAY, JUNE 8, 7:30 P. M.
A. H. VINCEN, Pres. ADA B. WILLIAMS, Sec.
PROGRAM.
MUSIC.
Chorus.......................................“Beautiful Rain.”
PRAYER.
Chorus.......................................“The Maiden's Choice.”
Oration.......................................“What Shall the Harvest Be?”
S. W. Armstrong, Dallas.
Essay.......................................“Life Cannot Be Hidden.”
Nettie V. Fairchilds, Houston.
Instrumental Music.......................................Lee's Quick March.
Fannie A. Washington, Corpus Christi.
Recitation.......................................“The Polish Boy.”
Ada B. Williams, Waco.
Declamation.......................................“Christianity in History.”
R. T. Thompson, Waco.
MUSIC.
Duett.......................................“Love Shall Guide Thee.”
Misses Ewell and Skinner.
Reading.......................................“Guilty or Not Guilty?”
Lizzie F. Reed, Denison.
Essay.......................................“A Trip to the Moon.”
Emma Jones, Brenham.
MUSIC.
Chorus.......................................“Greeting to Spring.”
Debate—Resolved: That Texas was Justified in Declaring Her Independence.
Affirmative—A. E. Gibbs, Anderson.
Negative—P. A. Stamps, Waco.
MUSIC.
Chorus.......................................Mortgage the Farm.
BENEDICTION.

Figure 9.1. The oldest surviving commencement program for Prairie View A&M University, then known as State Normal School for Colored Youth. (The site is Hempstead, TX because the incorporated area that is now the City of Prairie View did not come into existence until the late 1960s.) Photo provided courtesy of Prairie View A&M University's Special Collections and Archives Department.

who are assisted by several part-time student workers. Many of the PVAMU's most cherished historical artifacts await cataloging and processing for public access. By 2016, the mountain of backlogged work due to understaffing and the lack of an expert in website development and digitization had forced SCAD to postpone much of the work dealing with digital platforms.[10]

This idea informed our initial approach. During the fall of 2016, SCAD staff met again with PVAMU's history faculty to assist with preserving these endangered items and to create a joint service-learning program where students would gain a meaningful experience doing archival work and engaging in historic preservation.[11] Our first task in creating a sustainable collaboration was establishing an ongoing project between history faculty and the SCAD staff

Figure 9.2. PVAMU Extension Agents in March of 1940. These agricultural extension workers assisted communities of color throughout Texas, by providing instruction in the latest farming techniques and best practices. Photo provided courtesy of Prairie View A&M University's Special Collections and Archives Department.

where PVAMU students were at the center. By the fall of 2017, the team had conceptualized an approach and was ready to implement the plan. The project was facilitated through the "Intro to Historical Methods" and "Senior Capstone" research courses. Our approach involved connecting the classroom to the archive, and then to the local community. Ultimately, it was important to our team that our approach be as thorough and strategic as possible. We also considered there had been no formal existing channels that gave the local community members more access to the archive.

Archivists, librarians, curators, and historians have long been working against the challenges of access to archival materials.[12] PVAMU's Classroom–Archives–Community (CAC) approach, as we later termed it, is built on creating sustainable relationships among students, faculty, archivists, and community partners. The "CAC Approach" is focused on providing students with service-learning opportunities while conducting archival research, engaging faculty and archival staff in joint research projects that lead to publications, and forming lasting relationships with community partners while preserving the local area's history (see Figure 9.3). The formulation of our methods is influenced by a wide array of works by archival scholars including Andrew Flinn, Jeanette Bastian, Kelly Pereira, Laura Visser-Maessen, and Isto Huvila.[13] Our approach is to provide all groups with a role in decision making regarding the project, and gain reciprocal benefits from participating in the project. PVAMU's CAC project, focused on PVAMU and the local community's history, involved establishing collaborations across all three levels—classroom, PVAMU's SCAD, and the local community in Prairie View, Texas. The primary leaders were Marco Robinson (historian) and Phyllis Earles (archivist). Our initial concerns were providing PVAMU students with meaningful instruction and service-learning opportunities.

"Participation from the community hinges on the recognition that the community's stories have not been well documented and on a desire to make its experiences known."[14] Thus, from the

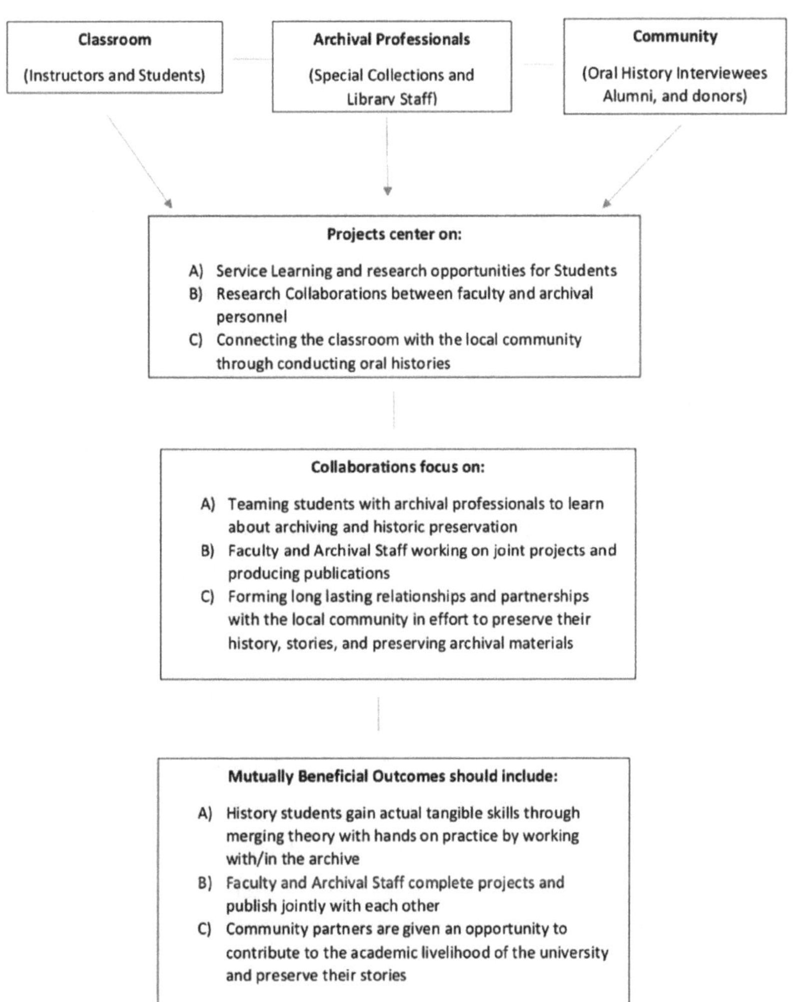

Figure 9.3. Classroom–Archives–Community (CAC). Diagram developed by Marco Robinson.

beginning of the project, the focus was on student learning outcomes and building connections with the community members to document their history. The project leader kept in mind this question: "[when] looking at regional [or local] archives and their silences…whose story gets told?"[15] Our commitment was to tell the community's story in tandem with its relation to the university and likewise items deposited into the archive. As it relates to the history program, this project served as a research opportunity for our students to gain experience working with archival sources, conducting oral histories, and engaging in public history by documenting the community members' experiences. Additionally, archival staff benefited because the students provided them with much-needed assistance with lingering tasks in the department ranging from cataloging to collection processing to display building.

Integration of preservation and access, and an understanding of the social and other benefits of supporting democratic processes through transparency and accessibility of government records is important for social development, whether at a regional, national, or international level.[16] We wanted our students to get firsthand experience of this through their participation. Students were able to network with a number of community stakeholders including university graduates, local citizens, and experts from other universities and archives who conducted trainings and workshops. The sessions dealt with conducting oral histories, utilizing archival materials in research, and using digital tools to document lived experience. The presenters included Adrienne Cain, Assistant Director of the Baylor University Institute for Oral History; Perky Beisel, Associate Professor of Public History at Stephen F. Austin University; and Anne Chao, manager of the Asian American Archive at Rice University. The partnerships with these individuals and groups were essential to reaching our curricular and archival goals.

HBCUs have a long-standing history of preparing students to engage communities of color that are likely to be underserved.[17] Following aspects of Kelly Pereira's community service-learning model, all of our CAC project activities were created to "fuse academic content, meaningful service, and reflection activities." Therefore, to connect the classroom with the archive at PVAMU, the history faculty and archival staff formulated activities that gave students opportunities to utilize primary sources in various ways and to gain hands-on experience processing collections and using the materials as primary sources for their research papers (see Figure 9.4). The second part of the service-learning component of the course required students to conduct oral histories with local community members (see Figure 9.5). As Kelly Pereria argues, "Community-engaged students need a learning approach and activities that encourage them to make connections between their service experiences and the course materials, themes, and discussions." The first time this approach was implemented was during the Fall of 2017 ("Intro to Historical Methods") and the Spring of 2018 ("Senior Capstone" research course).[18]

Figure 9.4. Lisa Stafford, a member of PVAMU's special collections and archives staff, and Chanel Williams processing a collection. Picture courtesy of Marco Robinson.

Figure 9.5. Marco Robinson and Jimmie Poindexter, PVAMU graduate and member of the local community, during an oral history interview. Picture courtesy of Marco Robinson.

Once the activities were agreed upon by CAC stakeholders, the courses were formulated with the aforementioned criteria in mind. The Fall course had fifteen students and the Spring course had eighteen. Archival professionals and scholars who want to engage in this approach, please be mindful of keeping students aware of balancing their time between their academic and service work. As an instructor, much of my time was spent facilitating both areas of work. According to Pereira:

> The instructor must occupy less the role of expert and more the role of facilitator, aiding students in the learning process, as they move from completing their service activities in the community, to reflecting on their experiences and making connections to their life experiences, skills, and knowledge, to applying what they've learned back to their lives and the lives of those in their communities.

This insight was true for PVAMU's CAC project. Our students immensely benefited from our having thoroughly planned from the beginning of the project so that the instruction and archival activities were consistent and correlated with the proposed class outcomes.[19]

The third portion of PVAMU's CAC project involved establishing relationships with members of the local community in the City of Prairie View and PVAMU alumni with whom students could conduct oral histories and collect potential historical items such as rare photos. The project leaders took into consideration that "historical abuses of communities and systemic inequities present formidable challenges for those who seek to develop partnerships with vulnerable populations."[20] From the outset of the project, we wanted to establish relationships with these individuals that gave them assurances that there was shared ownership of the project, their input was vital to any decisions made, and the products from the project would focus on highlighting their experiences and insights. Key to establishing a relationship with this community of individuals where they were equal stakeholders was including them in meetings and making sure final decisions for activities reflected their insights. Because of our vesting shared authority with the community participants, we gained a mutual respect, which opened doors for participants trusting us with personal photos, documents, and collectibles we could digitize. The trust gained also built a strong relationship and sustained the community's interest in the project.

Phyllis Earles, university archivist, played a pivotal role in the process of building trust with community members due to her over thirty-year tenure at the University. Earles was able to introduce my students and me to local graduates of Prairie View and facilitate other introductions to local community institutions so that we could document their history. After making these connections, we unofficially designated community liaisons—individuals who were our go-to persons for leads to individuals to interview and potential research areas. Jimmie Poindexter quickly became one of those liaisons. Poindexter was born on Prairie View's campus, taught at the university, and was a lifelong member of the local community (see Figure 9.6). We understood that with community archives and community-based projects like ours it was important to allow the "community to make collective decisions about what is of enduring value to them, shape collective memory of their own pasts, and control the means through which stories about their past are constructed."[21] Throughout the process of building trust with community members, we explained to the community participants the potential of the project extending past the semester and establishing lasting relationships with the local community. We also provided information about the items the archive had from the local community and offered access to all trainings (on digitization and conducting oral histories) to community collaborators. Our students were able to gain much from the in-classroom instruction and the skills learned in the archive. More than this, they gained valuable lessons in organizing and working

Figure 9.6. Picture of Daren White at Penn State University. Courtesy of Daren White.

with the local community. The most frequent community meeting attendees, including Mrs. Poindexter, served as community liaisons who directed students to individuals to interview who played integral parts in local historical developments. During the process of collecting the oral histories, the student participants applied the information learned in the trainings and workshops. Additionally, students gained an expanded sense of community beyond the campus by establishing relationships with the local community and conducting oral histories. This experience had a profound impact on many of the student participants.

The CAC project directly affected our student participants' ideas of community and conducting research, their place in the community, and the ways they can contribute to preserving the history of the local community. As it relates to the academic goals of the project, students gained proficiency in conducting historical research. Student Daren White expressed, "Before I took the senior level research course I knew very little about research....In saying that, I understood how to do research online and search for credible sources but my research skills were limited." This project gave our students a firsthand opportunity to conduct archival and field research through oral histories. From engaging in training for and applying their obtained knowledge in the field, the students were able to gain a meaningful research experience. Daren recalled, "When I enrolled in the course I expected to gain an in-depth understanding of the many different ways to conduct research, but I gained more." The "more" was practical experience in conducting historical research, a more in-depth understanding of the local community's history, and skills he could leverage for employment and graduate school preparation.

During the summer of 2018, Daren was able to leverage his experience and the skills he learned in an application to a summer research program at Penn State University. Daren recalls, "That experience in the archives really showed me what type of work historians and archivists do." Daren was accepted to the program at Penn State and he credited his experience working with the CAC project as one of the reasons why he got into the summer program.

Out of the 33 CAC students, six secured internships and were able to transition into their summer positions as a direct result of their experience with the program. Most importantly, student participants gained a greater understanding of professionalism, research protocol, and ethical practices within their discipline. Daren reflected, "I learned from Dr. Robinson that in preparation for your interview, it's important to get approval from PVAMU's internal review board, follow the Oral History Association's best practices, and send the person being interviewed the questions you're going to ask beforehand."[22] In addition to the students gaining hands-on experience as researchers from the project, the university archive gained new avenues for outreach and instruction on campus and in the local area.

THE IMPACT OF THE CAC PROGRAM AND THE FUTURE OF ARCHIVING AT HBCUS

Grassroots archives that actively involve communities have the potential to complement traditional archival collections.[23] The PVAMU CAC project's influence on the work and direction of SCAD was tremendous. Terry Cook poses the question "What roles do the archive or archivists play?"[24] Indeed, the traditional functions of archivists have been acquiring, describing, and preserving documents as evidence. However, in consideration of these traditional functions and the contemporary demands of the academy and the needs of the local community, PVAMU's archival staff sought to reconfigure the department's roles at the university, in serving academics, and making connections to the community. The CAC project was a major step toward PVAMU's SCAD obtaining a new identity. This new identity is shaped by not only preserving, but producing scholarly knowledge from and about the processes for maintaining its holdings. It was apparent to the SCAD staff that the focus on producing knowledge was only obtainable through committing to an emphasis on interdisciplinary collaboration and community engagement. The commitment to interdisciplinary collaboration gave the staff an opportunity not only to aid researchers, but also to be active contributors to scholarly works within the archival discipline. PVAMU's SCAD understands its commitment to collaboration and community engagement is the only way the archive will continue to be an integral part of university and community affairs. Taking the work outside of the archive's walls by teaming with scholars to produce works is central to the ways the unit seeks to transform the authority of the archive. The CAC project set this process in motion.

The effects of the project were broad and encompassed establishing connections with a number of parties that SCAD had no formalized dealings with. The project wedded SCAD more intimately with the academic programs at the university, connected the department with a cadre of community members willing to assist, and created an inroad to a lasting relationship with the local community. The content collected from the project is a rich array of information ranging from oral histories to rare photos. Oral histories collected through the program speak to the experiences of local Blacks living through segregation and helping to implement changes during the civil rights era. These items were tapped to potentially contribute to the core collection related to the history of the City of Prairie View. In addition, the rare photos are exhibited in SCAD's display areas at the entrance of the main campus library. Community members proudly viewed the displays during the Fall semester of 2018.

Moreover, the results of PVAMU's CAC project were far-reaching and impacted lives on and off campus. New pedagogical approaches were integrated into PVAMU's history courses which provided our students with tangible skills and revamped the history curriculum. Most importantly, a lasting collaboration with PVAMU's SCAD was established which is mutually beneficial to both areas. SCAD was able to create access to a number of the unprocessed collections and digitize items that lay in obscurity. Also, a collaborative team was formed that is actively publishing and seeking outside funding to support the important work underway at PVAMU. To date, two scholarly works are in circulation.[25] More importantly, connections were made with the local community, which have built bridges of mutual aid to and from campus. The relationships formed have positioned PVAMU to become a true "communi-versity." Ultimately, developing sustainable collaborations at Prairie View has enhanced the academic life of the university, provided PVAMU students with meaningful service-learning opportunities, and re-connected the local community to the school. In addition, the students were essential partners, played a significant role in expanding the reach of the archive into the community, and changed the way SCAD builds collections through their community work. All of these are ways that PVAMU is seeking to transform the authority of the archive.

The benefits of taking the CAC approach, though applicable to all institutions of higher education, can be particularly rewarding for special collections and archival departments at HBCUs. The strength of the archive is found in its ability to best aid its patrons. In many cases for HBCUs, these patrons are members of communities that are economically deprived and lacking resources. Historically, Black colleges and universities have always formed relationships with the communities in which they are located in order to address these issues. Therefore, in many instances HBCU archival staff members have an opportunity to highlight this history and to document new social justice movements in the community. This level of community engagement further transforms the traditional role of the archive and its relationships with its patrons. Whether they be researchers, students, donors, or consultants, an archival department should be ready to contribute on demand. By engaging with these parties in new ways by being more active in the production of knowledge, historic preservation, and promoting public history, HBCU archives center themselves as important community institutions and vital support departments for the academic programs at any university. Moreover, the potential of HBCUs to serve as regional repositories that have primary source materials that document the nation's racial and social history position these archives to make a significant contribution to the larger discipline.

Considering the challenges HBCU archives face documenting and preserving the past, there is still much work to do. John Berry articulated this challenge in the form of this statement: "HBCU's should archive the African American story."[26] Rightfully so, the historical connections of HBCUs to communities of color dictate that these institutions are likely candidates to be among the primary places for preserving, documenting, and interpreting the Black experience in the United States. To fully take on this task, HBCUs will have to invest more in preserving and highlighting their individual collections along with aggressively procuring noteworthy archival collections from within their communities and from alumni. Most importantly, HBCUs must center students' learning and the needs of the community at the heart of this work by using methods like the CAC approach. Prairie View is stepping forward to lead the way in engaging in this type of work. New initiatives housed in the recently established Ruth J. Simmons Center for Race and Justice such as the Epa Committee initiative, a research collaboration between the center and the university archive, employs the CAC approach (see: https://www.pvamu.edu/simmonscenter/our-work/the-epa-committee-on-the-legacy-of-slavery-and-the-impact-of-segregation-at-prairie-view-am-university/). Through engaging in this important work, HBCUs join colleges and universities across the country who are transforming the authority of the archive on campus and in communities.

NOTES

1 Thomas Peace and Gillian Allen, "Rethinking Access to the Past: History and Archives in the Digital Age," *Acadiensis* 48, no. 2 (2019): 217–29.

2 Gabrielle Blais and David Enns, "From Paper Archives to People Archives: Public Programming in the Management of Archives," *Archivaria*, no. 31 (January 1990): 102.

3 Blais and Enns, "From Paper Archives to People Archives," 102.

4 Andrew Flinn, "Archives and Their Communities: Serving the People," *Comma*, no. 1 (2008): 157–59, https://doi.org/10.3828/comma.2008.1.23.

5 See the following books that document this history: Jelani M. Favors, *Shelter in a Time of Storm: How Black Colleges Fostered Generations of Leadership and Activism* (Chapel Hill: University of North Carolina Press, 2019); James D. Anderson, *The Education of Blacks in the South, 1860-1935* (Chapel Hill: University of North Carolina Press, 1988); Harry G. Lefever, *Undaunted By The Fight: Spelman College And The Civil Rights Movement, 1957-1967* (Macon: Mercer University Press, 2005); Merline Pitre, *Born to Serve: A History of Texas Southern University* (Norman: University of Oklahoma Press, 2018).

6 John M. Berry, "HBCUs Should Archive the African-American Story," *Diverse Issues in Higher Education* 34, no. 15 (August 24, 2017): 36.

7 Danielle Alio, "Princeton University Library Partners with HBCUS in Inaugural Archiving Program," *States News Service*, July 30, 2018, https://www.princeton.edu/news/2018/07/30/princeton-university-library-partners-hbcus-inaugural-archiving-program.

8 Sandra Edmonds Crewe, "Education with Intent—The HBCU Experience," *Journal of Human Behavior in the Social Environment* 27, no. 5 (2017): 360–65, https://doi.org/10.1080/10911359.2017.1318622.

9 Dana R. Chandler, "Lifting the Veil: Digitizing Black Archives at Tuskegee University," *The Public Historian* 40, no. 3 (2018): 232, 239, https://doi.org/10.1525/tph.2018.40.3.232.

10 Marco Robinson and Phyllis Earles, "Engaging the Public with and Preserving the History of Texas's First Public Historically Black University," *KULA: Knowledge Creation, Dissemination, and Preservation Studies* 2, no. 1 (2018): 1–13, https://doi.org/10.5334/kula.33.

11 Robinson and Earles, "Engaging the Public," 8.

12 Peace and Allen, "Rethinking Access to the Past," 217.

13 Flinn, "Archives and Their Communities"; Jeannette A. Bastian and Ben Alexander, eds., *Community Archives: The Shaping of Memory* (London: Facet Publishing, 2018), https://doi.org/10.29085/9781856049047; Isto Huvila,

"Participatory Archive: Towards Decentralised Curation, Radical User Orientation, and Broader Contextualisation of Records Management," *Archival Science* 8, no. 1 (March 1, 2008): 15–36, https://doi.org/10.1007/s10502-008-9071-0; Laura Visser-Maessen, "'The Background for Our Future': Locating The Black Archives in the Netherlands in Black Atlantic Traditions of Archival Activism," *The New Americanist* 1, no. 4 (Summer 2020): 59–100.

14 Grace I. Yeh, "The Re/Collecting Project and Rethinking Archives and Archival Practice," *Verge: Studies in Global Asias* 1, no. 2 (2015): 33–34, https://doi.org/10.5749/vergstudglobasia.1.2.0031.

15 Yeh, "The Re/Collecting Project and Rethinking Archives and Archival Practice," 34.

16 Nancy Bell and Dinah Eastop, "Learning from Archives: Integrating Preservation and Access," in *Heritage Conservation and Social Engagement*, ed. Renata F. Peters et al. (London: UCL Press, 2020), 141–54, https://www.jstor.org/stable/j.ctv13xps1g.16.

17 Belinda Davis Smith et al., "A Partnership Forged: BSW Students and Service Learning at a Historically Black College and University (HBCU) Serving Urban Communities," *Journal of Human Behavior in the Social Environment* 27, no. 5 (2017): 439, https://doi.org/10.1080/10911359.2017.1295005.

18 Kelly Lowther Pereira, *Community Service-Learning for Spanish Heritage Learners: Making Connections and Building Identities* (John Benjamins Publishing Company, 2018), 140–50.

19 Pereira, *Community Service-Learning*, 140.

20 Amy E. Earheart, "Can We Trust the University? Digital Humanities Collaborations with Historically Exploited Cultural Communities," in *Bodies of Information: Intersectional Feminism and the Digital Humanities*, eds. Elizabeth Losh and Jacqueline Wernimont (Minneapolis: University of Minnesota Press, 2018), 369, https://doi.org/10.5749/j.ctv9hj9r9.23.

21 Michelle Caswell, Marika Cifor, and Mario H. Ramirez, "'To Suddenly Discover Yourself Existing': Uncovering the Impact of Community Archives," *The American Archivist* 79, no. 1 (Spring/Summer 2016): 61.

22 Daren White, Course Reflection, 2018.

23 Krista McCracken, "Community Archival Practice: Indigenous Grassroots Collaboration at the Shingwauk Residential Schools Centre," *The American Archivist* 78, no. 1 (Spring/Summer 2015): 182.

24 Terry Cook, "Evidence, Memory, Identity, and Community: Four Shifting Archival Paradigms," *Archival Science* 13 (2013): 97, https://doi.org/10.1007/s10502-012-9180-7.

25 Marco Robinson, Farrah Gafford Cambrice, and Phyllis Earles, "Telling the Stories of Forgotten Communities: Oral History, Public Memory, and Black Communities in the American South," *Collections* 13, no. 2 (June 1, 2017): 171–84, https://doi.org/10.1177/155019061701300211; Robinson and Earles, "Engaging the Public."

26 Berry, "HBCUs Should Archive the African-American Story," 36.

BIBLIOGRAPHY

Alio, Danielle. "Princeton University Library Partners with HBCUS in Inaugural Archiving Program." *States News Service*, July 30, 2018. https://www.princeton.edu/news/2018/07/30/princeton-university-library-partners-hbcus-inaugural-archiving-program.

Anderson, James D. *The Education of Blacks in the South, 1860–1935*. Chapel Hill: University of North Carolina Press, 1988. https://www.jstor.org/stable/10.5149/9780807898888_anderson.

Bastian, Jeannette A., and Ben Alexander, eds. *Community Archives: The Shaping of Memory*. London: Facet Publishing, 2018. https://doi.org/10.29085/9781856049047.

Bell, Nancy, and Dinah Eastop. "Learning from Archives: Integrating Preservation and Access." In *Heritage Conservation and Social Engagement*, edited by Renata F. Peters, Iris L. F. den Boer, Jessica S. Johnson, and Susanna Pancaldo, 141–54. London: UCL Press, 2020. https://www.jstor.org/stable/j.ctv13xps1g.16.

Berry, John M. "HBCUs Should Archive the African American Story." *Diverse Issues in Higher Education* 34, no. 15 (August 24, 2017): 36.

Blais, Gabrielle, and David Enns. "From Paper Archives to People Archives: Public Programming in the Management of Archives." *Archivaria*, no. 31 (January 1990): 101–13.

Caswell, Michelle, Marika Cifor, and Mario H. Ramirez. "'To Suddenly Discover Yourself Existing': Uncovering the Impact of Community Archives." *The American Archivist* 79, no. 1 (Spring/Summer 2016): 56–81.

Chandler, Dana R. "Lifting the Veil: Digitizing Black Archives at Tuskegee University." *The Public Historian* 40, no. 3 (2018): 232–51. https://doi.org/10.1525/tph.2018.40.3.232.

Cook, Terry. "Evidence, Memory, Identity, and Community: Four Shifting Archival Paradigms." *Archival Science* 13 (2013): 95–120. https://doi.org/10.1007/s10502-012-9180-7.

Crewe, Sandra Edmonds. “Education with Intent—The HBCU Experience.” *Journal of Human Behavior in the Social Environment* 27, no. 5 (2017): 360–66. https://doi.org/10.1080/10911359.2017.1318622.

Earheart, Amy E. “Can We Trust the University? Digital Humanities Collaborations with Historically Exploited Cultural Communities.” In *Bodies of Information: Intersectional Feminism and the Digital Humanities*, edited by Elizabeth Losh and Jacqueline Wernimont, 369–90. Minneapolis: University of Minnesota Press, 2018. https://doi.org/10.5749/j.ctv9hj9r9.23.

Flinn, Andrew. “Archives and Their Communities: Serving the People” 2008, no. 1 (2008): 157–68. https://doi.org/0.3828/comma.2008.1.23.

Huvila, Isto. “Participatory Archive: Towards Decentralised Curation, Radical User Orientation, and Broader Contextualisation of Records Management.” *Archival Science* 8, no. 1 (March 1, 2008): 15–36. https://doi.org/10.1007/s10502-008-9071-0.

Lefever, Harry G. *Undaunted by The Fight: Spelman College and The Civil Rights Movement, 1957–1967*. Macon: Mercer University Press, 2005.

McCracken, Krista. “Community Archival Practice: Indigenous Grassroots Collaboration at the Shingwauk Residential Schools Centre.” *The American Archivist* 78, no. 1 (Spring/Summer 2015): 181–91.

Peace, Thomas, and Gillian Allen. “Rethinking Access to the Past: History and Archives in the Digital Age.” *Acadiensis* 48, no. 2 (2019): 217–29.

Pereira, Kelly Lowther. *Community Service-Learning for Spanish Heritage Learners: Making Connections and Building Identities*. John Benjamins Publishing Company, 2018. https://books.google.com/books?id=I4l8DwAAQBAJ&dq=+Kelly+Pereira.+2018.+Community+Service-Learning+for+Spanish+Heritage+Learners%E2%80%AF:+Making+Connections+and+Building+Identities.+Issues+in+Hispanic+and+Lusophone+Linguistics+(IHLL).+Amsterdam:+John+Benjamins+Publishing+Company.+http://search.ebscohost.com.pv&lr=&source=gbs_navlinks_s.

Pitre, Merline. *Born to Serve: A History of Texas Southern University*. Norman: University of Oklahoma Press, 2018.

Robinson, Marco, Farrah Gafford Cambrice, and Phyllis Earles. “Telling the Stories of Forgotten Communities: Oral History, Public Memory, and Black Communities in the American South.” *Collections* 13, no. 2 (June 1, 2017): 171–84. https://doi.org/10.1177/155019061701300211.

Robinson, Marco, and Phyllis Earles. “Engaging the Public with and Preserving the History of Texas’s First Public Historically Black University.” *KULA: Knowledge*

Creation, Dissemination, and Preservation Studies 2, no. 1 (2018): 1–13. https://doi.org/10.5334/kula.33.

Smith, Belinda Davis, Isiah Marshall Jr., Brian E. Anderson, and Kevin K. Daniels. "A Partnership Forged: BSW Students and Service Learning at a Historically Black College and University (HBCU) Serving Urban Communities." *Journal of Human Behavior in the Social Environment* 27, no. 5 (2017): 438–49. https://doi.org/10.1080/10911359.2017.1295005.

Visser-Maessen, Laura. "'The Background for Our Future': Locating the Black Archives in the Netherlands in Black Atlantic Traditions of Archival Activism." *The New Americanist* 1, no. 4 (Summer 2020): 59–100.

Yeh, Grace I. "The Re/Collecting Project and Rethinking Archives and Archival Practice." *Verge: Studies in Global Asias* 1, no. 2 (2015): 31–36. https://doi.org/10.5749/vergstudglobasia.1.2.0031.

CHAPTER TEN

REIMAGINING THE WORLD THROUGH COMMUNITY-BASED MEMORY WORK: THE TEXAS AFTER VIOLENCE PROJECT

Jane Field

The Texas After Violence Project (TAVP) was founded in 2007 to document the impact of the death penalty on Texas, Texan communities, and Texans themselves. The first staff members (and interns) traveled around Texas interviewing family members of people who had been executed, family members of murder victims, defense attorneys and prosecutors, members of juries, media witnesses, scholars, and activists. They conducted hours-long oral histories with people who had been deeply affected by their experiences of the death penalty, no matter what their personal beliefs about it were. I started working for TAVP in 2016 and have served a variety of roles at the organization (now, as the community archives director, I run our documentation and archiving activities). During my time at TAVP, this core work has expanded to encompass a broader view of state violence, one that recognizes the death penalty is just one facet of a criminal legal system that wields many forms of violence as methods of social control. These other forms of state violence include police brutality and murder, the dehumanizing nature of the criminal legal system, as well as incarceration. We ground our work in the firsthand experiences of those who have encountered violence at the hands of the state, and aim to pull those experiences into a collective, recorded history narrated by and for those who are most directly impacted by state violence. In order to document these stories effectively, we've come to rely on radical empathy and an ethics of care, which helps us sustain our work and those we work with.

We have long been inspired by the work of Michelle Caswell and Marika Cifor, who have written about bringing radical empathy to the archive and explored the various affective relationships present in archival work.[1] This analysis is particularly important for projects like ours, which aims to build an archive centered around the shared experiences of a group of people and is part of a growing movement of community-based archives. Community-based archives have always existed in various forms, but in recent years they have gained more mainstream support, with recognition—and funding—from institutions like the University of North Carolina at Chapel Hill and the Andrew W. Mellon Foundation, both of which have recently established grants to fund community-based archives like the TAVP.[2] In 2019, TAVP also partnered with the South Asian American Digital Archive (SAADA),[3] Densho: The Japanese American Legacy Project,[4] and Interference Archive[5] to form the Community Archives Collaborative (CAC), a network dedicated to sharing knowledge and resources among community archives. In the announcement of the CAC, SAADA wrote:

> Community-based archives hold some of the most valuable materials documenting the lives of marginalized people, and mostly reside in spaces outside of traditional academic and government-run cultural heritage institutions. By disrupting the hierarchical models in place in traditional archives, these repositories prompt

community members to view collections as belonging *to the community* and challenge dominant practices and conceptions of custody, description, and ownership. In community archives, archival work is done *by* and *with* the community, and not just *for* the community.[6]

This statement is grounded in further research by Caswell (adviser to CAC), who has written extensively about the way community archives counter symbolic annihilation (the "absence and misrepresentation" of communities in media, archives, and other contexts) through these disruptive models.[7] By viewing collections as "belonging *to the community*" (as stated in the CAC announcement quoted above), she finds that community members also find a sense of meaning and personal belonging as their stories are preserved within archival spaces.

At TAVP, our entire work is formed around disrupting these hierarchical models, not just as they exist in traditional archives, but also as they exist in our everyday interactions, and, of course, as they exist in our interview space. As my colleague Gabriel Solis has written, "the principles and ethics of oral history make it an effective method to document the impacts of violence and trauma because it rejects the power dynamics and adversarial nature of forms of interviewing that typically occur in the aftermath of violence."[8] In many ways, this disruption is crucial to our ability to record these long-form life history interviews with people who have experienced deep trauma at the hands of the state. Often, they or their loved ones have been portrayed as fatally criminal—the worst of the worst—and deserving only of the highest forms of retribution: death by execution, police shooting, or violent, long-term incarceration. Our primary goal is to create a safe space for the interviewee to tell their own story in their own words, without fear of judgment or reprisal—in complete contrast to experiences they may have had sharing their stories with media, legal teams, and sometimes even their (geographic) communities. Disrupting the hierarchy of a more formal research interview can help create that safe space for an interviewee to share their story in a way that feels authentic to their experience, and, we hope, does not expose them to unnecessary retraumatization.

We build this disruptive space by emphasizing close, empathic listening to the people we interview, and together with them, creating a record of their experiences that reflects *their* understanding of *their* story. It is a collaborative creation in that we ask certain questions to provide some direction, but part of our interviewing ethos is to let the storyteller guide the conversation wherever they choose. The process does not end after the interview is over—instead, we continue to work with interviewees, and have them review their transcript and request any changes they would like to make to the interview before it is published. These edits can be simple factual corrections, and sometimes substantial cuts to the interview to make sure that sensitive personal information revealed during the intimacy of the interview space is not published.

TAVP interviews are hard to conduct, because the stories are hard to tell, and hard to listen to. Our interviewing approach, which draws heavily on trauma oral history research methods, requires a great deal of patience, empathy, and compassion on the part of the interviewer—it takes incredible trust for someone to tell you about a terrible harm they suffered, and we have a responsibility to meet that trust with respect and care. We try to hold onto the story being told, while holding back from expressing judgments or disbelief, frustration with details, or becoming overcome with emotions. We try to avoid imposing a narrative on someone else's story, and we try to let go of any expectation of how the story ought to be told, instead choosing to be open to messy narratives and contradictions; unresolved feelings and loose ends.

When I conduct these interviews, or sit in on them as a videographer, I try to work from a place of mindfulness. I believe becoming a better listener requires ongoing practice—we are always slipping along a spectrum of doing better and falling back while trying to hear the other person and remain open to every part of their story, even the parts we do not like, or that we disagree with. This is a far cry from the work I did as a graduate student at the School of Information at the University of Texas at Austin, where I studied archives and preservation. While there, I learned the ins and outs of archival work, from processing and appraisal work to current archival theory about community archives and how they disrupt archival centers of power. But this work within the space of the interview to develop a practice of mindful listening has had a substantially greater impact on my understanding of memory work beyond the academy. It is with this mindful listening that we can, and do, foster incredible connections with interviewees, build a trusting space where they can do this transformative storytelling, and craft an alternate—and arguably more authentic—version of history.

This skill of listening openly can be learned, and while it is not the primary objective of our interview work, I truly believe that the interviews are also a powerful tool to teach others how to practice this mindful listening and create these transformative moments elsewhere in the world. Furthermore, a person does not have to participate directly in the interview itself in order to hone this skill. Our work with undergraduate interns demonstrates this constantly.

These interns have been a vital part of ensuring the interviews we record become public. Charlotte Nunes has written about the pedagogical benefit of undergraduate students processing oral history archival collections, drawing from her experiences incorporating TAVP materials into her classroom, and having her students experience archival labor as they engage with critical theory in the humanities. Nunes also notes the rise of post-custodial archiving, where custody of physical archival materials remains with the creator and institutions provide the creator with digital support and labor to ensure their sustainability (oftentimes, a community-based archive like TAVP). Ideally, post-custodial arrangements allow community-based archives to accept substantial support for their collections without giving control over to institutions. Often, this support is in the form of archival labor: digitization, description, digital archiving.[9] Without question, the labor of student interns has sustained the TAVP archive to varying degrees over the past fourteen years we have been conducting oral histories.

They spend hours working on transcripts of these interviews, listening to each sentence repeatedly until they are sure the written record reflects what was actually said. They use software to make sure the videos of the interviews are synced with the transcripts, so researchers and other viewers can explore the interviews in whatever way suits them the most. They create metadata: abstracts, tables of contents, and other descriptive material to make the interviews as accessible as possible. This work is the tedious, often thankless reality of so much of archival work, but it is critical to what we do—and every video we upload, every transcript we sync chips away at the control of institutional archives, which routinely wield their versions of historical memory to uphold corrupt systems of power.

And yet there remains a complex tension at the heart of this arrangement. Through our engagement of undergraduate student interns—regardless of benefits they may realize as a result of their work with us—we are still relying on institutional support of local universities, even if that support is not (directly) financial. Samip Mallick and Michelle Caswell make clear the central difficulty of partnerships like this, arguing that "true fiscal sustainability for community archives coalescing around marginalized identities must be rooted in support from within the community rather than from dominant institutions and funding agencies."[10] We have tried to financially compensate interns when possible, and recently moved to paying them an hourly rate for a small number of hours each week. Often, they contribute more labor to our organization than we pay them for, but our hope is that every slow movement toward compensating institutionally-affiliated labor is a step toward independently sustaining our work in a way that centers the needs of our community over the needs of any institution.

Of course, this begs the question: are members of our community ever interns? The answer is complex, because our community is difficult to define by simple boundaries such as geography, language, or identity. We define our community the same way we define who we consider interviewing: individuals who have been directly impacted by certain forms of state violence—the death penalty, mass incarceration, in-custody deaths, police brutality. We do not ask students to give us any personal information like this—an existing understanding of the prison industrial complex is not a prerequisite to becoming an intern at TAVP. However, several students over the years have self-identified to me or others about their experiences with some of the topics we cover. Most frequently this involves a loved one who has been or is incarcerated—after all, almost 50 percent of Americans have family members who have been incarcerated.[11]

A notable encounter with an undergraduate student took place with a colleague, Celeste Henery, who spoke poignantly about the experience during a recent talk at the New Story Festival in Austin. She told of the student attending a lecture she gave (which included excerpts from a TAVP interview), then later setting up a meeting with Celeste. Their meeting began with a lengthy period of idle conversation, until finally,

> She began to tell the story of one of her parents' murder by a person with mental illness and the fraught political, social, and familial world in which the homicide occurred. She had come to my talk, for only the first part, before having to leave, but it had compelled her to come speak to me, to share her desire to help save her parent's killer ... She told me I was the first person she could share her story and terrifying dilemma with.[12]

"I now understand our encounter as several forms of rendezvous," Henery said in her talk. For Henery, these points of rendezvous (the moment in the office, the moment at the lecture, during which the student watched a recording of a previous encounter that took place during a TAVP interview) build up, layer after layer. I, too, have seen the way stories in our interview collection intersect with moments in the present, impacting the trajectories of the people who engage with them.

This brings me back, again, to our interns. Who are we in conversation with when we sit down with undergraduate students, sent to us by institutions such as the University of Texas at Austin? What is being sustained by our dependence on their labor? Young interns, in their late teens or just out of them, do not always see their tasks within the framework of the power struggle between community-based archives and institutional archives over the writing of history. In fact, since most of our interns come to us from within academia, they often start their internships viewing the world through a hierarchical lens that places academia and institutional archives above community-based archives. They expect their excellent education to allow them to go out after graduation and change the world.[13] Part of our work is demonstrating to these undergraduate students that their visions of change are empty without a deeper engagement with other peoples' stories, and a substantial disruption of their understanding of who is capable of creating change. Of course, I believe that intervention comes through engaged listening to the interviews in our collection—not only because it introduces them to the ideas and experiences of others, but because it inherently requires them to sit back and relinquish control of whatever narratives they are forming in their minds.

We ask them to dig down into the words of each interviewee, and to become experts in a discrete world created during the span of a single recorded dialogue. It can become a kind of devotional to replay a segment of a recording again and again, trying to ensure its translation to written word is as accurate as possible, and in fact, interns often become devoted to the stories of one or two narrators whose story they work with repeatedly over the course of the semester. It is not walking a mile in another's shoes, exactly, but it is something close to that, this repeated deep listening. Something that might have seemed, at first, like tedious, repetitive grunt work instead develops into an intensely personal experience, and still requires them to do that hard work of listening without judgment and creating a space for these messy, complicated stories to breathe. These are lessons people spend lifetimes learning, and our students are not experts at the end of a single semester working with us. But I hope that this work provides the foundation of a skill that will have a cascading impact on their ability to move through the world wholeheartedly and openly to the experiences of others.

For this foundation to take, though, it must be bolstered by a safe environment where people can engage with these stories with time and support. The interviews we ask our interns to listen to contain so much pain, and there is a very real risk that these young students will experience trauma simply by spending so much time listening to them. There is also the risk that these young students will experience *retraumatization* by listening to these interviews, depending on previous encounters in their lives that they might bring with them to their work. Thus, the other critical element of our internships is to bring the same ethos we bring to every interview into our office every day. We try to make sure that our interns feel safe discussing their listening experiences and free to track and honor the very real emotional impact of this work. It would be irresponsible to simply expose them to these interviews without providing the necessary support for them to process the stories they are hearing.

As it happens, physical sites of community archives are incredible locations for transformative experiences, as described by Caswell, et al. in "Imagining Transformative Spaces: The Personal-Political

Sites of Community Archives."[14] This article discusses a series of focus groups with users of community archives, through which the authors determined a theme of "community archives as home-away-from-home." In the focus groups there were various meanings ascribed to users' concepts of home, encompassing safe spaces, places for intergenerational dialogue, and "extensions of or alternatives to the domestic spaces of home, where previously taboo conversations could be started." All of the versions of "community archives as home-away-from-home" described in "Imagining Transformative Spaces" resonate for our work, and have implications for the work we ask interns to undertake. By engaging with our archive, interns become members of our broad community, and we therefore encounter them with the same intention we try to bring to our encounters with the individuals we interview.

We try to bring empathy, compassion, and a willingness to listen to all our interactions with interns. Just as it is during interviews, this can be difficult, although for different reasons: we are busy and distracted by the details of the day (this is never a problem with interviews, where we are sure to set aside the full day for an interview and we pick a location that is as distraction-free as possible). Sometimes, we feel impatient with their ideas of the world—and sometimes their ideas of the world are a painful reminder of old ideas we used to carry. Sometimes, we feel we just need a finished transcript immediately, or the pull of other deadlines makes it hard for us to step back and remember the true value of these internships. We want students to learn how to engage with these stories in a way that is authentic and sustainable, so that they can continue to practice this good-listening and space-making after the internship is long over.

So, I turn off the part of my brain that wants quick results and independence, and I put my listening skills to work to find out what they are going through. Sometimes there is a breakthrough—they learn new skills, or a new idea seeps into them about the world that could be—and sometimes, we realize that the only way to have a future breakthrough is to take a break in that moment.

I send them home, or they decide to take a walk, or we just sit and drink tea and discuss whatever is bothering them. And it is in those moments that the most valuable transformations happen because we give ourselves the grace to be human and have needs beyond productivity. This sets the stage for a greater capacity to learn, explore, and offer up similar grace in their interactions with others—even when those interactions are mediated through the pages of interview transcripts.

We need people who know when to listen and know when to make space for their own emotions so that in the future, they can make space for the emotions of others. This radical empathy and ethics of care—extending from ourselves and our interns all the way to the narrators we collaborate with—allows us to hear complicated stories without trying to force them to conform to the existing—and flawed—narratives of violence in our society. These troubling narratives lure us in with their simplicity, dividing us into neat binaries: victim or perpetrator, innocent or guilty, a witness for the prosecution or a witness for the defense. But then they fail us. They fail us over and over again. From Trayvon Martin to George Floyd, from the earliest lynchings to modern lethal injection, our society is good at projecting narratives of criminality onto the people it wants to destroy. In fact, it depends on it. No amount of innocence can stand up to the current mythmaking of the criminal legal system. One powerful way to start countering that system is to foster deep, empathic listening that centers the experiences of those most impacted and opens space for nuanced narratives that shatter deadly myths of criminality.

NOTES

1 Michelle Caswell and Marika Cifor, "From Human Rights to Feminist Ethics: Radical Empathy in the Archives," *Archivaria* 81 (May 6, 2016): 23–43.

2 In 2019, TAVP became a member of the first cohort of community-based archives to receive funding from the Andrew W. Mellon Foundation as part of their grant opportunity for community-based archives.

3 South Asian American Digital Archive (SAADA), https://www.saada.org/.

4 Densho: The Japanese American Legacy Project, https://densho.org/.

5 Interference Archive, https://interferencearchive.org/.

6 "Community Archives Collaborative," South Asian American Digital Archive (SAADA), October 30, 2019, https://www.saada.org/project/community-archives-collaborative.

7 Michelle Caswell et al., "'To Be Able to Imagine Otherwise': Community Archives and the Importance of Representation," *Archives and Records* 38, no. 1 (January 2, 2017): 5–26, https://doi.org/10.1080/23257962.2016.1260445.

8 Gabriel Daniel Solis, "Documenting State Violence: (Symbolic) Annihilation & Archives of Survival," *KULA: Knowledge Creation, Dissemination, and Preservation Studies* 2, no. 1 (November 29, 2018): 4, https://doi.org/10.5334/kula.28.

9 Charlotte Nunes, "'Connecting to the Ideologies That Surround Us': Oral History Stewardship as an Entry Point to Critical Theory in the Undergraduate Classroom," *The Oral History Review* 44, no. 2 (2017): 348–62, https://doi.org/10.1093/ohr/ohx042.

10 South Asian American Digital Archive (SAADA), "Against Precarity: Towards a Community-Based Notion of Fiscal Sustainability," *Sustainable Futures*, *Medium*, July 30, 2018, https://medium.com/community-archives/against-precarity-towards-a-community-based-notion-of-fiscal-sustainability-815d1d889309.

11 "Half of Americans Have Family Members Who Have Been Incarcerated," Equal Justice Initiative, December 11, 2018, https://eji.org/news/half-of-americans-have-family-members-who-have-been-incarcerated/.

12 Celeste Henery, "Oral History as Rendezvous: Memory and Story in the Aftermath of State Violence," *Texas After Violence Project*, *Medium*, October 8, 2020, https://medium.com/texas-after-violence-project/oral-history-as-rendezvous-memory-and-story-in-the-aftermath-of-state-violence-bf4d726318d1.

13 The motto of the University of Texas at Austin being "What starts here changes the world."

14 Michelle Caswell et al., "Imagining Transformative Spaces: The Personal–Political Sites of Community Archives," *Archival Science* 18 (2018): 73–93.

BIBLIOGRAPHY

Caswell, Michelle, and Marika Cifor. "From Human Rights to Feminist Ethics: Radical Empathy in the Archives." *Archivaria* 81 (May 6, 2016): 23–43.

Caswell, Michelle, Joyce Gabiola, Jimmy Zavala, Gracen Brilmyer, and Marika Cifor. "Imagining Transformative Spaces: The Personal–Political Sites of Community Archives." *Archival Science* 18 (2018): 73–93.

Caswell, Michelle, Alda Allina Migoni, Noah Geraci, and Marika Cifor. "'To Be Able to Imagine Otherwise': Community Archives and the Importance of Representation." *Archives and Records* 38, no. 1 (January 2, 2017): 5–26. https://doi.org/10.1080/23257962.2016.1260445.

South Asian American Digital Archive (SAADA). "Community Archives Collaborative," October 30, 2019. https://www.saada.org/project/community-archives-collaborative.

"Half of Americans Have Family Members Who Have Been Incarcerated." *Equal Justice Initiative*, December 11, 2018. https://eji.org/news/half-of-americans-have-family-members-who-have-been-incarcerated/.

Henery, Celeste. "Oral History as Rendezvous: Memory and Story in the Aftermath of State Violence." *Texas After Violence Project, Medium*, October 8, 2020. https://medium.com/texas-after-violence-project/oral-history-as-rendezvous-memory-and-story-in-the-aftermath-of-state-violence-bf4d726318d1.

Nunes, Charlotte. "'Connecting to the Ideologies That Surround Us': Oral History Stewardship as an Entry Point to Critical Theory in the Undergraduate Classroom." *The Oral History Review* 44, no. 2 (2017): 348–62. https://doi.org/10.1093/ohr/ohx042.

Solis, Gabriel Daniel. "Documenting State Violence: (Symbolic) Annihilation & Archives of Survival." *KULA: Knowledge Creation, Dissemination, and Preservation Studies* 2, no. 1 (November 29, 2018): 1–11. https://doi.org/10.5334/kula.28.

South Asian American Digital Archive (SAADA). "Against Precarity: Towards a Community-Based Notion of Fiscal Sustainability." *Sustainable Futures, Medium*, July 30, 2018. https://medium.com/community-archives/against-precarity-towards-a-community-based-notion-of-fiscal-sustainability-815d1d889309.

Author Biographies

Hannah Alpert-Abrams writes and speaks on topics including higher education, labor, and the humanities. She has taught students ranging from third graders to doctoral students, in college classrooms, outdoor classrooms, virtual classrooms, and special collections reading rooms. She is a vice president of AFGE Local 3403. She wrote this chapter in her free time.

Mary A. Armstrong is Charles A. Dana Professor of Women's, Gender & Sexuality Studies and English, and chair of the Women's, Gender & Sexuality Studies Program at Lafayette College. She teaches and does research in LGBTQ+ Studies, with an emphasis on Queer Theory and narrative representations of Queer identity. She has published widely on issues of diversity and equity in STEM fields, strategies for institutional change in higher education, and inclusive pedagogies. Mary is co-founder and faculty director of the Lafayette College Queer Archives Project, in which role she coordinates project design and development with colleagues in the College Archives and Digital Scholarship Services, as well as with amazing Lafayette students.

Gianluca De Fazio is an Associate Professor in the Department of Justice Studies at James Madison University. Gianluca's research interests include the study of political violence in Northern Ireland and lynching in the US South. He has recently released the website *Racial Terror: Lynching in Virginia*. Gianluca is also a member of the History of Lynching Working Group at the Virginia General Assembly.

Phyllis Earles is Archivist and Head of the Special Collections and Archives Department at Prairie View A&M University. Earles' tenure in the library and information sciences started in January 1979 at Prairie View A&M University. In July 2000, she was reassigned as University Archivist, Head of

Special Collections/Archives Department. Phyllis was appointed to the Texas Historical Records Advisory Board, February 2020 and in February 2022, she was appointed to the CLIR and HBCU Library Alliance Authenticity Project Advisory Committee. She has coauthored two publications, "Engaging the Public with and Preserving the History of Texas's First Public Historically Black University." *KULA: knowledge creation, dissemination, and preservation studies*, 2(1), p.24 OID: http://doi.org/10.5334/kula.33 and "Telling the stories of forgotten communities: oral history, public memory, and black communities in the American South," Marco Robinson, Farrah Gafford Cambrice and Phyllis Earles, *Collections: A Journal for Museum and Archives Professionals* 13 (2, Spring 2017): 171–84.

aems emswiler is the founder of the Inside Books Project Archive and the community archivist for the Arizona Queer Archives (AQA). They are a PhD student at the University of Arizona, Tucson, School of Information, where they research and participate in grassroots archives and anarchist organizing. They have a chapter in the edited volume, *Surviving the Future: Queer Abolitionist Strategies* (PM Press, 2022).

Jane Field worked for Texas After Violence Project from 2016-2022, where she managed the oral history program, built the digital After Violence Archive, and oversaw day-to-day operations. As part of her work with TAVP, she was deeply involved in the development of the Community Archives Collaborative, a peer-support network for community-based archives in the United States. She is a co-founder and core-organizer of Mourning Our Losses, a community memorial project that began at the start of the COVID-19 pandemic, dedicated to honoring and remembering those who died while living or working behind bars. Her interests include trauma-informed memory work, grief and archiving, as well as anti-oppression memory work documenting legacies of violence in the American south. In 2022, she began working as an independent contractor for small community-based archives seeking support building digital archival collections, developing community-centric fundraising practices, and growing capacity.

Myranda Fuentes is the former Institutional History Research Specialist at the Dartmouth Library in Hanover, New Hampshire, where she coordinated the Historical Accountability Student Research Program. In her time at Dartmouth, she oversaw the research of twelve Historical Accountability Student Research Fellows and laid the groundwork for students to conduct part-time and off-site research under the auspices of the Historical Accountability Student Research Program. She received her BA in English Literature from Columbia University in 2018.

Andi Gustavson is the Head of Research Services at the Harry Ransom Center at The University of Texas at Austin. She teaches primary source literacy with the collections and has published on ethics, archives, and pedagogy, most recently in *Teaching with Archives*, ed. Nancy Bartlett, Elizabeth Gadelha, and Cinda Nofziger (Ann Arbor: The University of Michigan Press, 2020).

Michele Hardesty is Associate Professor of US Literatures and Cultural Studies at Hampshire College. Her research focuses on the crosscurrents of social movements and literary cultures during the Cold War era, with a focus on the cultural politics of international solidarity. Her work appears in *boundary 2*, *Critical Quarterly*, *The Monthly Review*, *Archive Journal*, *Radical History Review* and edited volumes including *Transnational Beat Generation* (2012) and *Neocolonial Fictions of the Global Cold War* (2019). Her website is www.michelehardesty.com.

Christopher Jones is the Special Collections Librarian and Archivist of the College at Grinnell College in Grinnell, Iowa. He earned a bachelor's degree in French from the University of Northern Iowa, a master's degree in information and library science from the University of Illinois at Urbana-Champaign, and a certificate from the Center for the Book at the University of Iowa. Prior to his current position, Chris worked as a library assistant in special collections at Grinnell, a scanning center supervisor for the internet archive, and as an assistant to the curator of special collections at the University of Illinois Urbana-Champaign.

Sam Koreman is a PhD candidate in political theory and American politics in the Department of Politics at the University of Virginia. She graduated from Dartmouth College in 2020 with a double major in government and philosophy. Her research currently focuses on subjects ranging from political obligation, state authority, philosophy and law, and ethics and public policy.

Alana Kumbier is a research and instruction librarian at Amherst College. They are the author of *Ephemeral Material: Queering the Archive* (Litwin Books, 2014) and coeditor, with Maria T. Accardi and Emily Drabinski, of *Critical Library Instruction: Theories and Methods* (Library Juice Press, 2010).

Elon Lang is Associate Professor of Instruction at the University of Texas at Austin, where he teaches a variety of undergraduate literature survey courses on ethical topics, medieval and early modern studies, dramatic literature, and experiential learning courses based in archival research. In addition to the class described in his contribution to this volume, in 2020–2021 he led two classes of students to bring archival techniques to bear on a real-world social justice issue facing the East Austin, Texas, community: the closing of one of Austin's historically Hispanic elementary schools, 106-year-old Metz

Elementary School. This class built an online archive and website for the school's history in partnership with former staff and parents associated with the school. In the process, undergraduate students learned about the importance of amplifying the voices of communities that have often been neglected by civic institutions and the municipal government, while developing meaningful relationships with members of the affected community.

Nora Claire Miller is a poet and multidisciplinary artist based in Western Massachusetts. They are the author of the chapbook *LULL* (2020), and their writing has appeared in *Bennington Review*, *Bat City Review*, *TYPO*, *Tagvverk*, *Hobart*, and other places. Nora is the editor in chief of Ghost Proposal. They hold an MFA from the Iowa Writers' Workshop and a BA from Hampshire College.

Elise Nacca is a librarian at The University of Texas at Austin where she leads a unit of teaching librarians who partner with faculty to integrate information literacy skills into courses across disciplines. Inspired by her own experiences as an art historian, she has built expertise in facilitating meaningful engagements with archives and special collections in the courses she supports.

Charlotte Nunes is the dean of Lafayette College Libraries. She is interested in the role academic libraries can play facilitating undergraduate research opportunities that center on archives, oral history, and community partnerships. In her previous role as director of digital scholarship services at Lafayette College Libraries, she played contributor and project manager roles in such digital archives initiatives as the Queer Archives Project, the Lehigh Valley Engaged Humanities Consortium Digital Archive, and the Modernist Archives Publishing Project. Her work has appeared in the *New Review of Academic Librarianship*, the *Oral History Review Portal: Libraries and the Academy*, *Literature & History*, and *Archive Journal*, among other venues.

Dr. Marco Robinson is a historian, archival and qualitative methods specialist. Marco is an assistant professor of History and the Assistant Director of the Ruth J. Simmons Center for Race and Justice at Prairie View A&M University (PVAMU). Robinson's recent coedited book, "Contemporary Debates in Social Justice: An Interdisciplinary Approach to Exploring the Lives of Black and Brown Americans" explores the complexities around Black and Brown communities and social justice issues. Additionally, his most recent book chapter "We were all we had": Transcending Race and Forging a Community of Mothers in the Post-Civil Rights Era South" explores the contours of Jim Crow life in north Mississippi and the pivotal role both Black and white women played during the integration of DeSoto County Public Schools. Marco specializes in historic preservation and facilitating projects that engage in the digitization of historical pictures and documents. Robinson's 2018 article "Telling the Stories of Forgotten Communities," explores the efficacy of oral histories and working on collaborative teams to document the histories of Black communities. Marco is a strong advocate for community studies and organizing community archives. His current research projects deal with the impact of COVID-19 on Black church congregations in Waller County, TX, the Texas Domestic Slave Trade Project, and exploring the legacy of slavery and impact of segregation at PVAMU.

Elizabeth Rodrigues is Associate Professor, Humanities and Digital Scholarship Librarian, at Grinnell College, where she co-leads the Vivero Digital Fellows program. Her research focuses on life writing and critical data studies. She is the author of *Collecting Lives: Critical Data Narrative as Modernist Aesthetic in Early Twentieth-Century U.S. Literatures* (University of Michigan Press, Digital Culture Books Series).

Rachel N. Schnepper is the director of academic technology at Wesleyan University in Middletown, CT. She holds a PhD in European history.

Jennifer Wellnitz is a computer science masters student at North Carolina State University, with a research focus on computational narrative and artificially intelligent characters with emotion and personality. Her work has been published under the proceedings of the Intelligent Narrative Technologies workshop of the Artificial Intelligence and Interactive Digital Entertainment conference. She is currently a part of the POEM lab at NC State.

Daren White earned his bachelor's degree in history from Prairie View A&M University in 2019. Mr. White is currently a graduate student in the Sports Industry Management Master's Program at Georgetown University.

Temitayo Wolff is an alumna of the Grinnell College Vivero Digital Fellows program and an aspiring public librarian. She holds a BA in classical languages and literature from Grinnell College, where she worked in the special collections and archives while completing her degree. At the time of publication, Ms. Wolff is collections assistant in the Art Collection at Xavier University of Louisiana and is applying to graduate programs in library and information science.